NEW AMERICAN PLAYS

New American Plays

Edited and with an Introduction by
WILLIAM M. HOFFMAN

❧

VOLUME 2

A MERMAID DRAMABOOK
HILL AND WANG • NEW YORK

Copyright © 1968 Hill and Wang, Inc.
Standard Book Number (clothbound edition): 8090–7251–3
Standard Book Number (paperback edition): 8090–0741–X
Library of Congress catalog card number: 65-14530

. FIRST EDITION APRIL 1968

4 5 6 7 8 9 10

Manufactured in the United States of America by
The Colonial Press Inc., Clinton, Massachusetts

For Joe Cino

For Joe Cino

CONTENTS

INTRODUCTION

The plays in this collection have nothing in common with one another—except that they are good plays and that their authors are American and relatively unknown. In choosing the plays I did not feel that the collection should be "representative" of various schools or of this particular decade. I followed no principles in my selection, only my taste and intuition: here is a good serious play, here is a good humorous play; let a good serious play follow a good humorous one.

It turned out, however, that most of the plays were first performed in New York, more specifically, Off-Off-Broadway. My selection is due to no New York or coffee-house prejudice but only to the fact that most of the theatres willing to present new American plays are still in New York and the center of this kind of activity in New York is Off-Off-Broadway. Although there is much good theatre outside New York, there is very little good *new* theatre outside New York (or on Broadway, for that matter). To the exclusion of new drama, most theatre in this country is devoted to such safe bets as Shakespeare, Murray Schisgal, Molière, Tennessee Williams, Edward Albee, Brecht, Arthur Miller, Jean Anouilh, Thornton Wilder, Arthur Kopit, Neil Simon, and Sophocles. To perform certain of these playwrights is for some reason still considered daring in some places. I have no ready solutions, for the excuses that are given for not performing the works of new playwrights are often legitimate: poor box-office appeal, the poor quality of some of the writing, local censorship problems, the lack of skilled directors and actors. Nonetheless, it does seem disingenuous of such places as Lincoln Center, Arena Stage, the Alley Theatre, and most university theatres to tout themselves as centers of "living art" when they devote themselves almost entirely to the works of the past, or near past.

In the world of "living theatre" even new movements are old if they are thought of as answers or ends. Theatre of the Absurd, Theatre of Cruelty, happenings, mixed media are all already old hat. Schools and movements are valuable only insofar as they add to the existing repertoire of dramatic techniques, situations, and advertising gimmicks. "Living theatre" should be devoted to the performance of good new plays regardless of school, rather than to aping the latest fashions of theatre as described in *TDR*, *The Village Voice*, or the drama section of the Sunday *Times*.

This is not to say that the plays I have chosen belong to no school or have no antecedents, but by labeling them and classifying them I would, I believe, misrepresent them. To what extent a play conforms to any pattern and to what extent it deviates is only of academic interest; what is important is how and in what way a play is profound, or funny, or wise—and this can only be experienced by seeing or reading the play. In this light I would agree with Artaud's advice to burn the masterpieces, if this were taken also to include the works of Artaud.

—W.M.H.

FUTZ

by

ROCHELLE OWENS

Now concerning the things whereof ye wrote to me: It is good for a man not to touch a woman.

I Corinthians 7:1

CHARACTERS

NARRATOR
CYRUS FUTZ
MAJORIE SATZ
OSCAR LOOP
BILL MARJORAM
PRISON GUARD
ANN FOX
SHERIFF TOM SLUCK
FATHER SATZ
MOTHER SATZ
BROTHER SATZ (NED)
MRS. LOOP
WARDEN
BUFORD
SUGFORD

Futz was first presented (for one performance) at the Tyrone Guthrie Workshop, Minneapolis, on October 10, 1965. The play was first presented in New York City by Ellen Stewart on March 1, 1967, at the La MaMa Experimental Theatre Club, with the following cast of the La MaMa Troupe:

NARRATOR	Beverly Atkinson
CYRUS FUTZ	John Bakos
MAJORIE SATZ	Beth Porter
OSCAR LOOP	Seth Allen
BILL MARJORAM	Michael Warren Powell
ANN FOX	Mari-Claire Charba
SHERIFF TOM SLUCK	Peter Craig
FATHER SATZ	Robert Thirkield
MOTHER SATZ	Mari-Claire Charba
BROTHER SATZ (NED)	Victor LiPari
MRS. LOOP	Marilyn Roberts
BUFORD	Peter Craig
SUGFORD	Michael Warren Powell

The music and direction by Tom O'Horgan, set by Saito, lighting by Laura Rambaldi, technical assistant Howard Vishinsky.

FUTZ

SCENE ONE

NARRATOR. Let's give it a strange passion to a story, some handyman handy in the barns with animals—"someone to watch over him"—somethings, the udders of the moo-moo especially. No stupid pretty girl to rely on him, like a homemade stunt between his feet, to knock up his knees—bad onions—spoiling him eternally.

Small fetid room, obvious barnlike but still a small room with lots of oily automobile rags and other signs of the terrible city existence, brewed still more stinky with the worst the country has to offer: dead grassy worms; horseshit; small portions of a moldy outhouse; summer brooms; women's drawers; rubber suits for working in the water; etcetera. Anything you can think up naturally. Cy Futz, a Scandinavian sort of big fellow, wearing new dungarees, bell bottom—they could be overalls—comes in filled with a sexual dream; it does not bear in the least to anything real in terms of yours or Cy's world. It's pure sickness but in its pureness it's a truth. Sitting down on a wet broken step he says:

CY. O the cow's tits are bigger and I know it's wrong, but young uns never know the difference between an animal's or a woman's hipbones, so soft like my socks, freshwashed like new kids' hoofs. O I could sing. OOOOOoooOOO-OOooooooOOOO LooLoooooooooLoooooooo Looy [*Loud.*] Looy loy Lord Lord I love you God. [*Normal voice.*] And I have no hate for anybody, but wanting to love the animals the way I do. *They*, mean folks, hate my face. I turn around the corners and make fun on their asses, no tickle does theirs feel like my own good one as I sing tears in the sow's belly. With their fried eggs for wives, they know no song.

NARRATOR. Again he sings his ooos and looooos intermingled with a belch and a mock fart and ending with three very loud "Lords." All the time he's buttering his wrists with his red hands, making bird and other noises, he is very excited and seems absolutely certain to explode all his love or whatever over the world which is the room where he is in now. Now she comes in, Miss Majorie Satz, about twenty-seven years old, tall with a square, worldly, insulted once maybe, body. Her coarse red hair is combed up in a sophisticated way which is sweetly silly in retrospect to her food-stained gingham, typical farm girl get-up.

MAJORIE. Hello, bastady man. Yus big man-bloke, I missed you at the greengrocer, yus said that you would come, yus said so, and I painted my big toe too for yu. [*Giggling.*] Yu man-bloke, old Swede man.

NARRATOR. Cyrus is looking at her and is vexed at her, probably Cy was always squinnied by her, probably because she obviously is a woman in the very dreamy sensual way which he only wants his animals to be. Gentle sick man he is. He hoots at her.

CY. Hallas, Majy, ya French dancer! You woman of ten beds and manure heaps, yus stinking human woman with only cat mouths for tits and a baby paw for your arse. I did not want to see you; you told me a foul story the last time that I saw you. Not again, mind you, do I want that shit! Always you are pretending to be my friend and better yet a hole for me to dive in, but I'd rather sink my pick in turd, cleaner, my Lord, more than you, Maj!

NARRATOR. Majorie moves backwards and starts to hum the French anthem.

MAJORIE. I'll pick up my skirt right now if yu want, I'll get on my heels and elbows, old farmer, yus not so old yu know, only forty, there are whut's younger men than yu who'd like to take me to a movie, strongir and slimmir than yu, so why make me hurt your chest—an' don't I buy you fodder for your sick love, Amanda the sow, so she could be a better one for yu? Even I know, who likes yu, how bad it is to sleep with a pig! Unnatural, like in the Bible, it's piggish—that's where the word comes from yuo know piggish—from a pig yugh yugh sooo evil. Yu smell so baad it is no joke——

CY. Go forget about it and your cheeks won't be nervous—
put your nose out of my business, disgusting girl. I like
Amanda because she's good. Pig or not. And I don't stink
that's your lie—any much more than you or the boys
that take you in the fields.

MAJORIE [*hatefully*]. That's your awn dirtty story 'nd it
makes me nasty towards yu—I can't feel bad for your
dread and doom—yu sleep with the unimals bitter bitter unholy unholy.

NARRATOR. Cy pushes her from behind, then stoops and
picks up a dirty broom, begins to sweep her flanks with
a mock lust, also singing a very low song in a Celtic
tune. She covers her ears and shrieks.

MAJORIE [*shrieking*]. Yeeeiiiiiey oyu big man-bloke!

NARRATOR. He snaps her rope belt with his left hand and
slaps her face—not hard—with the right. He pushes her
ahead of him and they both go behind the half-rotten
wall which was once an old outhouse.

Animal grunts sound and lights are dimmed.

SCENE TWO

NARRATOR. Look at the old rotten wall—behind it, here
are Cyrus and Maj and yugch! a sow. Amanda! The
animal that's sure to steal forever Cy's heart never to
marry yus, her, Maj, sweet flower, woman with a wholesome grin, and no hair on the chin, sallow woman with
a cantaloupe seed in her belly and toes that are canary
yellow. Ooopph.

NARRATOR *shapes his hands into a cup form and feeds the
sounds of grunts and human voice to the audience.*

MAJORIE. Pechhh *so* indecent, I'd live in shame if the village ever knew what I'd done.

CY. Fahhh my woman the people need never know what
you done, anyways they would want the full freedom to

be able to do what you done. Girl, peachy sweet currant stop being afraid, even the sow won't tell!

NARRATOR. Maj tears, she's sore afraid.

MAJORIE. Yu make it wus tan it is mentionin' the pig— she does not know anyting about it, and she did not feel soft like you said but like an old razor on my feet. O O O *so indecent I am,* and now the filty dreams'll come. O Gods help meee that we shoulda both laid with a sow.

NARRATOR. Maj carries about awhile with hands scratching out her Lord from the sky, pushing him into her soul, trying to wring his sweat from the skinny body, trying hard hard to have his water wash the dinny sin from her wretched body. Lust for animals is like a run in spring rain, sniggle. Lewd lewd, foosh foosh, and she calls on all the idols and the true God to make the slop go away.

CY. Now fish stop, stop fish, nobody knows and the pig won't tell.

MAJORIE [*loud*]. Stop stop stop! Yus mean rat, your modern sin has killed me!

CY. Isn't no modern sin, old as your Bible, lay down with a calf somebody did and did get no punishment from God, like your village will give you, Cluck, if you don't stop your sirens blowing. Shit your mouth up, Majorie, you're makin' me sound funny in my own ears and I have faith for my love of the animals with hoofs and corncob appitite, can't you really see—it is no wrong. They laugh more real than the mayor and your mother. *Brooey* to the devil for the bad conscience you feel, say *phat phat* to it. It don't pay.

MAJORIE. Your diggnitty is like sloppy ole shoes, but good luck to me, soon as I get away from evil—never again. Os os never agin piggying myself like that.

NARRATOR. She gets up from the bed of wet paper and rags, smoothing her clothes and wrapping her hair in her fists. Cy watches her with pickles in his eyes. He spies the pig and on the knees and hands jerks towards her, sticking his fingers out like stone worms, his tongue lolls like mice in his mouth, he sticks his leg out banging his shoe on the pig's ass (not cruelly though) just enough to make the animal turn and be conscious of him, for in that white flesh no blood brain she remembers pleasure. And she backs towards him you know and he grabs her body. Maj is watching with bloody senses, then tears out shrieking.

SCENE THREE

NARRATOR. In an old-fashioned prison cell with the traditional water-pot, hammock, etcetera, two men are talking O everything is the same with these two as with a hundred other yolts, the jailbird Oscar Loop is skinny and wears the prison suit like he was a fallen priest, the other man is Bill Marjoram, squat, strong, sweaty, and typical in workclothes, fat shoes, etcetera, how can well I go describing on?

LOOP. O breakfast is not much, I mean breakfast is not much, two pieces of bread, glass of water, and a sausage, not real you know, something to think about anyway, sometimes I think like a motherless child, I mean take the tiny spices out of the sausage and grow them like small insects, I mean if they get watered and sun on them they might get life and then they'd be like insects.

MARJORAM [loud]. Shut up, Loop! Stupid, talking 'bout insex and maybe hanging tomorra! Your riddles too! Make me sick.

LOOP. Listen, they would be spice-insects, so you could eat them—they would even be medicinal, cure a palsy helpfully, jerk a dead newborn back to life. O I hope it would do all those things.

MARJORAM. *Shut up, Loop*, I said! Stupid. Don't you know you gonna die?

LOOP. I mean a dead newborn could have been Mozart— I care in a great many ways for life, that's why the good sausage seed-spice might work—[*He whispers.*]—without the evil eye, I bet Siva would help me, Siva is beautiful with her lovely hands, she's picked the mosquitoes out of my head. I've read greatly about her.

MARJORAM. You keep blabbing on 'nd on 'bout things that don't stop you from dying!

LOOP. How do you know? What makes you be so sure? Anything cun help a man maybe, a rock hit a devil in the Bibledays and a devil sucked out the blood of the thrower of that rock in hell. Somebody made that devil draw out all the blood in the man. Hmmmmmmmmmmmmmmmm I'll have to write that on the sausage. Mustn't forgit all the marverlous thoughts I git lately.

MARJORAM. Mavilous thoughts my foot! Swear you're gonna hang on Monday. Man, think, Loop! Think! Whut did you do?

LOOP. Whut did I do? Flah! A woman saw me, she bought me a mitten, tole me to put it on, said that the feeling would come through better. She looked like Mary in a story, but not the Lord's mother you know. No she looked like the whore. But then like *Him* I changed her.

MARJORAM. Whut do you mean changed her! Speak it up truthfully. You killed her!

LOOP. I made her fall asleep on the ground. Put a bad blueberry in her mouth, Satan was a grub, and when he got inside of her he ate her innards out but that was God's wish.

NARRATOR. Loop is smiling like a good king.

MARJORAM. How did she die? And if it's too bad a story, you bitter not tell it in your crazy way. Tell me how you killed the girl, nobody dies with fruit-bugs, tell it sound and real.

NARRATOR. Now there are keys and chains sounds, the prison-keeper comes in and Loop, eyes frightened, begins to stretch. He is afraid that he has been heard.

Everybody cringes.

LOOP. I mean to say that what I tole Bill wasn't all so. [*He points to the* GUARD *and ropes his arm toward him-*

self.] You come here, guard, O I'm gonna tell you how I killed the girl, but in the beginning. Hoos! In the beginning was purity, and cleanliness was a big garter-belt.

NARRATOR. The keeper is sniffing in his giggles, feeling his bone, trying to see garter-belts.

GUARD. Tell us what happened and maybe you can get a reprieve, hhah ha ha ha hiss— Did you put the garter-belt round her small throat?

LOOP. I met Ann Fox in the greengrocers. I saw her skirt swing frisky, and I knew that her father was a good farmer and Baptist. I knew that everybody in the village liked that family. And no young fella would treat her disrespectfully. I could not just get married to a girl, without her being like Ann, I knew that I wouldn't get married and be normal—so I asked her out, and she went with me, she said she liked the smell of leather. You know I have a good leather belt and jacket that a handcrafts woman sent me. Well, Ann liked that jacket, she said she'd take it from me when I was asleep. Sometimes I think she meant it too. Her father was a rich man, he could buy her all the leather clothes she wanted but she'd say she wanted my jacket too. Well, I'd get mad thinking about it, though I knew too that she was playing. But I took her one night near the field where Cy Futz's barn is and we horseplayed a little bit, nothing but some hunky-punk.

SCENE FOUR

NARRATOR. A small dark field, nighttime, a blanket on the grass, a leather jacket spread perfectly out. Oscar Loop and Ann Fox are sitting opposite each other cross-legged.

LOOP. Little good cat, ooph, you knock my eyes out of my head, you're so pretty.

NARRATOR. He sticks out his forefinger and strokes her nose.

ANN. Buford Skark says I'm pretty too—too bad to mention another fella? You both think the same, that I'm pretty.

NARRATOR. Loop hops on his knees hooping himself towards her. If it's possible lights should shine green on top of his hair.

LOOP. Little rat, stop thinkin' of other men! Dogs'll crawl up your back if you do.

NARRATOR. He puts his hands on her hips and she falls at him laughing. They both move at each other like beachballs. Her foot catches in the jacket and he pushes at her ankle with two hands. She meanly slams her shoe into the precious leather.

LOOP. Crazy rich girl, cut that out!

ANN. Hang it!

LOOP. Whut d'yu mean, "Hang it!" Have respect for a man's garment. I wear that on Sunday!

ANN. On Sunday the people laugh at you too just like on Monday. OOOOBles you're serious, so, so serious. Why'nt you kiss me? I'm a girl.

LOOP. I—I—I will kiss you—I would like to learn to dance, so that I can go with you to fancy places.

NARRATOR. She moves her hip closer to his and takes his hand laying it on her stomach. He grabs her mightily and they kiss.

ANN. I hear something, is it my head? There are crazy bees inside of it, you kiss crazy. [*There are sounds, animal sounds, like an animal in heat.*] Listen—I hear grunts! And I think someone cussing. Don't it sound strange?

LOOP. Yus, I hear them too. Don't know why somebody should beat their animals. Terrible to do that—I would never do that.

NARRATOR. Loop and Ann move very close to where the noises come from. Futz's barn. The barn is not seen though. The noise is a human and animal one. And both people are dumfounded at what in all heaven's holy name is happening. Something equally weird is happening to Loop, he looks insane. He pushes himself at Ann and starts to pummel her, his voice is croaky.

LOOP. Gonna rid the place of evil, gonna make you sleep a long time till your soul becomes clean.

ANN [*loud*]. Stop it stop it! Let me be! [*She screams.*]

NARRATOR. She tries to get away but he drags her around in a small circle.

LOOP. Gonna bury you in that evil dress, stink will in a hundred years be covered up by the sweet grass, hell isn't as bad as a whoring girl. May your father and mother not mourn you too long.

NARRATOR. Ann cries in soulful anguish. Loop drags her off. He comes back in terribly bloody clothes and sits cross-legged in the moony night. The animal sounds are louder but he shows no life, just sits with his arms folded and the hands covering his eyes. Then he slowly takes off his shoes and with a monkey's grace raises his feet to his nose and whiffs deeply.

SCENE FIVE

NARRATOR. Cy Futz's barn again just like in the beginning. Cy is sitting with his kneebones high like the two hemispheres. The pig Amanda is sleeping on her side.

CY. *Flahfy Amanda ya faymale!* Four ugly legs you got, Zeus, wot hams. Lucky luck that I'm in love with you otherwise you'd be hanging in my pantry. Heeeehhhhehehehe when you're old you'll be sitting in my granny's rockin' chair readin' the Bible. Amanda, you are of the world, known two kinds of male animals, pig and man! Sow, I know you love me but I wonder whether you'd rather be with your own kind? Piglets I can't give you you know though I am a healthy man.

NARRATOR. Cy licks his hands passionately and praises God for making him a husbandman. Silent is his worship but the world enters his barn now. Bill Marjoram and the Sheriff Tom Sluck, slowly they go up to him. Futz yawns one eye open.

MARJORAM. There's the creep!

SLUCK. Y'all be quiet now.

MARJORAM. Quiet in hell, the biggest sinner in the world is here. If we weren't fair he'd be dead now by our own hands.

CY. I'd break them off like they were rabbits' necks.

SLUCK. Nothing is really proven yet. There will be justice.

MARJORAM. Men can make men insane!

SLUCK. Nothing is really proven yet.

MARJORAM. He drove a fella whacky!

CY. Fitz on you both, boys! I know no man well enough to make him nuts. Tell me who's crazy?

SLUCK. A man's in jail now for murdering a girl he killed because he saw something very evil.

CY. Very sad thing. But there's lotsa evil here in the world.

MARJORAM. You're the satan here in our village!

CY. I'm not anybody's keeper. I'm never near anybody. Except when they come here to see me. I just work on my little plot of land raisin' vegetables for me and my pig. What sort of evil could I have done?

NARRATOR. Cy plays a tom-tom with his feet, and salutes the sun. This is done subtly, the men not being aware of the ritual. Lord, these two are blind.

SLUCK. The man who murdered an innocent girl says he did it because he was under an influence, a spell he says, because he's a simple man. Now, Mr. Futz, I'm going to be blunt. People say here that you are an unnatural man.

CY. Am I?

SLUCK. Well, aren't you?

MARJORAM. Gods, he bangs pigs!

CY. I never do. Why my mother didn't bring me up like that. I'm a Bible-man.

SLUCK. If you're not serious you better become it. Very many people talk about your way.

CY. They're all wrong, Mr. Sluck. An animal is something to care about, not to committeth a sin with. Soos!

MARJORAM. See what he says! Soos!

SLUCK. Soos! Soos! What does it mean?

MARJORAM. It means he be guilty and pulling our feet.

CY. Why why I never would go with an animal! I'm a village man and the sun is good on me, why I say that fellow has a devil in his head. [*He points at* MARJORAM.]

MARJORAM. Devils, you bastud!

NARRATOR. He lunges at Cy and throws him down, he should not have done that though because Futz is quick and kicks his legs out, cracking Marjoram's guts hard. The sheriff fires his pistol a warning shot into the air. Both men relax like drugged sheep.

SLUCK. There will be a trial for the man who killed the girl and he'll probably hang! The day will be Monday!

CY. I do wish they, folks, wouldn't be mean toward each other.

MARJORAM. Mean! He talks about not bein' mean! Whut about Majorie Satz? She's wretched. She's become a bigger tart than she was. She's yapping always about what he did with her and the pig with him, at the same time too he was with her. Crazy evil! Heaven help us working people with Lucifer here in our village!

NARRATOR. Futz is laughing hard.

SLUCK. What are you laughing for? It ain't funny when a man's going to die.

CY. I'm not killing. I'm not a judge or lawyer, just a farmer who lives poorly mindin' his own business.

MARJORAM. Well my word! You live here in the town with us. Where's your duty and responsibility?

CY. In my hands. I use them only on my land and in my barn.

SLUCK. I'm gonna tell you that I hate you myself. It isn't right that I as a lawman feel that way. The Constitution says that there should be fairness. But you ruined women and animals, and a man's going to die because of you. Futz, I'm gonna do something that my sweet guts don't want. I'm gonna lock you up in the prison because the people might come here, my choppers say yes to your head under their feet, taking good revenge. But I'm gonna lock you up. You'll be safe.

CY. Who'll feed my pig and water my vegetables?

SLUCK. That's not our thought to care about your land and animals. My duty's gonna be lockin' you up in a cell.

MARJORAM. I think he needs death, not just bein' locked up. Futz has done so much harm.

SLUCK. He'll be locked up.

NARRATOR. Futz throws up his arms as though ready to receive lightning sticks from his friend God and crash them down on the heads of his judgers who want to see him minus, with nothing, no bliss.

CY. I'm a helpless man now, a partridge run after by turkeys!

MARJORAM. Bastud! Lecherous bastud! You'll get yours for spoilin' our lives!

SLUCK. I'll be easier when you pay up your debt to us. You've done a wrong, man.

NARRATOR. Futz, in the middle, walks out with the men, maybe sad jazz could be played now, not too much though.

SCENE SIX

NARRATOR. Majorie Satz—it's another day—is in the field with two men, father and brother. Father is father and brother is brother. The first is simple. The second is complex.

FATHER. I don't know what about anything but Futz should hang though.

BROTHER. Like Loop, Dad. And the corpses hosswhipped.

NARRATOR. Majorie is quiet with her arms hard against her body. She's listening like water.

FATHER. My dotter Majie is a good girl. Frisky like her reverent mother. [*The old man slaps her face.*]

MAJORIE. Git away from me, ya old creep. Nothing was my fault!

BROTHER. Dad cut it out! Nothin' is the girl's fault. She's just crazy.

FATHER. She is crazy! Should be put away!

MAJORIE. Can't be solved this way, nothing can, important thing is that I get revenged.

BROTHER. Nobody gonna revenge you! Nobody really cares that much.

FATHER. I care. Who's gonna marry this tramp if somehow we don't save her honor. Nobody'll git the bitch off my neck if Futz is allowed to get away with what he done. She's gotta get married off or I'll have her around our shack forever.

NARRATOR. The old man is sick by this fact of life.

FATHER. She's just got to be made respectable.

BROTHER. Don't Bill Marjoram want to marry her? I get the idea he'd be willing to have the ole slot machine.

MAJORIE. Shet up, ya bastud. Don't call me names.

FATHER. Control that trap! It's a wonder you haven't been killed yet being whut you are. Majorie, you're a poisonous snake. And if I didn't have to live in this village I'd kill you myself. Your daddy or not—[*Loud.*]— I hate you!

NARRATOR. Does Satz mean it? I don't know.

BROTHER. The both of you really get me! Spoiling with fight when we got to think of something. Something where we can get Futz. I mean he should be killed! Loop is gonna be killed and Futz should also.

NARRATOR. Brother does not have much feeling when he says this. Does he have a reason for Futz's death? Yes. His sister's honor? No. Well——

FATHER. I don't want a ruckus and yet there's gotta be something to happen.

MAJORIE. What he does with animals is dirty.

BROTHER. HAHAHaaaahshhhhhushy yeah yeah.

FATHER. Craziest thing I ever heard of.

BROTHER. Maybe it's good?

MAJORIE. OOOOOOOOOOOOooooooooohhhh I'm sick!

FATHER. Stop your yellin', tramp. You've muddied yaself with every bloke in the village.

MAJORIE. So I have. But it's with men!

FATHER. Quit up your braggin'. Slut!

BROTHER. She sure is. [*He hunches over with jackal laughter.*]

SCENE SEVEN

NARRATOR. Oscar Loop is in his cell, his mother is there. She looks like Loop, smaller of course, and wearing old things. It's the day of her boy's death.

MRS. LOOP. Oscar, sweet good boy. I didn't do nothing but —but good for you I thought. I told you 'bout God when you were small and polished up your shoes for you when you went to school. I did my best for you, my son. [*She weeps.*]

LOOP. Mama, I know you did, Mama, I know you did. But let's make some plans for the wonderful things that I have. [*He takes from his pocket tiny specks of something.*] Mama, these are holy bits of something good. They can cause miracles. Make people that are sick well. You know. They can even make a dead thing come alive again.

MRS. LOOP. Let me hold some in my hand, maybe it'll cure my arthritis. What are they, my son?

LOOP. I call them spice-seed insects, they're alive.

NARRATOR. Mother flings her arms to the north and south, letting the insects fly. She squelches a shriek letting something dawn on her. Her son's dream.

MRS. LOOP. O Son, I'm sorry. But those wonderful seeds are potent, they cured my arthritis so quickly, my hands tingle!

LOOP. I knew it would work. I'm so happy! Take care of them I only have a handful. Mother, use them wisely, don't give them to no pretty women, only old people and dead things. It's a gift from Siva.

MRS. LOOP. Siva? Who is Siva?

LOOP. A holy thing with lots of arms. She couldn't die with her lots of arms, even if ten brutes tried to do her in. Siva lives and lives.

MRS. LOOP. Siva sounds like she's a good Christian woman. None around here like her. My son hates evil so he justly killed it. Oh Son, oh Son, that you should be killed by the villagers is fair though you're my precious blood, it's right. And that you should have killed an evil girl, is right too. No! Nobody—no woman is good, all want one thing from a man, his lust-stick!

LOOP. Mother mother mother—[*He is weeping sickly.*]— mother mother mother, why couldn't I find you? Why couldn't I ha' been my own father.

MRS. LOOP. Stop it, my son—[*She is slightly smiling.*]— that is not a thing to say, but we two are godly and there shall be rest for us both. A son and his mother are godly.

LOOP. A-son-and-his-mother-are-godly. Everything you say is beautiful. Mother, you are like the Holy Virgin.

MRS. LOOP. That is blasphemy, Son. Never say that. Look! Look! Look at me, my boy, watch me. Don't talk— just look at me. See my eyes and nose and lips? Remember my face good so that you see it on the inside of the black hood— Oooo I shouldn't say that but it's all so important to me, that when after—when you are dead they'll come to be with me and grieve. But if they don't? I couldn't stand it, I must feel them all around me, they must be a loving family—all around me, they must feel so sorry for me—because I am a mother with no son.

Loop. Nothin' nothin' nothin'. . . .

Mrs. Loop. Whut?

Loop. I'm gonna be nothin'—[*He rubs his feet on the floor.*]—nothin'—so? Mother, who's gonna be with you? The folks you like?

Mrs. Loop. Yes. But they've made my life very hard. I need them though. You wouldn't know, being a man. You're my son and if you were a minister I couldn't be more proud. I'm saying everything now. I remember when you got tattooed. You said it was manly. I wasn't more proud. [*She opens her raggy bag and lifts out a square package.*] I remember when Howard bopped me. Take some fruitcake, Son. Your father was jealous of me, you wouldn't dream that I was a good-looking girl to look at me now, but I was, and Howard was very jealous of me. You look like me you know, when I was young. And he would say he'd kill me too you know, even before you were born when you was just the fruit of my womb. I'm an old woman now and have not one bit a thing. When I was young I coulda had a lot, cause of my looks. I didn't want anything, just to be happy.

Loop. Mom—wouldn't it be wonderful if I could make myself invisible? Then I could go away. They couldn't find me. You and me would finally be let alone.

Mrs. Loop. Yes, it would be wonaful. [*She's almost in a trance.*] Oscar, I forgive you for wanting me to die.

Loop. Mama, I never meant that really.

Mrs. Loop. I know you didn't. I'm sorry I said that.

Loop. You couldn't die anyway, 'cause I've given you the spice-insects.

NARRATOR. They look at each other as if he's a tot learning to walk. Noise is heard, it's time for Loop to die. When he's dead he won't see anymore.

WARDEN. Hello, Mrs. Loop and Oscar. Mrs. Loop, go to my cousin Hattie, she's outside waiting to take you home with her. Oscar, you come with me to the middle of town. Right?

LOOP. Right, yes yes, right. I'm bad. But I'm gonna keep my feet together when I swing like a soldier.

MRS. LOOP. He's gonna look like a minister high on the pulpit above the congregation. I'm going to dress respectably!

SCENE EIGHT

NARRATOR. Majorie in a whorey mood, walking with two drunken blokes in the field.

MAJORIE. Runnin' bastad. Futz's so scared now.

SUGFORD. Aaaaa harrrr that's good.

BUFORD. Pooos. Scared yella. Uuuuuuuuuuuuch my stomach hurts.

MAJORIE. You have your stomach—Cy's not gonna have his.

SUGFORD. Yeah yeah.

BUFORD. Gal, that was a *creazzy* thing to do with you. I wouldn't ha' done that. I'm bagged.

SUGFORD. You bagged? I'm alive.

MAJORIE. I'm alive too.

NARRATOR. She sits on the grass, the two get down on her sides.

MAJORIE. I'm wanting excitement.

SUGFORD. Maybe you need to get banged.

BUFORD. Me too.

MAJORIE [*laughing high*]. What for?

BUFORD. Wha' ya mean wha' for? For fun.

NARRATOR. He picks up a stone and throws it at her. She catches it and starts playing with it, hands cupping it like it's a baby chick.

MAJORIE. Let's go nuts, us three, then clean up somehow.

SCENE NINE

NARRATOR. A little time later.

MAJORIE. Noooooot enough noooot enough!

SUGFORD. We gotta fix it good.

BUFORD. Gal you're a pig!

SUGFORD. Yeah she's a pig. We should chop her up with the other one.

MAJORIE. It's too late and I'd be dreary eating. I'm revengeful. Look I know where it is! His sow. Let's kill her. Let's kill his pig!

BUFORD. So what for? So? Fat pig wants to kill a pig.

SUGFORD. Wouldn't that be like killing yu sister?

MAJORIE. Both of you are like mice! Just wanting——

BUFORD. Git off it.

SUGFORD. Girly, git off it. You're just askin' for it.

BUFORD. You don't know how you could end up.

MAJORIE. *You don' have to do nothin'.* I'll just do it.

SUGFORD. Why?

MAJORIE. Because I want to.

SUGFORD. Buf?

BUFORD. Okay.

SCENE TEN

NARRATOR. Everything is the same.

SUGFORD. Who wants it?

MAJORIE. She's a dirty dirty thing.

SUGFORD. I'm getting away from totty. You don' want to stay here anymore, do you?

BUFORD. No. Let's just gooooo.

BUFORD *and* SUGFORD *run off.*

MAJORIE. Come back, ya chicken bastads!

NARRATOR. Hell hath no fury like a woman scorned by a man—for a pig.

SCENE ELEVEN

NARRATOR. In the prison cell Futz sits very hard. He's blowing out his cheeks and binding his nostrils close to the bone.

CY. Huh-uuh-huh-hh-uuh— Oooooook huuhhhhoooookii-ooook huuuuuh—uuuuhuh—huuuuoook oooK *Amaaaa-anddddaaaaa I miss you soooooo. My Molly Amaaaa-andaaaaa I miiiiiiiissssss youuuuuuu.* Tain't faih, my faymale. You were good to me 'nd I was sooo good to you. You ate corn 'nd sleep beside me. We tried to go to church but they wouldn't let us in so I'd read you the Bible at home. *My mother was a good Protistin,* she'd love you too. *Mother, get back in your grave you're stinkin' up the green world!*

WARDEN *comes in.*

WARDEN. Behave yourself. Isn't there any decency in you? Dishonorin' your parent's memory screaming out blasphemies in prison.

CY [*loud*]. Warden, you look like a bad drawing of God!

WARDEN. Futz, I should let the folks take you. I should hand you over to them. They'd teach your dead body manners.

CY [loud]. You want a war!

WARDEN. I want you legally killed.

CY. You don't have to fear I'll rape your mother, she's too old. Or your daughter she's got your bad teeth. [Loud.] Warden, why don't you kill your wife and kids? You know that you're unhappy.

WARDEN. I'm a normal man, Futz. It's you that's unhappy. And you've caused treachery.

CY. I wasn't near people. They came to me and looked under my trousers all the way up to their dirty hearts. They minded my own life. O you're making me be so serious. And I'm only serious with my wife!

WARDEN. Your what?

CY [loud]. My wife my wife! And how many tits does your wife have? Mine has twelve!

WARDEN. You're ranting, animal.

CY. If I was wi' her I'd be grunting.

SCENE TWELVE

NARRATOR. It's Satz's place. Dirty. The old man, son, and mother are there.

MOTHER. Majorie's such a bitch.

FATHER. It must ov been the bug's fault when she was born.

MOTHER. What d'ye mean?

FATHER. I saw a bug on your stomach when she yipped.

MOTHER. I was clean when the child was born.

FATHER. Clean as a swamp.

MOTHER [loud]. Swamp! Swamp! No. It was pure water that they had on me.

FATHER [*loud*]. Pig piss it was. Why, Woman, you're still slying and lying.

MOTHER. I'm not gon' to say the story anymore.

FATHER. Look. Look. The girl is not mine. Not my dotter.

MOTHER [*loud*]. She is she is she is.

FATHER [*loud*]. She is my dotter? Then why did the bugs sit on your knees crying prayers to heaven?

MOTHER [*loud*]. It didna happen.

FATHER [*loud*]. It could ov been you with the pig and him —like it was her.

MOTHER. I'll call my son. [*Screaming.*] Ned! Ned!

BROTHER *comes in.*

FATHER [*loud*]. Ned Ned—be dead!

MOTHER [*loud*]. Hear him!

FATHER. Everythin's made her nervous, Ned. She's mad again.

BROTHER. Don' be mad. Majorie'll get her honor back again. I'm goin' to kill Futz.

FATHER. Don't do it alone, take someone with you.

BROTHER. I want to do it myself.

MOTHER [*crying*]. But wash with pure water, don' leave the blood.

FATHER. He could leave the blood. There's no disgrace in fightin' for his sister.

BROTHER. *Hah*uuuhahahashus hahhas hohaaahh— Mother, don't fret I won' leave the blood.

MOTHER. Before you go will you have somethin' to eat?

SCENE THIRTEEN

NARRATOR. He's in the prison with Cy. Ned.

CY. Boy boy boy. You want to kill me. Why?

BROTHER. My family.

CY. I've got none just a sow.

BROTHER. You make my brains red.

CY. I'll tell you peace.

BROTHER. *Shut up shut up!* I don't want to *know you!*

CY. You don't have to know me—just let *me be.*

BROTHER [*in cold fury*]. Your neck should be boiled!

CY. That's what I don't want to happen to my sow.

BROTHER. She'll die too.

CY. Now why, Ned, why do you want to kill the animal?

BROTHER [*seething*]. You make my brains red!

He stabs CY.

NARRATOR [*ironical*]. Amanda—there's someone here he needs you. Yes.

End.

UNTIL THE MONKEY COMES

A *Play in Two Acts*

by

VENABLE HERNDON

For Lawrence Wunderlich

CHARACTERS

CASSY. *In college. Tall with a hollow-cheeked, high-fashion face.*

SONNY. *In college. Shorter than Cassy, with a Chaplin-imitating-Hitler mustache.*

JACK. *In the last year of prep school. British-aping son of an art-and-auction gallery owner.*

LUKE. *Just out of college. Irish-tinted son of a well-known radio couple.*

BILLIE MAE. *Works as a secretary. Daughter of a Harlem preacher.*

PHILIP. *In college. Son of a lady New Yorker writer.*

SCENE: New York City. Living room (with a spectacular view of the East River) in the Sutton Point South, an apartment house built over the East River Drive at the very edge of the water. Two massive couches, back to back, dominate the room. One faces the great window over the river. Other important objects: a bar, several hippopotamus-sized lounge chairs, a big stereo set, a small TV, a medium-sized bright-balled Christmas tree, and a large animal cage (with vertical bars) on casters. The cage has been rolled against a rear wall to become an unobtrusive part of the furniture. Its top may even be covered with plants and books. The total effect of the room is that of wealthy clutter. Door right leads to the kitchen. Door left leads to the bedrooms. Door down left leads to the entrance hall.

TIME: The last day of the year.

———

Until the Monkey Comes was first presented on June 20, 1966, at the Martinique Theatre by Slade Brown and the Mannhardt Theatre Foundation, Inc., by arrangement with David Black. The cast was as follows:

CASSY	Susan Tyrrell
SONNY	Philip Carlson
JACK	Don Amendolia
LUKE	Russell Drisch
BILLIE MAE	Norma Donaldson
PHILIP	Gordon Addison

The play was directed by Robert Haddad and designed by Bil Mikulewicz.

UNTIL THE MONKEY COMES

ACT ONE

Late afternoon. Light behind closed curtains. CASSY, *under a zebra skin, is asleep on the couch that faces the audience.* SONNY, *invisible to the audience, is asleep on the couch that faces the window.*

CASSY [*waking, languid, exhausted*]. Sonny? [*No answer.*] Sonny! [*Pulls zebra skin.*] Son-n-n-n-n-n-nceeeee! *Sonny!*

SONNY [*long yawn*]. Not now, Julie! ʼ

CASSY. Sonny?

SONNY. I said, "Not now, Mary!"

CASSY. Hey!

SONNY. What?

CASSY. Can I have some new names? I'm sick of Julie and Mary all the time.

SONNY. Not until I decide, Julie! Not until it pleases me, Mary! [CASSY *lights cigarette without sitting up.*] How can you? Before breaking fast, ugh! [CASSY *inhales deeply.*]

CASSY. That's a notion.

SONNY. Huh?

CASSY. A dumb notion.

SONNY. What? What's a dumb notion?

CASSY [*exasperated*]. That you shouldn't smoke before breakfast.

SONNY. Birdie smokes five fat black Frenchies before she ever puts claw one out of the rack.

CASSY. What?

SONNY. Not what? A bed, Julie. A bunk, Mary. A cot, Julie. A sack, Mary. You're just not with it, are you? A rack is a bed, is a bunk, is a cot, is a sack, Rose.

CASSY. A new name. Rose. That's nice! Well I never thought I'd like that one. In grade school I knew this girl . . . her name was Rose . . . she slobbered.

27

SONNY. I am very tired of your childhood, Mary.

CASSY. I am very tired of your Birdie, Sonny. I do not at all enjoy thinking about her or about how many fat black Frenchies she lights up before she puts moldy toe one out of the sack.

SONNY. Rack, Rose. Rack!

CASSY. And I should sometimes enjoy something, don't you think?

SONNY. I am depressed to hear that you do not enjoy thinking about the beautiful, blue-feathered birdie who egged me out into this cluck-cluck world, lo, those nineteen years ago.

CASSY. Cheep-cheep! Cheep-cheep!

SONNY [annoyed]. No, Rose, no! Cheep-chirp! Cheep-chirp! Now let's hear it loud and clear from the top, Rose!

CASSY. I cheep-cheep . . . do not . . . chirp-chirp . . . have any cheep-cheep, chirp-chirp reason to discuss Birdie with you at this or any other time. We have discussed her enough forever!

SONNY. You're really asking for it, Julie. Tonight is your night, Mary. You're going to spend it a-lone. New Year's Eve is very lonely a-lone. The loneliest night of the year a-lone! In a lonely hotel room.

CASSY. You wouldn't dare.

SONNY. Oh, and why wouldn't I dare, pig person.

CASSY. Because, Adolph, you wouldn't be anywhere without all these pretty blond people to shout at.

SONNY [shouts]. Silence!

CASSY. Exactly.

SONNY. Now for a few wake-up hymns. Ready, set, sing! [Sugary singsong.] When the wind blows . . . [Waits for CASSY to join him; she doesn't.] When the wind blows, Rose! [Violent.] Rose!!

CASSY [pathetic]. Aw, come on, you know my name is Cassy. You used to call me Cassy.

SONNY [ominous]. The cradle will fall . . .

CASSY [*singsong*]. And down will come Sonny, cradle and all.

SONNY. Oh that's good, Rose. Let's try another one. [*Chant.*] Bye Baby Bunting . . .

CASSY [*resigned*]. Bye Baby Bunt— Uh . . . this one always makes me sad.

SONNY. Daddy went a-hunting . . .

CASSY. *Cruel* Daddy went a-hunting . . .

SONNY. Rose! To get a 'ittle wabbit skin . . .

CASSY [*refusing to use baby talk*]. To get a little rabbit skin.

SONNY. No, Rose! Say exactly as I say: To get a 'ittle wabbit skin . . .

CASSY. To get a 'ittle wabbit skin . . .

SONNY. To wap his—*Rose!* To wap his—???

CASSY. To wap his Sonny Bunting in. . . . [*Plaintive, painful, trying for contact.*] Good morning, Sonny. [*No response.*] Good morning?

SONNY [*suddenly allowing contact, lazy, coy, loving*]. Oh, not so sure it's so good. It's afternoon. Late afternoon.

CASSY [*luxurious yawn*]. Yep. Maybe it is. It's got to be gooder than yesterday, than last night. [*Stretches.*] Oh, boy! Kiddies shouldn't drink so much.

SONNY [*yawns*]. I'm still sleepy, Cassy.

CASSY. Ah, my real name. That's nice.

SONNY [*beginning to disconnect again*]. Sorry, I slipped.

CASSY. I'm not sorry. I reckon it's time to get up.

SONNY [*harsh again*]. If you get me my morning Coke it may be time to get up, Rose, or at least time to wake up.

CASSY. Coke! First thing in the morning. That's blaugh!

SONNY. Now, Sally, that is only a notion, a dumb notion! However, if you want to stall you can tell me a wake-up story. How about little Cassy Meek-Cheek, Girl Orphan. That's my favorite wake-up story.

CASSY. I don't feel like it.

SONNY [*breezy, nasty*]. Oh, that's okay. I'll start it for you. [*Documentary.*] Orphaned at eight, little Cassy Meek-Cheek grew up a lone and lonely child——

CASSY [*interrupting*]. At nine . . . nine and a half. That's
when Cassy's mummy did her bright red bit in the indoor
dip.

SONNY. Oh good. That betters it much. The indoor dip.
Posh. Elegant. Now tell your sad orphan story, Miss
Meek-Cheek, and Sonny will wake.

CASSY. Really, I don't feel like it.

SONNY. Don't "really" me! I said it was all right that you
don't feel like it. Tell your sad story or I don't wake up
and that will leave you lonelier even than you would be
if I exiled you to a hotel room.

CASSY [*caving*]. Once upon a timey my mummy——

SONNY. Yes——

CASSY. Once upon a timey my mummy met a man on the
beach at East Hampton——

SONNY. That's right, dear. Go on.

CASSY. And it was a hot tanny day and Mummy and the
man got to talking the way people do at the beach, and
especially with Mummy because she was very friendly as
well as gloriously, glamorously beautiful. Yes, except that
she was getting a little older just then, you know how it
happens, all in a flash, and suddenly you are *instant older!*
Well, it was nothing really . . . just a few slight, shadows of darkness, nothing but slight, invisible little wrinkles. But to Mummy they mattered. They marred the
perfect face in the glass. Me. I was born with them . . .

SONNY. Please no embroidery, Rose. Back to the man, the
man who's talking to Mummy on the beach.

CASSY. Yes, well, during the course of their flirtatious en-
counter he happened to mention that he was a doctor.
A specialist. In cosmetic surgery, as a matter of fact. Well,
after a little more seductive chitchat Mummy just couldn't
resist showing the man those tiny little almost invisible
wrinkles. She pointed them out to him ever so casually,
ever so carelessly, and he assured her that he would never
have been able to see them at all if he weren't a professional skin man. But, in any case, should Mummy ever

want those tiny little invisible wrinkles to be completely invisible, all she had to do was drop in for an afternoon at his office—no need to go to the hospital even—*zip!* That would be it! That's all there was to it! *Zip!*

SONNY. Go on, Rose, that's good. I can feel my eyes opening.

CASSY. Well, he wrote his name in the sand so Mummy would be sure to remember it. And guess what? When she got back to town that fall she did somehow remember it and she went to the good doctor's office one afternoon and he operated. *Zip!* Except that was not all there was to it. She did not come home the very same evening. Or the next. Or the next. And finally Daddy told me that she was in the hospital . . . that we wouldn't be seeing her for a while. And then, after weeks and weeks and weeks she did come home, and she was wearing big black glasses—like owl eyes I called them—and she never took them off and she never came out of her room . . . her meals were sent up. And one night late I got out of bed. I couldn't sleep—you know how kids are—and I wandered down the hall . . . and Mummy's door was open a crack so I peeped in . . . she wasn't wearing those big black glasses . . . and there was something wrong with her face . . . it was stretched taut . . . like a mask— like a movie monster's mask—the eyes great big keyholes . . . too wide open . . . much too wide open . . . [*Hush.*] He had cut out *too much skin!* [*Laughs.*] *Zip! Zip! Zip!* [*Laughs again.*]

SONNY. Oooooooooooh . . . that is good. It's working. I'm waking.

CASSY [*caught up in the story*]. After that some other doctor came to the house and offered to graft some of Mummy's skin back under her eyes . . . and for free . . . that is if she would only exhibit herself at a plastic surgery convention in Atlantic City as an example of how not to do that particular type of operation. And so she went to Atlantic City and did exhibit herself and when she came back she was supposed to have the operation, but she

never did . . . or he never did . . . and then one afternoon she got hold of one of Daddy's big blue blades for
big blue beards and made bright red water all over the
indoor dip—looked like a thousand gallons of blood in
that pool.

SONNY [*claps hands in the air above the back of his couch*].
Very good, Miss Meek-Cheek. *Much* better with the
pool than with the bathtub. And . . . [*Yawns.*] I'm
much more awake now. God, if only your parents had
really been exciting people like that instead of two ac-
cidentally dead Lutheran liberals . . . may be that the
Great White Almighty didn't approve of their stomping
around down in darkest Alabama preaching all that broth-
erhood stuff . . . maybe that's why a lightning bolt came
out of the sky and struck their plane—

CASSY [*shrugs*]. Maybe . . .

SONNY. God, if only I had my morning Coke.

CASSY. In a minute.

SONNY. I can sleep right through till tomorrow if you like,
Joan.

CASSY. If you do I'll go shopping. That would be a good
thing to do with today, shop it away.

SONNY. No, I do not think you should go shopping. You
shopped enough at Christmas. Besides, one does not shop
for New Year's, one exchanges.

CASSY. Oh, I never exchange. I just keep shopping. I love
shopping.

SONNY. You spend too much. Eleven hundred and seventy-
five bucks for a sweater.

CASSY. Mink sweater. The Rich Kid by Chombert.

SONNY. Peggy Ann, can you guess how many little minks
they murdered to make you that . . . "poole-ovair"? How
many poor little innocent minks with their bright trusting
eyes?

CASSY. Now all of a sudden you feel sorry for minks? Sor-
rier than you do for your own little selfish self . . . aw
. . . that's sweet.

SONNY [*nagging*]. You should buy me a car. Yeah? Got it all picked out. A Ferrari. The 500 Superfast . . . and it's blood red and so dangerous—[*Makes a motor sound, basso profundo, vroom-vroom-vroom.*] Just so you'll dig it, too, we can order seats in mink. Hey, let's call up and order right now.

CASSY. But I don't know the Italian word for mink. How can I order?

SONNY. Well, that's perfectly all right, dear, just let your money do the talking, they'll understand.

CASSY. That's an awful pile of pullovers, dear, one teensy red Ferrari. Besides, your father would never let you have a car. Not with your grades.

SONNY. Tightwad! What's one little runabout to a person who's as extravagant as you are?

CASSY. I'm not extravagant. I've got money. Lots of it. Acres, barrels, yards, tons, scads of it.

SONNY. Sounds so crude.

CASSY. Crude?

SONNY. "I've got money."

CASSY. Would you prefer: "I'm rich!"?

SONNY. That sickens me, too!

CASSY. I spend *freely* to encourage *free* enterprise.

SONNY [*venom*]. Freely, eh? Well then, my little hot heiress, why don't you dispense your jack more jauntily in the cap department? You could use better biters—or do you imagine those big brown rot spots on your front choppers go with your big brown eyes? The way they once did with your beautiful chestnut brown hair—before you colored it whore. This is my hair! Color it whore! One could imagine that you were some tarty little typist . . . some Sally Strumpet or Harriet Harlot who just hasn't got the moolah to go to Harry Hollywood for a whole new movie mouth. But that's not you, baby! No! You're the Rich Kid by Camembert, or whoever. You could have a whole new keyboard installed if you wanted to, sharps and flats!

CASSY [*sincere*]. I'm afraid, Sonny! I'm afraid of the *pain!* Haven't you ever been afraid of *pain?*

SONNY. Jacket crowns were invented by an English dentist in the eighties or the nineties. Yes they were. And it was during a command performance at Victoria and Albert Hall . . . an American Jew's harp virtuoso harped the last coat of enamel off his incisors and ran screaming from the stage. Was there a dentist in the house? There was . . . and once more necessity was a mother . . . caps were born!

CASSY. You know, dear, too many movies can give you brain failure.

SONNY. My Coke, Rose. Get me my Coke!

CASSY. Glued to the boob tube right down to the wee wee hours of the morning.

SONNY. Saves "getting up in the night," as they say. I probably suffer from premature prostate.

CASSY. You're so anatomical.

SONNY. It's my daddy the doctor.

CASSY. Chirp-chirp! Cheep-cheep! Quack-quack!

SONNY [*angry*]. That will do, Rose!

CASSY [*lyrical*]. Ah yes, the horny old, corny old, corner gynecologist. On call for all call girls by day, on call for— [*Country twang.*]—all them worn-out Park Avenue widders by night. In the service of Hippocrates . . . and Mammon!

SONNY. Not so fast, Griselda. We can help ourselves to all the lullabye pills we want. That's nice, isn't it! Yes it is. And unless you get me my Coke immediately, the spantial effects of my current slumber drop will take me back to Freudland. And then I might dream, dear Charlotte, of those long gone, long after-school afternoons when you used to pay me as much as thirty dollars a dive. And sometimes I'd even get up a half-price bonus special! Yeah! But now the only time I ever think of doing it twice is before we've done it once. [*He shifts to self-reflection.*] Boy, that cash really used to boost my post-pubescent self-esteem. Teen stud! Some role, huh?

CASSY. Your performance isn't worth three bucks today.

SONNY. You don't much enjoy chatting about those dear old bygones, do you, dear?

CASSY [*musing*]. Four years ago . . . it' seems like forty.

SONNY. Bedroom is the perfect anagram of boredom. [*Scream.*] I'll have my Coke now, Sally.

CASSY [*not moving*]. Fine, I'm getting it now.

SONNY. Right now, Sally Ann, right this damn instant!

CASSY *yawns, stands up in the zebra skin, wraps it around her, and wanders over to the refrigerator-bar.*

CASSY. God, am I fagged.

SONNY. And don't forget the napkin.

CASSY [*rummaging around in search of a bottle opener*]. All right. All right.

SONNY. Remember the punishment meted out to Jackie-Lackey last summer when he forgot the napkin?

CASSY [*sudden cruel laugh*]. Right off the dock. Glug-glug! And he told us he could swim, too. [*Laughs again.*]

SONNY. Glug-glug! Help! Glug-glug! [*Laughs.*]

CASSY. And you wouldn't even help me get the poor baby out of the water.

SONNY. No napkin, no helping hand!

CASSY. He'll probably call sometime today. I'll bet nobody's invited him out for tonight.

SONNY. If he calls, I want you to disguise your voice. Tell him that "Marster and Modom are not to home!"

CASSY. He knows my voice. He also knows you don't have an English maid. . . .

SONNY. Then do Ernestine. [*Nasty whining Negro imitation.*] "Peace, dis is dee Boynton res-dence. No'um, Doctor Bo ain't heah jus' now if dat's who you want to speak wif." [*Shouts.*] My Coke, Rose! [*Phone rings.*] There. There he is now. Answer it, Julie! Run, Mary!

CASSY [*slams Coke bottle down on bar, runs to phone*]. 'Allo! 'allo! Oooo eees eeet? [*Pause.*] Ah'm sorree you 'ave zee wrahng noombear. *Au revoir.* [*Hangs up.*]

SONNY. You're no better at French maids than you are at French kisses. Well, who was it? Jackie-Lackey?

CASSY. Pretty sure.

SONNY. What do you mean you're pretty sure. Not good enough!

CASSY. Well it sounded like him.

Phone rings.

SONNY. Well, pick it up. *Pick it up!*

CASSY [*imitating* SONNY *imitating* Ernestine]. Peace, dis is dee Boynton res-dence. Huh? Oh, Dr. Bo. [*Uneasy laugh.*] I'm sorry, sir. We were just horsing around. We thought you were somebody else. We didn't recognize your voice.

SONNY. We?

CASSY. You want to speak to Sonny? . . . No? Still asleep I think. We'll get her some breakfast when she wakes up. You're sure you don't want to speak to Sonny. . . . All right. Yes, Doctor. Fine. Good-bye.

SONNY. Old horny on the horn, eh?

CASSY. Yes, and the next time he calls, you answer the phone.

SONNY. Now how will I know who it is, stupid?

CASSY. Well, he wanted to know how your mother is. How am I supposed to tell him that? We haven't heard a chirp out of her all day.

SONNY. Go and see how she is. Go on. Go!

CASSY [*going back to bar*]. I'd rather fix your Coke.

SONNY. They're not interchangeable actions. Go and see how she is!!!

CASSY. I will go in and I will see later.

SONNY. Bring me my Coke then. Perhaps if Daddy is so worried about Mummy we should phone the drugstore and order her coffee. . . . So it will be ready when she wakes up. Hand me the communicator.

CASSY. Why can't Ernestine make her some? And some for us, too.

SONNY. Because I always take Coke, you know that. And besides, Ernestine doesn't much like Mummy.

CASSY. Yeah. Who does?

SONNY. Hand me the communicator.

CASSY. The communicator, darling, is right under your snubby nose, at the tips of your pudgies there.

Phone rings.

SONNY. Ulloo. Yes. Who? . . . Oh, Jack. Okay. Fine. Lolling about. . . . What else should we be doing? Lolling. Is there anything else to do on vacation? . . . Yes, she's here. She's fine. Yes, except for one thing maybe. She's overshot her maiden moon now by about ten days. . . . Nah, Jack. It's something us older fellows are almost proud of. A youngster like you wouldn't understand. [*Wheedling.*] Huh? . . . Want to make yourself much more welcome? Stop off at your favorite deli and pick up a couple of six-packs of beer. We'd be much gladder to see you. No. There's no allowance check yet. It's Cassy's lawyer. Last visit to Forty Wall he tried to raid her panties on his how now brown couch. And she wouldn't, or didn't, now he's Mr. Molasses with the capital. You still thinking about that? . . . How do I know? Maybe her immaculate contraption is getting frayed at the edges. Yes, you're right. I should ask Daddy for the pills. But what good would that do now? . . . Okay, see you. Bye.

CASSY [*furious*]. You told me to disguise my voice.

SONNY. You have not learned yet, have you, dove, that the rules I make for your conduct are in no way intended to circumscribe my own? Jack is going to provide, I would like you to note, our minimum minimum—never a cover —two six-packs of brew.

CASSY. Screw! I think I'll go out and scare up a couple of minks.

SONNY. Be careful, mink frightens easy. Besides, this, Rose, is not a day of shopping!

CASSY. If it is not a day for shopping, Sonny, then what is it a day for?

SONNY. It is a day for a rapid bunny hop. I had a dream that makes me all eager.

CASSY. Don't tell me your dreams, dear. I don't feel the least little bit humpy.

SONNY. Not even for free!

CASSY. My contraption is not in.

SONNY. Of course it is. You put it in last night. But we didn't use it. Don't you remember anything? You're so forgetful. *Come here!*

CASSY. No!

SONNY. Jane!

CASSY. Maybe if you'd call me by the same name three times in a row.

SONNY. Jane. Jane. Janet.

CASSY. Almost. . . . Weeks and weeks and weeks with nothing and then all of a sudden it's *rabbit, rabbit, rabbit!*

SONNY [*kisses* CASSY]. Put the FM on.

CASSY [*annoyed*]. Why?

SONNY. You know very well I always like the FM on.

CASSY [*sitting up, visible to the audience again*]. You know very well I'm not pregnant, too. Why did you tell Lackey those lies over the phone?

SONNY. Gets him all hot. I could hear him panting into the mouthpiece. Fun! Don't you ever have any fun? Put the FM on!

CASSY. If I have to go away now I'm not coming back.

SONNY. And while you're up, shut off the lights and light a candle.

CASSY. No! Your radios and your candles. You can't be very eager.

SONNY. Well, I might be if you would shut off the lights and put the FM on.

CASSY [*standing up, rambling about*]. You're rotten. You can be very nice when you want to be. What's the matter with you?

SONNY. Where are you going? I thought we were going to engage in a pelvic peccadillo.

CASSY. I know . . . the only time you ever get hot pants for me is when you want to cool something off on your brain. So what's bugging you?

SONNY. Well, after all, what else should I think about? [*Bitter.*] Some people make it and others just don't. And it doesn't look like I'm among the making-it ones, does it?

CASSY [*exasperation*]. Nineteen and you talk like you're ninety!

SONNY. You're too goddamn filthy rich to know what it's all about anyway.

CASSY. Haven't you always told me, darling, that money is no substitute for success?

SONNY [*angry meditation*]. I read yesterday that he is being translated into seventeen languages.

CASSY. I knew it. I knew it. You're thinking about him again. You made Teen Stud. Now you want to make Teen Brain!

SONNY [*sick envy*]. Yes, well, all he did was parlay last summer's little seaside dicky dunking into an international name . . . that's all!

CASSY [*disgust*]. Oh, for God's sake!

SONNY. And they will probably make a movie out of it. Jesus! If only it was at least well written.

CASSY [*taking advantage of the chink in* SONNY's *ego armor*]. Well, dear, don't worry! You're famous to me, famous to your daddy, famous to your mummy—when she knows who you are—famous to good black Ernestine . . . that's not so bad. Lots of people are nothings even around the house. Besides, I haven't seen the manuscript of your epic gathering dust anywhere.

SONNY. What epic?

CASSY. Exactly.

SONNY. I'll write something this summer . . . at the beach . . . during the long vacation.

CASSY. Come on, you'll loll it away like you do every other summer. You'll never do anything ever, if you don't get out of that horizontal funk. [*Door chime rings.*] I think I hear somebody coming!

CASSY *slips under the zebra skin and pretends to be asleep.* JACK *enters through door, down left, carrying a six-pack of beer. British rhythm in speech.*

JACK. Hi! Hi, everybody! Ernestine let me in. She was scrubbing the hall.

SONNY [*indifferent*]. Deposit your offering, Jack. You know where.

CASSY [*pretending to wake up, yawning*]. Huh? Oh . . . oh, it's you, Jack.

JACK. Hi!

CASSY [*mocks* JACK's *British intonation; enters Mommy role*]. How did you ever manage to get over here so speedily, Son?

JACK. I rang up from a sidewalk booth, Mother.

SONNY [*mocks* JACK's *British intonation; enters Daddy role*]. That was sneaky of you, Son.

JACK. Do you and Mother always sleep like this while I'm away at school . . . in the drawing room, with the lights on and the shades down. You should pull them up. It's beautiful outside. The river's all white with ice.

SONNY. One doesn't question the window shades of one's parents, boy.

JACK. Sorry, Dad.

SONNY. That's all right. Your mother and I are perfectly delighted to have you home with us over vacation, but you will understand that we cannot tolerate any meddling in our lives.

JACK [*obedient*]. Yessir, Dadsir.

SONNY *and* CASSY. Yessir, Dadsir.

Sonny. Perhaps you'd care to tell us how things are at school? Lord knows it costs a mint to send you there.

Jack [*serving himself a beer*]. Yessir, Dadsir.

Sonny *and* Cassy. Yessir, Dadsir.

Sonny. And you might have the courtesy to offer your mother and me a drink, too. Are these the manners we sent you to that expensive school to acquire?

Jack. Yessir, Dadsir.

Sonny *and* Cassy. Yessir, Dadsir.

Jack. Would you care for a beer, Mumsie?

Sonny. Mumsie? I insist that you call your mother "Mother," until you're old enough to know better.

Jack. Yessir, Dadsir.

Sonny *and* Cassy. Yessir, Dadsir.

Jack. Do you wish a beer, Mother?

Cassy. No, thank you. Not just now, I do not wish a beer. I wish a coffee.

Jack. I'm sorry, we don't serve coffee—only beer at the bar.

Sonny. But I want a beer, Son.

Jack *takes a bottle of beer, carefully wraps it in a paper napkin, hands it to* Sonny.

Sonny. Ahhhhh, now that's better. Well, Son, tell us how things are going down at that gold-plated educational institution.

Jack. Things are fine, Dad.

Cassy. There, you see, Hugo? Things are fine.

Sonny. Well, I'm glad that things are fine, Son. Not a single demerit, eh?

Jack. Well, Dad, there is one thing.

Sonny. Yes. . . .

Jack. It's chapel. . . .

Sonny [*immediate indignation*]. The chapel? What's wrong with the chapel, boy? It's one of the finest in any prep school in America, boy . . . practically a cathedral . . .

why, it's modeled directly after Westminster Abbey. . . .
It's a little smaller, of course, but not much!

JACK [*fearful*]. No, Dad. Not the chapel. Chapel. The practice of going there. You know, every morning, every Sunday. I object to being forced to——

SONNY. Aha, so that's it. You've become an atheist this
semester. Is that all? Whew, and I thought it was something serious.

CASSY [*to* SONNY]. It's just a stage he's going through, dear.
[*To* JACK.] It's just a stage you're going through, dear.

SONNY. That's right, Son. Your mother is right. . . . Why
—[*Nostalgic laugh*.]—why, I lost my faith at school,
too. For six whole weeks once. [*Chuckle*.] Know what we
called the chapel, boy? Huh? . . . The Million Dollar
God Box. . . .

CASSY. Oh, really. [*Laughs oh, oh, oh*.]

SONNY. Oh . . . I hope I haven't shocked you.

JACK. A little, Dad, I'll admit.

SONNY [*pushing on*]. Used to actually read the funnies in
the balcony during the service. Gee, did I feel sinful.

JACK. Gosh, Dad, would you mind very much telling us
what led you back to God?

SONNY. Well it sure wasn't Little Orphan Annie . . .
[CASSY *laughs oh, oh, oh*.] huh-huh . . . huh-huh. . . .
No, it was that beautiful music. We had an old organist
named Theo Weincellar . . . and could that fellow tickle
the ivories . . . [*Hums a snatch of Bach's "Jesu, Joy of
Man's Desiring*."] Know it, Son?

JACK. No.

SONNY [*snaps out of his reminiscences*]. No. So things are
fine down at the old school. Well, that's fine.

CASSY. Well, that's fine.

JACK. Well, Dad, there is just one other thing.

SONNY [*clouds*]. Oh. . . .

CASSY [*fou*]. Oh. . . .

JACK. This is something I think I'd best discuss with Mumsie.

SONNY. Mumsie?

JACK. Mother.

SONNY. That's better. Well, if you must. I suppose there are certain trivial things a boy can best discuss with his mother.

JACK [*going over to* CASSY, *whispering loudly in her ear*]. Well, Mum, I'm not . . . I'm not just home on vacation this time.

CASSY. Oh?

JACK. I was . . . er . . . dismissed.

CASSY. *Oh!*

JACK. I've been bounced.

CASSY [*shriek*]. Oh, my baby. What to do? What to do? Let's not tell your father. He'd kill us! What have I done to be dealt a blow like this? Haven't I been a good mother? [*Groan.*] Ohhhhhhhhh.

SONNY. What's this?

CASSY. Oh!

SONNY. What are you telling her?

CASSY. Oh, oh.

SONNY. She seems a bit upset.

CASSY. *Oh, oh!*

SONNY. I think I can guess. Must be some female thing.

CASSY. Oh, oh.

SONNY. You've gotten some little girl in the family way.

CASSY. Oh, oh, oh, oh, oh.

SONNY. That's it. Well don't fret! I practically put Dr. Whataknabe in business around here . . . we'll work something out. [*Nostalgic laugh.*] Why, I remember once when I dated a little girl from Allentown.

CASSY [*wailing*]. No Sam, no. This is much worse. Much worse.

SONNY. Worse? What could be worse?

CASSY. Our boy has been . . . expelled. There. I've said it. [*Tears.*]

JACK. Gee, Mom, I thought we weren't going to tell Dad.

SONNY. Well, Son, don't you worry. [*Fury.*] Either you graduate from Quagminster or there'll be no new Sports House. No hockey rink, no pool, no squash, tennis, or basketball courts, no showers, sinks, toilets, or urinals . . . not a stick . . . not a stone . . . not a damn cent of mine!

JACK [*pleased*]. Gee, Dad, suddenly you're rich?

SONNY [*beaming*]. Right, Son, I'm loaded.

CASSY [*incantation*]. I'll just bet Penny Barnstable had a hand in this. Head*mistress*, indeed. Slept with half of every senior class since nineteen-aught-seven. Stuffs her brassiere with pink kleenex for the proms. The slut! Waltzes around like she was sixteen again. The bitch! Did she proposition you, Son?

JACK. No, Mum. It was smoking. They caught me smoking in the shower . . . and . . . and it was after lights out.

CASSY. Is that all?

JACK. They're very strict, Mum.

SONNY. My God, the shame of it. That this should have happened to a son of mine.

JACK. Shame?

CASSY. I should think that a cigarette would get soaking wet in the shower. What a hell of a place to smoke!

SONNY. Exactly, Grace. Exactly. I'm afraid our son wasn't smoking in that shower at all.

JACK [*suspicious of the direction in which* SONNY *is taking the "scene"*]. What?

CASSY. Why, whatever do you mean, George?

SONNY [*nostalgic laugh*]. Well, dear, to me it all sounds pretty much like a mess we had back at school in my day. Kid named Paddy Dietweiler . . . sort of a pretty, blond, soft-faced kid . . . and he was always going to the showers to "smoke" after lights out . . . and one night old Gritty Dingwald, our headmaster, caught him

. . . and he wasn't smoking at all . . . he was in there with one of the assistant house masters . . . and . . . aha . . . [*Shouting at* JACK.] There was someone in that shower with you, wasn't there, boy?

JACK. No, no, no, that's not true.

CASSY. Oh, my baby!

SONNY. Well, Amantha, there you are.

CASSY [*shriek*]. Oh, what to do do, what to do? Can Dr. Whataknabe fix it? He's been the family doctor for years. Can he be trusted?

SONNY. I'm afraid Marian, that *this* is something placebos can't cure.

JACK [*making his hand into a revolver*]. All right, Dad, if that's the attitude you're going to take you're going to die.

SONNY. No, no. Son! Son! Put that thing down!

JACK. Bang!

SONNY. Oh.

JACK. Daddy is dead. Bang.

SONNY. Oh.

JACK. Bang.

SONNY. Oh.

JACK. Bang.

SONNY. Oh.

JACK. Bang!

SONNY. Ohhhhhhh. [*Sinks dead to sofa.*]

JACK. Shot five times through the head.

CASSY. Why, Son, I never knew you carried a gun. How chic. I've been wanting to do that to Daddy for years.

SONNY [*dropping Daddy role*]. All right, Jack, now that you've disposed of Daddy, would you get *me* another beer?

CASSY [*dropping Mommy role*]. And while you're at it would you bring me my pants? I can't pretend I'm a zebra forever, can I?

SONNY. Yes, Jackie, do be good enough to hand Mademoiselle her trousers . . . which she seems to have abandoned in a moment of abandon.

CASSY [*to* SONNY]. Stop that!

SONNY. Daddy was getting perilously close to something you told the draft board recently, wasn't he, Jack?

CASSY. For Christ's sake, Sonny, can it!

SONNY. Well, Jack?

JACK. Oh, leave me alone.

SONNY [*taunting*]. Of course, you did it only on your auction gallery father's advice. So you could stick around to learn store minding, of course. No smart merchant would waste the fruit of his loins on warfare, right?

CASSY. Lay off!

SONNY. Well, Jack certainly did not like that scene in the shower, I could see that.

CASSY. One might wonder why you invented it. Some fantasy of *yours* perhaps.

SONNY. Now *you* lay off!

JACK *hands* SONNY *a beer with napkin and then gives* CASSY *her slacks.*

JACK. Here.

CASSY. Thanks. Hey, don't go away, lover. You know I've always liked you. Why don't you and I go out for a little stroll along the river? How about that for a proposition?

JACK. Well, yes, but what about . . . uh . . . [*Nods toward* SONNY'S *couch.*]

CASSY. Oh, him . . . why, it's none of his business . . . we're not married, are we? Besides it's so stuffy in here I don't think I can swallow another lungful.

JACK [*looking over at* SONNY'S *couch again*]. Well sure, I'd love to . . . uh . . .

CASSY [*loud to* SONNY]. Good. Good. Good. Well, my Lord and Master, Master Jack and I are going out for a little stroll along the river. A little daylight does a girl good once in a great while.

SONNY. You do, and I'll lock the front door and you won't get back in.

CASSY. Maybe we won't want to get back in, will we, Jack?

JACK. Well, I——

SONNY. Hey, Jack, come here. There's something I want to tell you about Cassy. She's terribly high strung, you know. And it's been particularly difficult for her since she found out . . . well . . . since she learned that——

JACK. Since she found out what?

SONNY. Well it was terribly difficult after so many years of thinking she was the other.

CASSY [getting into her clothes]. Other what?

SONNY. I'll never forget the look on her face when she came back from her lawyer's that day . . . after they told her.

CASSY. I suppose that was the same supposed day my lawyer supposedly molested me on his how now brown couch.

SONNY. Yes, it may turn out to have been. It was a difficult day.

JACK [smutty]. Wow!

SONNY. It was the day they read the will, her father's will. That's the day she found out.

JACK. Found out what?

SONNY. That she was an adopted child!

JACK [surprised]. You're an orphan?

CASSY. So what?

JACK. Well, I mean it makes me feel awfully sorry for you, that's all. Your real parents are dead too. Huh?

CASSY [almost to herself]. Everybody's dead.

SONNY. You see, Jack, she really doesn't know. That's the point. All she does know is that she was adopted from a Jewish foundling home.

JACK. You Jewish?

CASSY. Never!

JACK. Well, why not? I'm Jewish.

CASSY. Well, it just doesn't happen to be the case in my case, okay?

SONNY. Well, now who can say really? I mean it wouldn't absolutely prove that you were Jewish—being adopted from a Jewish home—on the other hand, wouldn't you think it highly likely?

CASSY [to JACK]. Oh, yes. I can see you already believe it.

JACK. Well, it does seem probable, doesn't it?

CASSY [pointing at SONNY]. He's always inventing things . . . like all that crap he told you over the phone, about my not having my period.

JACK. Oh?

SONNY. I'll bet now that Jack knows you're Jewish, Rebecca, he—[Yiddish accent.]—vouldn't be heff as interested in teking you for a stroll along the river, vould you, Jeckie?

JACK [shock]. That's disgusting.

SONNY [loud]. Oh is it now? Well, why else do you assimilate with us every vacation, huh? Even though we're in college now and you're still in school. Wouldn't it be a little more natural for you to spend time with people of your own class, and I mean that both ways. You don't have to tell me why you come over here all the time. I know. It's because you can't bear—absolutely cannot bear—being the son of a Jewish art peddler, read high-class hock shoppe. You don't go for that six-pointed star stuff . . . or the three balls bit either.

CASSY. Come on, Jack, let's get out of here.

JACK [ignoring CASSY]. You want to know why I come over here. I'll tell you why. Because somehow you two get away with living more or less like grown-ups. Because your mother, Sonny, your Mummie-Birdie, or whatever you call her, is too sick to notice what goes on around here, and your father, your dear Doctor Daddy, apparently doesn't care. At my house they're forever watching me . . . forever telling me what to do. You'd think I was taking violin lessons in life or something.

SONNY [*slightly reached*]. Oh well, what can I say? Welcome. Stay as long as you like.

CASSY [*annoyed with* JACK *for ignoring her*]. You came over here today because you know goddamn well you won't be invited anywhere tonight! Right? And you also know goddamn well that we're too soft-hearted to throw you out.

SONNY [*suddenly cozy and intimate with* JACK]. Hey, Jack, look! The moment anybody mentions my Mummie-Birdie she starts to chirp. I don't know how she knows she's being talked about—her room's way at the other end of the apartment—but she knows. It's uncanny.

CASSY. What new nonsense is this?

JACK [*delighted by* SONNY'S *unexpected warmth*]. Sick people are often telepathic.

CASSY [*disgust*]. Oh, come on.

SONNY. Crazy people, you meant to say, didn't you, Jack?

JACK. No, I—

SONNY. Well, she's not really crazy, you know. Just awfully, awfully depressed. That's all.

MRS. BOYNTON'S VOICE. Sonneeeeeeeeeee. . . . Sonny-Birdie? Where are you? Where are you? Your Mummie-Birdie is awake.

SONNY. What did I tell you?

MRS. BOYNTON'S VOICE. Birdie-dear, where are you? Where are you?

SONNY [*suffering*]. Christ!

JACK [*shaken by the voice*]. What? What does she want?

SONNY. Coffee, that's all.

JACK. Well, shouldn't someone get it?

SONNY. Yes, shouldn't you, Priscilla?

CASSY. Why not Ernestine?

SONNY. No dice. You, Olivia.

CASSY. If you come along I will. I'm not going alone.

SONNY. Jack, go out into the kitchen and ask Ernestine to make Miz Boynton's coffee.

CASSY. Yes, that's a great idea, Jack!

JACK. I'm not the butler.

CASSY. No, that is true, and you are free to leave any time you choose.

JACK. Kitchen is woman's domain.

CASSY. I said, dear, that you were free not to stick around here. We make the rules here. And you are here and you will follow them or not stay here. We'll follow your rules in your house, if we ever come over to your house, won't we, Sonny-Birdie?

SONNY. Yes, Jack, why don't you go and take your sister to a matinee concert 'at Carnegie Hall . . . or go have tea and matzohs with Mother out of some battered old samovar from some battered old Russian prince's estate? Go, go, raggle-taggle merchant o!

JACK. My mother drinks coffee . . . instant coffee.

SONNY. Now so does mine. So why don't you go out into the kitchen and ask Ernestine to make her some.

CASSY [indicating door right]. The kitchen is that way. Home is . . . [Indicating down left.] Got it?

JACK. Okay, okay. [Goes out door upstage right.]

CASSY. God! He eats it up! The more you kick him the more he licks.

SONNY. And now, Sally Ann, let's take up our little game of double-backed beastie where we left offee.

CASSY. With Lackey here?

SONNY. He might make a wonderful audience.

CASSY. Not to mention the fact that your stark raving mother may come chirping through here any minute.

SONNY. She'd probably just think she'd stumbled in on one of Daddy's little knock-up-a-nurse parties. That's probably what loosened her screws in the first place.

MRS. BOYNTON'S VOICE. Sonny-Birdie, I'm awake. Your Mummie-Birdie is awake.

SONNY. Yes, sir. Wake and the world wakes with you. Christ, she'll go on like that for hours now.

CASSY [*produces a small blue bottle of sleeping pills*]. She needn't.

SONNY. Oh?

CASSY. Perhaps we should share some of our snoozing pellets with her, you know . . . just one or two in her cupacawfee and she'll be out for the remainder of the year.

MRS. BOYNTON'S VOICE. Sonny-Birdie, your Mummie-Birdie is awake.

CASSY [*sighs*]. Just once I'd like to spend a day here without Mad Mother Muzak in the background.

SONNY. You would. . . .

CASSY. Yes.

SONNY. You honestly would. And I thought your kind feelings toward her were just another lovely way of saying thank you to a kind family for taking you in off psycho street . . . for offering you the warmth of our hearth and our hearts.

CASSY. Easy on the home life, boy . . . that's dangerous stuff in big doses. Do you remember our friend Debbie Olsen who excused herself from her family's Thanksgiving table and jumped out the window—Eighty-eighth and Park— Splat!

SONNY. I don't like turkey either.

MRS. BOYNTON'S VOICE. Chirp-cheep. Chirp-cheep. Cheep-chirp.

CASSY. There she goes for real. Just a couple of morpheus drops in her cup-a-java and rock-a-bye Birdie. . . . Okay?

MRS. BOYNTON'S VOICE. Cheep-cheep, cheep-cheep, cheep-cheeeeeeeeeeeeeeee . . .

CASSY. No wonder Doctor Daddy keeps a push pin full of coke around to knock her out with.

SONNY. We're not giving any injections, Nurse, if that's what you've got in your tiny terrible mind.

CASSY. Where is Lackey with her coffee?

SONNY. Probably out giving Ernestine his latest civil-rights spiel. [*Telephone rings.*] Answer that, Jessica, do you mind?

CASSY [*answering phone*]. Hello . . . Oh. Hi! Oh, we're right around the corner. Forty-five Sutton Point South. Oh please. See you soon. [*Hangs up.*]

SONNY. And to whom have you given permission to trespass?

CASSY. You told Lackey he could come over, didn't you? Maybe we can have some of my friends.

SONNY. Lackey is your friend. Now who was that?

CASSY. Well, you'll just have to curb your curiosity until he-she-it gets here. [*Sees* JACK *in doorway with coffee tray.*] Ah, there you are.

JACK [*tries to hand* CASSY *the coffee tray*]. Here. End of the line.

SONNY. Oh no, Jackie. Half begun is only half the fun. Now you take the coffee into Mummie-Birdie. Cassy will go with you, won't you, Rhoda?

CASSY [*seductive*]. Yeah. Come on, Jack darling, we can neck in the hall. Dalliance . . . you'll love it.

JACK [*tries again to give* CASSY *the tray*]. Take the tray. I'm not coming with you.

SONNY. Go with her, boy, go!

JACK. Yeah, maybe I would if she were even half-serious about necking.

SONNY. Knowing her as you do, can you be sure that she's not *all* serious?

CASSY. Yeah . . . [*Opens her mouth pin-up fashion.*] Yeah, big boy, how do you know? Well, come on, come on. . . .

JACK. All right. All right.

SONNY [*calling after* CASSY]. Easy on the potion, Lucretia, love. Beauty sleeps can last too long, you know. [*To himself after* CASSY *and* JACK *have been gone for a few seconds.*] Ah . . . yes. . . . "My life was lost on the little roads that led to Zelda's sanatorium." [*The door chime rings.*] Here comes he, she, or it. [SONNY *ducks down as he hears sounds of somebody being let in at the front door.* BILLIE MAE *enters, looks around, and thinks she is alone.*] Hi, there! [*Still lying down.*]

BILLIE MAE. Hi, there.

SONNY. I hurt my back skiing.

BILLIE MAE. Nothing serious, I hope.

SONNY. Do you like to ski?

BILLIE MAE [*shifts to a Negro voice*]. Now, where would *we* go to ski?

SONNY [*sits up*]. Oh, I'm sorry. You're a friend of Cassy's, aren't you?

BILLIE MAE. Yes, I am.

SONNY. I mean we've never met before, though, have we?

BILLIE MAE. Not that I remember.

SONNY. Where'd you meet Cassy?

BILLIE MAE. At a rally.

SONNY. What?

BILLIE MAE. At a rally. A rally. You know, like "rally round the flag, boys."

SONNY. You rally a lot?

BILLIE. Sure. It's chic. It's sec.

SONNY. Sec?

BILLIE MAE. That's a new word for cool.

SONNY. And what's the rally all about? Communism?

BILLIE MAE. No, clothes.

SONNY. Is that all girls ever think about, clothes?

BILLIE MAE. For Mississippi.

SONNY. Did Cassy turn in one of her mink sweaters maybe?

BILLIE MAE [*offended for* CASSY]. I don't know about that. I do know that she's very generous with what she has.

SONNY. So you do know *that* she has, eh?

BILLIE MAE. She's never kept it a secret.

SONNY [*fake confidential*]. Say, how do you know when people really have money? Maybe Cassy's putting you on. Maybe I'm supporting her.

BILLIE MAE. I doubt it. She has money all right. She has that special sort of . . . relaxed attitude about everything.

SONNY. Rich people are always afraid that you'll like them for their money and not for themselves.

BILLIE MAE. Takes a hell of a lot of self to match a million dollars. [SONNY *groans a little.*] Your back hurt you?

SONNY. Only when I shift around. Say, Miss—perhaps you should tell me your name.

BILLIE MAE. Y.

SONNY. Huh?

BILLIE MAE. Miss Y. Billie Mae Y.

SONNY [*with a smile*]. Now I suppose I should tremble for my lily-white life. . . . But, I'm not gonna. Okay? Say, what was your name before it was Y?

BILLIE MAE. That's not a well-bred question.

SONNY. I'm just curious.

BILLIE MAE. That's what kills cats, baby. [*"Cats" pronounced jazz way to mean people.*]

SONNY. Yes, I know, but like what was your hand-me-down white name before you changed it to Y?

BILLIE MAE. Boyndon.

SONNY. No kidding? How do you spell it?

BILLIE MAE. B-o-y-n-d-o-n.

SONNY. That's a variant of my name, Boynton, with a "T." God, do you suppose your great-great-great-granddaddy was a field hand on my great-great-great-grand-daddy's plantation?

BILLIE MAE [*firm*]. I have no past, all right?

SONNY. Wow! Yeah, sure, but there wasn't room for everybody on the *Mayflower*.

BILLIE MAE. I know, we came over on the *Simon Legree*.

SONNY. Do have the kindness to get me a beer, Miss Y. And why don't you have a drink?

BILLIE MAE *goes to bar, gets beer for* SONNY, *and pours herself a Scotch.*

BILLIE MAE. Thank you. I'd love one. Say, where is Cassy?

SONNY. Off on a little side trip.

BILLIE MAE [*disturbed*]. But she was here a little while ago when I called.

SONNY. She will return, Miss Y, never fear. She's just in giving my mother a Mickey Finn.

BILLIE MAE. Giving her a what?

SONNY. Well, Mother cheeps and chirps like a bird and it's very annoying. Disrupts the party.

BILLIE MAE. What party?

SONNY. The floating party we have here every vacation.

BILLIE MAE. If I'd known we were floating, I'd have worn my inner tube.

SONNY. Yes, and I must warn you that you're not the only minority representative on deck today. Although, I must admit that with you people stealing the scene all over the place his problem doesn't even make conversation anymore. He didn't change *his* name. It's Geltmann . . . Jack Geltmann.

BILLIE MAE. Cassy's mentioned him I think. . . .

SONNY. Yeah, his papa [*French "papa."*] runs an art gallery on Third Avenue.

BILLIE MAE. Oh, how chic!

SONNY. You know. Art like Friday and Saturday at one o'clock. [*Yiddish accent.*] "Jack, heng out the fleg!"

BILLIE MAE. Oh, cut it out, Bwana! [*Laughs.*]

SONNY. My, you are handsome, aren't you?

BILLIE MAE. You may have hurt your back, but there's nothing wrong with your eyes, is there?

SONNY. And whose little mocha delight are you, anyway?

BILLIE MAE. Well, at the moment I'm being hankered after by a charming prince from Princeton named Luke.

SONNY. So Biblical.

BILLIE MAE. Luke van Cuylenberg.

SONNY. Van who?

BILLIE MAE. Van Cuylenberg. Luke van Cuylenberg.

SONNY. He sport a monocle?

BILLIE MAE [*dreamy*]. Billie Mae van Cuylenberg. How does that strike you?

SONNY. As improbable. Say—van Cuylenberg—isn't that the name of that radio couple. Penny and Patch van Cuylenberg? What do they call the show? "Coffee and Croissants"? Yeah, that's it, and she pecks and pecks and pecks at his tail till it's a wonder he got any feathers left on it.

BILLIE MAE [*laughs*]. Yes. That's about right.

SONNY [*impressed*]. And this kid you know is their son, eh?

BILLIE MAE. The very same.

SONNY [*envious*]. Their son . . . huh . . .

BILLIE MAE. I do believe.

SONNY [*getting his "cool" back again*]. Very interesting. And what does that make you—some sort of celebrity-chaser?

BILLIE MAE. You'll find, I think, that he's the one who's doing the chasing. [SONNY *tries to kiss* BILLIE MAE *and succeeds.*] You're one of those unreconstructed whites who thinks dark meat is sweeter, is that it, Mister Sonny?

SONNY. They say you ain't a man till you splits a black oak.

BILLIE MAE. Just let yourself go, Big Boy. They say you never feel self-conscious in front of pets or servants. Which category am I earmarked for?

SONNY. The first, pet, of course.

BILLIE MAE. You know, you might find me terribly dull in bed. Remember what Kinsey found out?

SONNY. Can't say that I do.

BILLIE MAE. He found out that ladies of color are actually quite inhibited. They're afraid of living up to all those tales about spade maids being so hot and loose.

SONNY. You make it much with Luke, Billie, uh, Miss Y?

BILLIE MAE. Why don't you ask him when he gets here?

SONNY. Because— He's coming here?

BILLIE MAE. A little later on, yes, coming over to pick me up. There's something he wanted to finish working on.

SONNY. Something?

BILLIE MAE. A poem.

SONNY. Because he's a poet?

BILLIE MAE. Yale Younger last year.

SONNY. I thought you said he went to Princeton.

BILLIE MAE. It's a prize, sweetie, that Yale puts out. And they publish your book and they give you a grant and they sponsor your readings all around. . . . It's a very big thing in the verse world.

SONNY. The per-verse world. All poets are fairies.

BILLIE MAE. A girl won it two years ago, for your information.

SONNY. Yeah, I know, Renny Luckman, her name was. And she's rich and she gives big fag parties and she even sacked out a few times with the great Richard MacDowell, and he just happened to be one of the judges. What a coincidence!

BILLIE MAE. So you do know about those things.

SONNY. What's Lukie's slim volume called?

BILLIE MAE. *Until the Monkey Comes* . . .

SONNY. A bestiary? How conventional! Tell me, Miss Y, is this your first bleached romance?

BILLIE MAE. No, I've had two proposals of miscegenation so far. . . . I think Luke will ask soon and that will make three.

SONNY. Yeah, let me get a fix on those two scenes, okay? Scene one: Jewish boy trying to insult his Orthodox daddy, right?

BILLIE MAE. Um-m-m-m-m-m . . .

SONNY. And scene two: some other kind of religious specialist, a Quaker maybe, hoping a mixed-up marriage would brown out his guilt about dodging the draft.

BILLIE MAE. You're just itching to meet my Lukie, aren't you . . . now that you've found out he's the son of name parents?

SONNY. I'll match our name, Miss Y, Miss ex-Boyndon, with his any day. Why my great-great-great-granddad was a member of Jefferson Davis's cabinet in Richmond.

BILLIE MAE. Yes, while my great-great-great-granddad was still perspiring on the auction block.

SONNY. I thought you had no past.

BILLIE MAE. Sometimes I do.

SONNY. And where did your mother go to school, Miss Y?

BILLIE MAE. She still does, to Sunday school, and she plays for the services there. It's my father's church.

SONNY. Your father is a preacher.

BILLIE MAE. Yes, and a very well-known one up in Harlem.

SONNY. But don't you find all that a little gauche? I mean all that hand clapping and thigh slapping and tooth flashing. Don't you think Christianity has sold you darkies far enough down the drain without you thumping up trade for it every weekend? Huh? I ask you . . . can you think of a more segregated hour in America than eleven o'clock on Sunday?

BILLIE MAE. Well, what do you want me to do about it . . . go off to Cuba and broadcast for Radio Free Dixie?

SONNY. Sure, you could call yourself Havana Billie . . . the new Tokyo Rose . . . maybe you've thought of it.

BILLIE MAE. Maybe I have.

SONNY. Yes, you probably have . . . because by now you're probably getting slightly disenchanted with your nice preacher daddy . . . you've probably discovered that he can't tell his good intentions from his good collections anymore . . . that he's gone soft at the middle . . . and joined the middle class . . . because no matter how hard you hold people down, a few of them always pop up to help you keep the others in line . . . the model prisoner bit!

BILLIE MAE. One could learn to dislike you.

SONNY. Oh, but I didn't want that. I thought maybe you'd get to hate me bad enough to want me. I mean, why do you couch around town with all those paleskins, baby? Because you despise them. Isn't that it? I figured my little seduction scene—memories of the Old South and so forth was getting you all warm and ready. . . .

CASSY *and* JACK *come in.*

CASSY. Hi, Billie, glad you could come over. Have you been chatting with my hero?

BILLIE MAE [*dead pan*]. Hi, Cassy. Yeah, we talked some.

CASSY. Yeah. He's quite a talker!

JACK. Hi, I'm Jack Geltmann.

BILLIE MAE. Hello, I'm Billie Mae Y.

JACK. "Y" that means you're a— Is your father a Black Muslim?

BILLIE MAE. Is your father a kosher butcher?

JACK. Sorry, I didn't mean to be nosy.

BILLIE MAE. You could hardly be otherwise.

SONNY. Rub-a-dub-dub, minority friction.

CASSY. Well, I can report that Mummie-Birdie took her pill and fell fast asleep. Now Sonny and Cassy and company can party happily ever afterward.

SONNY. Done well, Annabelle. [*The door chime rings.*] Jessica, see who's on bell. It may just be—[*Burlesque announcer's voice.*]—the young, the exciting, the ever-lovely Luke van Cuylenberg. . . .

CASSY. Ernestine'll get it . . . she doesn't have anything else to do.

SONNY [*warning*]. Answer the door, Bridget.

JACK. Oh, so I'll get it. [*Starts toward hall.*]

BILLIE MAE. Well, that's white of you, kiddo, mighty white of you.

PHILIP *enters.*

PHILIP. Ernestine let me in.

BILLIE MAE. Well, that was mighty white of her.

CASSY *embraces* PHILIP. *He responds with gooey "mother kisses" on both cheeks.*

CASSY. Why, Philip, how nice to see you. I had no idea you were in town.

PHILIP. I just got in.

CASSY. Jackie, get Philly a drink.

PHILIP. Yes, Jackie, do get Philly a drink. [*Pulling a script out of a manila envelope.*] I have the most exciting news——

BILLIE MAE [*brushing between* CASSY *and* PHILIP]. Pardon me, but my name is Billie Mae Y.

PHILIP. How do you do, Miss Y. Philip Armitage.

BILLIE MAE. Doesn't he write for the *New Yorker?*

PHILIP. No, *she* does, my mother, Phyllis Armitage.

BILLIE MAE. I rather like her work.

PHILIP. Yes, she's a very nice person.

SONNY. Hi there, fella. My name is Sonny.

PHILIP. Enchanté.

SONNY [*childishly eager*]. Phil, did you bring me something? Perhaps a lovely art book you just "picked up" at Brentano's, maybe?

PHILIP. It's a script . . . a script . . . I think I have a part in a TV thing and I came over to ask Cassy to consult the oracle for me. . . .

JACK. You'd have to quit school, wouldn't you?

PHILIP. Exactly. My mother would have puppies.

SONNY. I always thought it was kittens.

PHILIP. Not my mother.

CASSY [*pleased to be the center of attention*]. I'd be delighted to consult the oracle for you, Phil. Jack, my Webster, San, please.

JACK *gets out a Webster's unabridged dictionary and gives it to* CASSY *who has put the zebra cover over her shoulders.*

BILLIE MAE. What is he, Japanese or something?

SONNY. Yes, originally. It's usually done with a Kenkyusha dictionary. We use Webster.

JACK. There, O prophetess.

CASSY. Thank you, O master of the temple. [*Folds her hands on cover, concentrates.*]

BILLIE MAE [*sarcastic*]. I suppose you're going to look up the answer to Philip's problem?

CASSY [*as though slipping into a trance*]. Yes. . . .

PHILIP. Please stop irritating him, Miss Y, or he won't speak to us at all.

CASSY. O Webster, San, will it be wise for Philip to quit college for a part on TV? What advice have you for Philip?

CASSY *opens dictionary with a jerk, lets her forefinger fall on a page, reads from the definition the finger strikes.*

PHILIP. Well, what does he say?

CASSY. Patience, my son, he says: "for-mid'-ō-lōse, adjective——"

BILLIE MAE. Oh, what the hell?

CASSY, JACK, *and* PHILIP. Shhhh!

CASSY. "For-mid'-ō-lōse, adjective. (Latin *formidolosus*, from *formidare*, to fear, dread.) Filled with dread, greatly afraid. (Obsolete.)"

SONNY. In other words, you're scared witless, huh, Philly?

PHILIP. Well, he's right there. I am afraid. Try another, Cas.

BILLIE MAE. Oh, yes, let's see what prophetic remark he comes up with this time?

CASSY [*with her fingers on the cover, waiting*]. Don't insult the oracle. You may regret it. Same question, O Webster,

San. [*Opens to another page.*] This time it's: "ō′-lē-fin,
noun. (From French *oléfiant*, from Latin *oleum*, an oil,
and *-ficare*, from *facere*——"

BILLIE MAE. Latin sure can sound dirty, can't it?

CASSY. "——from *facere*, to make.) Any of a series of un-
saturated open-chain hydrocarbons containing one double bond and corresponding to the general formula
CnH2n——"

BILLIE MAE. Now I defy you to make any sense out of
that——

SONNY. The key is "double bond," Philip.

CASSY. You see, now that your father has left your mother,
you are doubly important to her.

PHILIP. Then she'll let me go on television. Thank you, O
Goddess born, for your words of wisdom.

BILLIE MAE. Cool it with a baboon's blood.

PHILIP. Black out!

SONNY. Jack, remove the oracle. [*The door chime rings.
JACK replaces the dictionary.*] Someone get the door. Ernie
takes forever.

BILLIE MAE. Not me. Don't think that doorman didn't try
to show me to the service elevator on my way up here.

SONNY. But it's probably your own darling Lukie, Billie.
Now he wouldn't mistake you for our maid, would he?

CASSY [*surprise*]. Lukie?

SONNY. Her boy friend.

CASSY. She has several.

BILLIE MAE. Luke van Cuylenberg.

CASSY. I don't think I've ever heard of that one.

JACK. Say, that's the name of that radio couple, isn't it? Is
he their son?

SONNY. According to Billie Mae he is.

PHILIP. I saw their pictures in the papers recently. She has
the longest, funniest ears and I've heard that . . .

LUKE *appears in the doorway, dressed in the severe black
suit of a seminarian.* BILLIE MAE *starts to introduce him.*

BILLIE MAE. Luke, that is my friend Cassy over there.

CASSY [*taking over the introductions*]. Yes, this is my friend Philip . . . and Jack and that's Sonny. . . .

BILLIE MAE. And I'm Billie Mae Y, darling. I'll get you a drink.

SONNY. Get me a beer while you're at it.

LUKE. The view from here must be terrific.

SONNY. Huh?

PHILIP [*eying* LUKE]. M-m-m. Hum-m-m!

LUKE. You've got the whole East River right outside the window . . . and over the river that incredible junk landscape. It's really part of the new aesthetic. All those Wordsworth hills and dales are over. Now, it's smoke-stacks, steel, and Pepsi-Cola in letters eighty feet high.

SONNY. I like Coke.

PHILIP. Pepsi is six full ounces more. In case you didn't hear my name, it's Philip Armitage.

CASSY. I gave you billing, Philip, dear.

PHILIP. I only heard my first name, darling.

SONNY. I'd love to play host, Luke, but my game is poor from prone. Hurt my back. Taxi door hit it.

JACK. Say, do you ever go on your parents' radio show?

LUKE. Excuse me?

JACK. Your parents do have a radio program, don't they?

LUKE. Yes! Uh-huh.

SONNY. Yes, uh-huh. Well, Jack asked you if you ever go on it?

LUKE. No.

JACK. No?

LUKE [*to* BILLIE MAE, *suspicion*]. Could it be that you've been advertising me, darling?

BILLIE MAE. The great name, Luke, they just happened to know it.

SONNY. She didn't do a single commercial, honest, Lukie. It's like she says, your famous parents preceded you.

JACK. My mother listens to Penny and Patch religiously.

PHILIP. How very devout of her!

JACK. And you're really their son?

LUKE. Pinch me.

PHILIP. Oh, I'd love to.

JACK. It's a pretty dull show actually.

LUKE [*reached in spite of his effort to seem as "cool" as the others*]. Oh?

SONNY. Yeah, I'm with Jack on that. The show sounds sort of like testimony from a divorce court I can never quite make up my mind which one should get the alimony.

CASSY. Yeah, it is a drag. Lucky it never reached Philadelphia.

LUKE. You live in Philadelphia?

CASSY. In my youth I did.

SONNY. Say, Luke, how old can you be and still be a Yale Younger Poet?

LUKE [*ingenuous*]. Forty, I think.

JACK. You don't act forty.

BILLIE MAE. He's twenty-eight.

LUKE. Twenty-four, actually. Billie likes older types.

PHILIP. So do I.

JACK. Once, on the program, Penny—your mother, I mean —mentioned my father's art gallery.

LUKE. Oh, your father runs an art gallery? Which one?

JACK. Geltmann's . . . on Madison in the Seventies.

SONNY. Funny, I could have sworn it was on Eighth in the Forties.

BILLIE MAE. You've got a lot of cracked thundermugs and dented pewter in the window . . . I've probably passed it. . . .

JACK [*proud*]. Maybe you have. . . . We get some wonderful things in sometimes. Once in Haarlem—in Haarlem in Holland, I mean—my father found a man who had a

Kandinski—a drawing—but the man didn't know it was a Kandinski . . . and my father bought it for something like eight or nine guilders—about five dollars—and back here it brought over a thousand——

SONNY. Guilders?

JACK. No, dollars.

BILLIE MAE [nasty-sweet]. Your father must be a man of exquisite sensibilities.

PHILIP [tired of hearing about JACK's father]. Speaking of exquisite sensibilities, Sonny, have you been following the adventures of your friend Sally Montague in the papers?

SONNY. I never read the papers . . . if something's important, people will tell you about it.

PHILIP. Oh?

CASSY. I've had my fill of Miss Montague. Stuck-up Baltimore bitch!

PHILIP. Now, now, Cassy dear, I'm sure Sonny's interest in her was just a thing of the moment.

CASSY. What moment? He was trying to get into her drawers all semester.

SONNY. Oh, now, Maggie, stop it. . . . Those future matrons are all alike . . . hot tops and cold bottoms . . . they save it up so long, it goes stale.

CASSY. So you finally did find out?

SONNY. Yes, dear, I finally did find out, but do you mind if we catch up on the latest installment in her biography just now? . . .

PHILIP. It's all over the papers.

LUKE. Is that the girl who flew off to Mexico after she shot her fiancé with one of her father's rifles?

PHILIP. Yes.

SONNY. Whew, maybe I was lucky.

JACK. Gosh.

CASSY. Sally?

PHILIP [gossipy]. Well, right after she got out of school she got engaged to another member of the horsy set down there—a nice young lawyer or stock broker—and the very next thing anybody knew she'd put some holes in his head with her papa's hunting gun. . . . [*Mysterious.*] And then she hopped a jet for Mexico City . . . as if she were running away from the whole thing . . . but then to everybody's surprise she hopped on another jet and flew back—all within a few hours.

LUKE. Yes, that's what I read . . . couldn't figure it out . . . if she was trying to escape, why fly back?

SONNY. Ho-ho-ho, our dear old upper crust is getting flakier every day.

CASSY. And I suppose you've got the real-real, inside-inside dirt, huh, Philip?

PHILIP [*pleased*]. Well, my mother's agent also agents for Sally Montague's father's brother . . . and Sally's father's brother—well, I bet you've seen him, Luke, in places like *Holiday* and the *Saturday Evening Post*—well, the agent told my mother and I overheard him telling my mother because we have an extension phone and I listen in a lot when I don't have anything else to do——

SONNY. Okay, okay. . . .

PHILIP. Well, it seems that La Montague did more than just pump lead into her lovey's temples . . . for an encore she carved off the offending organ. . . .

JACK. Huh?

PHILIP. That's right, with the traditional kitchen blade, and then she packed up his family jewels in a neat little box and without benefit of additional luggage flew off to Mexico. . . . And when she arrived there she took a taxi straight to the apartment of the little Mexican poodle her about-to-be spouse had been playing hacienda with—because that's why she plugged him in the first place, because she found out that all the time he had been courting her he had been humping another—and when she had delivered the box and its heart-curdling contents to the slightly brown concubine, she got back on a plane and flew back to Baltimore so that Daddy could put her away in some Freud peddler's private pavilion. . . . Nice?

SONNY. The rich are so lucky in law.

JACK. And now your mother's going to use that as a theme for a *New Yorker* story.

PHILIP. Are you kidding? Mother's stuff is always about her girlhood with a French grandmother in Columbus, Ohio.

CASSY. How exotic!

PHILIP. It's a living, don't knock it!

JACK. Well, that is the dirtiest linen I've seen on the line for some time.

BILLIE MAE. And I think we've taken in enough wash for one afternoon.

CASSY. Yeah, so do I. Well. . . . What are we going to do . . . sit around this trap all day and drink? Come on, Sonny, up and at 'em. Let's get out of here.

JACK. I promised my sister I'd take her to Bloomingdale's.

PHILIP. Oh my God!

SONNY. What? You let your sister lead you around department stores? Is that any way for a cat to spend his meowing time? You should be out making the scene, jumping chicks.

PHILIP. Ha.

SONNY. And all like that.

CASSY [*looking into a* New Yorker]. We could catch Lightning Hopkins at the Village Gate.

PHILIP. That's last week's issue, darling.

CASSY. Maybe he's been held over.

JACK. Well, Billie?

PHILIP. Yes, Billie, I bet you know all about Lightning Hopkins.

BILLIE MAE. No, I don't know all about Lightning Hopkins, and I don't keep track of every brown in town. Do you, for instance, know where Eddie Piano's son Pierre is playing tonight? You don't? You don't keep track of every wasp in the hive?

LUKE. I forbid you to speak that way, Billie.

BILLIE MAE. Sorry, dreary deary, you can take the girl out of Harlem . . . you know the rest, okay?

PHILIP. After Jack's telltale on his daddy, I'll always think of Harlem as a place in Holland.

SONNY. Is the Dutch Haarlem famous for bitter chocolates, too?

BILLIE MAE. Listen, Mister Sonny, you're not such a light white yourself, I notice. Maybe your great-great-great cotton-plantin' grandpappy got happy one night on some Delta dew and foun' hisself some coon-tang in the cane-brake.

LUKE. Stop it, Billie! Come on now. Let's get out of here. Harry's show closes at six. I don't want to miss it. This is the *vernissage*.

BILLIE MAE. That means they'll be serving varnish in paper cups, I suppose.

SONNY. Harry's show?

LUKE. A friend of mine named Harry who paints. Terribly talented, too.

BILLIE MAE. And I don't care much for Harry or his work. Besides, I've already seen everything he has . . . in his studio.

LUKE. Things look different in a gallery.

BILLIE MAE. Not to me they don't.

SONNY. Sure they do, ask Jack, our art expert.

CASSY. Well, let's get out of here. I don't care where, but out!

SONNY. I'm not going anywhere. I'm tired. I mean my back aches.

CASSY. Your aching back. There is nothing wrong with you. And everybody knows it. . . .

SONNY. Yes, except me.

BILLIE MAE. You're depressed, Cassy. I can tell. The whole gestalt here with King Couch depresses you.

PHILIP. Honey, he'd depress anybody.

BILLIE MAE. You should change your psychic scenery a bit.

CASSY. I've tried. I guess I haven't got the guts. I don't know. It probably wouldn't work anyway. Do you know last night I spent hours and hours just staring at an ad in here? [*Gets magazine with a Salem cigarette ad.*] Oh, yes, there they are. [*Holds up magazine.*] The cool young people in the green, green land of meadow, brook, and millpond. In the sunlight of a post-orgasmic afternoon. [*All react.*] Crock of crap! [*Throws magazine to floor.*] I don't believe it. Because I know that in real, real life she is some poor, over-coffee-ed clotheshorse who can't get a rise out of her Mad Avenue husband. And I know that in real, real life her handsome companion is just another closet queen who would love to cruise Third Avenue every night. Even though I know all that . . . even though . . . I keep hoping that they maybe really do have that magic. . . . But no matter how much I spend to get it, I just don't have it. Because somehow I was born wrong. Just a junk-toothed, dyke-shaped kid. And that's what I'll be forever and ever and ever and ever. Amen. Let's get out of here.

PHILIP. Well, I'm interested in whatever-his-name-is's art show. I just love painting. So why don't Luke and I go to the show for an hour or so and leave the ladies here to entertain Sonny?

SONNY. You wouldn't all go and leave me all alone now, would you?

CASSY [*takes six-shooter cap pistol from* SONNY's *couch*]. If we don't go out I think I'll shoot myself.

PHILIP [*to* LUKE]. Shall we go?

CASSY *spins chamber Russian roulette style, points pistol at her temple, pulls trigger, hammer clicks empty; repeats spinning, etc., and hammer clicks empty a second time.*

CASSY. Shucks, you're plumb out of ammo, Sonny.

LUKE. Bravo! That's a cap pistol.

CASSY. Well, thanks a lot.

LUKE. Well, it certainly looks like a cap pistol.

CASSY. It's Sonny's Two-Gun TV Shootin' Iron Set, podner. It's so's you can get the drop on your favorite badman. It's better'n readin' Marianne Moore any night of the week. [*Spins chamber again, points at her head, pulls trigger.*] I'm shot. [*Collapses toward* LUKE *with mock reel and stagger.*]

LUKE [*catching* CASSY *before she falls*]. Hey, be careful.

　　　CASSY *forces him into a clutch and kisses him.*

PHILIP [*seeing the prize snatched away*]. H-m-m-m-m-m-m-m-m. . . . Mouth-to-mouth resuscitation.

BILLIE MAE [*angry*]. Well, personally, I don't care much for this do-it-yourself whore's opera.

PHILIP. Well, since nobody's going out anywhere I know a brand-new parlor game. It's called Hamlet.

CASSY [*still clinging to* LUKE]. Lukie and I don't want to play any *parlor* games, do we, Lukie?

LUKE [*kisses* CASSY]. There's only one kind of game you know how to play, Cassy. [*He pushes* CASSY *toward* PHILIP.]

PHILIP [*gives* CASSY *a slap on the behind*]. And you'll like my game better, dear. [CASSY *throws gun to floor and crosses to stand before the window.*] Because it's a great, great game, with all the chance you could ask to release those poor—[*Kicks the magazine.*]—pent-up emotions of yours. You'll see. [*To* LUKE.] You'll just love it. Do you remember how Hamlet has the players act out the poisoning in the garden before the king. Well, we pick out something we suspect about another person, or his background—[*Looks at* JACK.]—something we've never dared mention—[JACK *rises and crosses the stage. He finds a tube of long Japanese matches, picks it up, and fiddles with it before replacing it.*]—and we act it out. And the ones who aren't acting, try to guess who the play is about.

LUKE. All right. I'll play one more game.

SONNY. That sounds fine.

BILLIE MAE. I'm not a bad actress, as a matter of fact.

PHILIP [*nasty*]. School plays? [*To* CASSY.] Cassy! Have you cards? We'll have a drawing to see who goes first.

CASSY [*defeated*]. There somewhere, I don't know where, really.

PHILIP. Well, those matches will do it. [*Picks up the tube of matches, strikes one, looks at it for a moment.*] Skeletons, skeletons, burning bright . . . [*Takes out all but five matches.*] There, five remain, and one burned one makes six. Now I'll just shake gently—and—[*Shakes tube.*]—we'll draw. Is everybody ready? Here we go! [*Offers the tube to* BILLIE MAE.] Miss Y?

BILLIE MAE [*draws a good match*]. Ah, excluded again.

PHILIP [*offers tube to* JACK]. Jackie-Lackey?

JACK [*draws good match*]. Likewise.

PHILIP [*offers tube to* LUKE *on bended knee*]. My liege.

LUKE [*draws good match*]. Me too, leaving three: one for Cassy, one for Sonny, and one for you, Butch.

CASSY [*draws dead match*]. Well, look who got burned!

PHILIP. Okay, Cas, pick your cast, not more than one other actor . . . if you can help it . . . and then go out of the room to prepare . . . don't try to think up the lines. . . . Just work it out right here in front of us . . . it's much more fun that way.

CASSY [*glancing around the room, her eyes hesitate for a moment on* SONNY'*s couch, then move on*]. Okay. . . . Okay. . . . Yeah, I think I have something.

SONNY. What is it you've got, syphilis?

LUKE. That was the name of an ancient shepherd.

CASSY. And now for casting, it's always a bitch.

BILLIE MAE. Cassy, got a part for me?

CASSY. I don't know.

BILLIE MAE. Just like Broadway around here. Our turn seldom comes on the Great White Way.

CASSY. I think I see how to do this. You, Jack! [JACK *starts to rise.*] You're going to do it with me. Come on, we'll get changed up in Sonny's father's room.

SONNY. You could go along as a chaperon, Philip.

PHILIP. *Him* she can have.

Curtain.

ACT TWO

The same scene, a few seconds later.

SONNY. Okay, everybody, let's have a drink. Phil, would you do the honors in my stead?

PHILIP [*wry*]. And to think I came over here to borrow Sonny's pony.

SONNY. I thought you came over to consult Cassy about your big TV part, sport?

PHILIP. Two birds with one stone, dear.

SONNY. If you've really been offered a TV part, and you're really going to leave college, you won't need my pony.

BILLIE MAE. Don't tell me that Sonny has a horse to go with his cap pistols.

PHILIP. What? . . . No, his trot, dear . . . his cheater . . . for Vergil's *Aeneid*. We're up to Book Two at the moment . . . about the horse the Greeks built outside the gates of Troy . . . oh, you know . . . *timeo Danaos et dona ferentes* . . . never look a Greek gift horse in the mouth—

SONNY. Very free translation indeed.

BILLIE MAE. I'm sorry I'm not tracking—

PHILIP. A pony is an English key to the Latin text, dear. Sonny rides through all his exams that way—it's easy—especially when you have the honor system. . . .

SONNY. Then why, pray tell, dear Philip, do you want to borrow my trot?

PHILIP. Because I want to lock up the answers *before* the exam, not *during* it.

SONNY. You wouldn't have the nerve *during*.

PHILIP. Oh, no?

SONNY. Well, why don't you just prove it sometime?

PHILIP. I prove my nerve in other ways.

SONNY. *What* ways?

PHILIP. Book lifting. That's much nervier than cheating on an exam. . . .

LUKE. I'm shocked. Really. [*To* SONNY.] You steal grades— [*To* PHILIP.] And you steal books—

PHILIP [*coy*]. I'm shocked that you're shocked, Luke, dear, but while you're at it, would you mind telling us which practice you find more reprehensible?

LUKE. An impossible choice!

BILLIE MAE. Oh, come on, Luke, now's your chance to dish out some preordainment wisdom. [*To* PHILIP.] Personally I find your crime worse——

PHILIP. And why is that?

BILLIE MAE. Because yours is not a matter of necessity.

SONNY. Because I suppose my cheating is a matter of necessity—I suppose that is what you're trying to say. Thanks a lot, bitch! Thanks a whole goddamn lot!

BILLIE MAE. Well, stealing books certainly can't be a necessity for Phil. . . . I'm sure his mother earns enough with her twice-told tales to buy him an occasional *McGuffey's Reader*, wouldn't you guess?

SONNY. It's not that I need to cheat . . . it makes exams a lot kickier, that's all.

BILLIE MAE. Okay, love, relax, don't justify yourself . . . nobody really cares.

PHILIP [*supercilious*]. That's right, love, nobody really cares. . . . If it gives you a little pleasure, why not?

BILLIE MAE [*mocking* PHILIP]. Why not?

LUKE. Why not? Because it happens to be—[*Disgust*.] Oh well, why try to explain. . . .

BILLIE MAE. You steal nice books, Phil?

PHILIP. Only. I'll pick you up a morocco-bound copy of Luke's poems the next time I do Brentano's.

BILLIE MAE. Thanks, but I've got several autographed copies as it is . . . but you could take me along on one of your capers one day . . . I'd just love to learn how to build my library.

LUKE. Really, Billie!

PHILIP. Well I just would love to take you, dear, but the trick with me is establishing rapport with a nice young clerk—you know—and then he sort of agrees not to notice. . . . I'm not sure I could work that with a lady along. . . .

LUKE. I don't understand.

BILLIE MAE. It's all right, dear, you don't have to.

LUKE. Well, I like to understand everything.

BILLIE MAE [to PHILIP]. You specialize in the big stores?

PHILIP [arch]. Of course, there's a bigger selection there.

LUKE. I wonder what scene they're going to do? They've certainly been out long enough.

BILLIE MAE. Long enough for what, love?

SONNY. Now, now.

BILLIE MAE. They are taking their own sweet time, aren't they?

SONNY. Yes, and why don't you come and sit beside Sonny, black beauty?

BILLIE MAE. I'd love to, darling, but I wouldn't want to hurt your bad back.

PHILIP [closing in on LUKE]. You know, Luke, you're really a very nice person.

LUKE. What?

BILLIE MAE. You know, Sonny, if you try hard enough you just might reach me after all.

LUKE. Maybe I should go

SONNY [pawing at BILLIE MAE]. Okay, sport, go!

PHILIP. Now, Sonny, don't tell him that . . . he can't leave just when the curtain is about to go up.

JACK. Okay. Clear the couch everybody. We're ready. [LUKE *crosses to a chair, downstage left, and* PHILIP *follows.* LUKE *notices* PHILIP *close at hand, takes the chair to below the bar, and offers it to* BILLIE MAE. *Meanwhile* PHILIP *has gotten the cage chair, which he places where the other chair originally was.* LUKE *freshens his drink at the bar and sits on the hi-fi chair.*] Philip, you yell, "Curtain!"

PHILIP. Curtain!

JACK, *now dressed in a white doctor's coat, with a stethoscope and a clipboard, sits on* CASSY's *couch, and pretends to be working at a desk.* CASSY, *in a vaudeville maid's apron, carrying a mop or broom, dustpan, and brush, knocks at an imaginary door.*

CASSY [*drawling*]. Knock, knock . . . Knock, knock . . .

JACK [*all his timidity gone now that he is in costume. Drawl, not as thick as* CASSY's, *mixed with some years of school in the North*]. Yes, what is it?

CASSY. It's me, suh, Ahletta.

JACK. Who? Huh, well do come in, do!

CASSY. Yassuh, thank you, suh. [*Comes in, singing, "Jesus loves me this I know, for the Bible tells me so."*] A fren' of mine, Flora, who wuk for Miz Doctuh up to de big house say, you lookin' fo' somebody tuh clean up down heah at yo' office.

JACK. Come in, come in, girl. Right here.

CASSY [*smiling and grinning*]. Yassuh, thank you, suh.

JACK. Well, what did you say you wanted, girl?

CASSY. My fren' Flora say you maybe wuz lookin' for a clean-up person down heah at yo' office.

JACK [*arrogant*]. She did, eh?

CASSY. Yassuh.

JACK. Well, it just may be that maybe I am.

CASSY [*shifting about painfully*]. I sho' would keep it mighty clean, suh. I needs wuk bad.

JACK. You do?

CASSY. Yassuh.

JACK. You from 'roun' here, girl?

CASSY. Yassuh.

JACK. You wouldn't be one of them what came up here from New Awlins or Birmin'ham or any of them places where the niggers are gettin' uppity, now, would you?

CASSY. Mah fathuh is a cropper out to Panthuh Buhn.

JACK. Panther Burn, pretty name.

CASSY. Yassuh.

JACK. How old are you, girl?

CASSY. Nineteen and some.

JACK [*pokes her with stethoscope*]. Not married yet, are you, girl?

CASSY. No, suh, but I hopes to git married. [*Smiles sweetly, forgetting her fear for an instant.*]

JACK. Who's going to marry you, girl?

CASSY. The preachuh. I hopes.

JACK. Now don't you get sassy! I mean who you going to be married with?

CASSY. I don't rightly know for sure, suh, he ain't asked me yet, but it just might be that boy what washes cahs for Mistuh Yancey down at the fillin' station.

JACK. Yes, I know the one you mean. A good boy, always smilin' and grinnin' at everybody.

CASSY. Yassuh, he does smile a lot.

JACK [*holds stethoscope out like an earphone*]. What's your name again, girl?

CASSY. Ah-letta.

JACK. That's a pretty name.

CASSY. Yassuh.

JACK. Tell me, Arletta, did you ever happen to speak to any of the ladies who happened to work for me before? I mean did any of them tell you how they came to get the job cleanin' up here?

CASSY. I don't recall askin' anybody at all, no suh. It was my fren' Flora up to de big house tole me to come down heah.

JACK. You never spoke with Susie, or Erma Jean, or Cleontha, or any of them?

CASSY. No, suh. Not that I remember, suh.

JACK. Well now that's too bad. Might have made things a damn sight easier. Now, if you ever had spoken to one of my girls, why, you'd know that you have to pass a medical examination before you can work here. It's a doctor's office, you know, and my girls must be healthy and clean.

CASSY. Flora didn't say nothing about no examination.

JACK. You've had a medical examination before, of course?

CASSY. No suh. My mothuh mostly took care of us when we wuz sick. They ain't no doctuh out to Panthuh Buhn nohow.

JACK. Aah. I'll just latch the door so we won't be disturbed. Latch! [Latches an imaginary door.]

CASSY. But I don't feel in the leas' sick. I'll be gettin' home now.

JACK. Well, now you just lie down there on the examining table. [Indicates couch.] And I'll help you with your clothes.

CASSY. Oh, Lawdy, Lawdy, I see what Erma Jean mean by takin' her wuk tes'.

JACK [excited, violent]. So you did speak to one of my girls. Well then, you know all about it, don't you? [Throws himself on top of her.] Ahhhhhhh. . . .

CASSY [struggling]. Oh . . . Oh . . . God-amighty! God-amighty! Ain't it shameful! . . . Shameful!

LUKE [yelling]. Curtain! Curtain! Curtain!

JACK and CASSY stop playlet.

PHILIP. But, Luke, you're not supposed to stop the show until you know who it is they're acting out.

JACK *and* CASSY *resume playlet.*

LUKE [*pulls* JACK *off* CASSY]. Stop it, you two! Stop it! Stop it!

JACK [*jumping up*]. Good audience tonight, my dear.

CASSY [*hysterical sexy laughter*]. We're a hit, Basil. A hit!

PHILIP. It was all over so fast. What do you two do for a curtain call?

CASSY. Come on, Jack, let's get changed. You know that doctor's smock almost made a man out of you. But you can't stay in costume forever, can you?

JACK *picks up clipboard, broom, dustpan, and brush, and goes out with* CASSY.

PHILIP. Well, it was a moving little piece of theatre, but we must remember it was only a play after all.

SONNY. Only a play after all, but oh, it brought back memories beyond recall. Well, not quite beyond recall . . . when there were kisses from Cassy in corridors, and in cars, and in bars, and in bathrooms, and in kitchens, and even in bedrooms. But I am indulging myself. I know who it is they were acting out, and I did not yell "curtain."

BILLIE MAE. I'm so glad I didn't get the part. It was Aunt Jemima from the word go.

SONNY. Yes, Billie, and besides you could never have gotten the accent right.

PHILIP. Well, Luke, since you brought the curtain down you must tell us who the little drama was all about.

LUKE. I don't know. I just know I didn't like it, that's all.

SONNY. If you didn't know, you had no right to stop the show. All right, Luke, you must answer, whom were they acting out?

LUKE. How would I know?

SONNY. You don't know anybody around here whose daddy is a doctor? That's a clue.

LUKE. No.

SONNY. Like you didn't notice the big fat name plate on the door—Dr. Boynton?

LUKE. Uh . . .

SONNY. Okay, now maybe you would care to guess who the other character in the drama is?

LUKE. What?

SONNY. Yes, the poor abused black girl.

BILLIE MAE. That's right, never say "Negro," it's not cool anymore.

SONNY [to BILLIE MAE]. See, I told you I was an okay ofay.

BILLIE MAE. You get the "T" for tolerance.

SONNY. All right, Luke, who was the black girl?

LUKE. Leave me alone, how would I know who those people were? It was supposed to take place in the South, wasn't it?

SONNY. You've actually been face to face with the black girl.

LUKE [incredulous]. Billie Mae?

BILLIE MAE. I have never been a maid. I am not a maid now. I am never going to be a maid. I'd rather be dead.

SONNY. Thank you, Billie, but what we want to know now, and from friend Luke, is who is the mysterious black girl in Cassy and Jack's production of "Delta Diary"?

LUKE [anguish]. I don't know, damn it, I told you I don't know.

PHILIP [putting his arm around LUKE]. Now don't you get upset, dear. Mother is here and everything will be all right.

SONNY. Ernestine! That's the answer: Ernestine.

LUKE. I was never face to face with any Ernestine . . . of any color!

SONNY. Oh no? She let you into this apartment.

BILLIE MAE. Well, I'll be a Georgia cracker.

SONNY. Somehow, after we moved North, Ernestine followed us up here and she tracked Daddy down, and she threatened to tell Mummy all about how Daddy had carried on with her . . . and she just wouldn't go away . . . and there were no Ku Kluxers to call out up here . . . and no red-necks to arouse . . . so Daddy hired her as sort of maid-in-perpetuity, you might say . . . but when Mummie-Birdie is carted off to a cage somewhere, I just wonder how much job security our Ernie will have.

PHILIP. And who told you all that?

SONNY. Cassy and Jack did in their play. At least part of it. I made up the rest to go along with the gag.

PHILIP. Well, maybe it's true what they acted out, and you're just hiding it by not hiding it.

SONNY. And how would I know if it is true? I was a baby then.

PHILIP. Because your daddy told you all about it.

SONNY. I suppose I should believe everything he tells me.

PHILIP. I see . . . and now we're in for an even more shocking revelation. You're going to tell us that you are actually the maid's illegitimate son, and your mother somehow suspects it, and that's why her brain is broken, huh?

SONNY. Never. Wouldn't I at least have kinky hair or something? Highly improbable! Besides, the cartilage in the end of my nose is split . . . I mean you can feel the separation under the skin. My father told me that Negro noses don't have that . . . that they're solid there.

BILLIE MAE. How many Negro noses have you felt?

SONNY. Well . . . well, none, actually.

BILLIE MAE. Exactly.

LUKE [seeing a way out for himself]. Let's stop this.

SONNY. Exactly. I'd like a drink. I'm bored with beer. Luke, get me a drink, will you? [LUKE hesitates, then rises and gets SONNY a drink.] Luke, I've been meaning to ask you, why do you wear that funny black suit?

LUKE. I am going to graduate school.

SONNY. That's why the funny suit?

LUKE. Graduate school for me is a seminary.

PHILIP. So you're going to be a man of the cloth?

SONNY. The whole cloth, no doubt. I suppose, Luke, that you go ape over Albert Schweitzer.

LUKE. He was a very great man.

BILLIE MAE. I liked him because he had a cat named Balthazar who was born on his desk.

SONNY. Say, Luke, would you mind a rather personal question?

LUKE. Ask it! You've been asking everything else.

SONNY. Can you actually manage to believe in God?

LUKE. No, as a matter of fact, I don't believe in God.

BILLIE MAE. You don't?

LUKE. No, I don't, but there are so many others who do . . . or who could . . . religion is a sort of social glue . . . and heaven knows society could stand some pasting together at this point . . . I mean, before the bomb blasts it apart forever. . . .

SONNY. You always think in slogans?

LUKE. I'm sure my life will be a little more useful than my parents' lives. . . . How much faith can you put in morning radio as a contribution to civilization?

BILLIE MAE. If you can't sincerely believe, Luke, you shouldn't play around with the pulpit. I thought you really admired my father for his work in Harlem and for the faith he gives people.

LUKE. But I do, darling. He gets them more boat rides and fried chicken than they'd ever see without him. Maybe God is fried chicken. How do I know? Fried chicken is good.

BILLIE MAE [ominous]. If you're not sincere, it'll show through the blackest suit.

PHILIP. Look who's calling the kettle . . .

LUKE. But I am sincere. I may come to believe one day.

SONNY. Hey, when Penny and Patch leave you their radio show you can turn it into a Gospel hour.

PHILIP. Hallelujah!

BILLIE MAE. We could all hop a jet for Alabama and join a march. There's bound to be a march going on somewhere.

SONNY. I don't think that's my scene . . . supporting white guys' guilt week. I don't even think that's your scene, Billie Mae.

BILLIE MAE. Oh, it's not. Those marches are nothing but big promiscuity parties. Did some of your best black friends tell you that? Night and day, everywhere, in the woods, on the grass, along the roads, up against fenders —everywhere.

LUKE. Well, I don't see what's so wrong with that. Segregation is mainly a sexual problem anyway, so we might just as well screw it right out of existence. Let everybody be light brown.

PHILIP. Well, it is a lovely color.

BILLIE MAE. You have no respect for anything, do you?

CASSY *sweeps back into the room in an expensive designer suit all ready to go out.* JACK *follows.*

PHILIP. Oh, you look ravishing!

SONNY. Well, dear, there you are. And how was it?

CASSY. Families that dress together repress together.

PHILIP. And strangers make the best lovers.

CASSY [*looking around the room*]. Hey, you're all getting pissed. Jack, get me a drink. We're falling behind here.

JACK *goes to the bar to get a drink for himself and for* CASSY.

SONNY. And why shouldn't we be getting plotzed? . . . You care to suggest anything better?

CASSY. Yes, I want to go out.

SONNY. Nobody's going anywhere. We're all going to play another game I know that's much better than Phil's substitute Shakespeare.

CASSY. Sonny, I don't want to play any more games. I want to go out.

SONNY. Arletta, if this game is going to be any good we all have to agree to play.

PHILIP. Well, what is it?

SONNY. The whole fun is agreeing before you know what the game is.

CASSY. Strip dominoes.

SONNY. No.

CASSY. Okay, okay, count me in. I always go along with everything anyway, no will power.

PHILIP. So what is it?

SONNY. Listen, after we play, Cassy will find you my Latin trot and you can keep it right up to the night of the next exam, okay? Now agree to play.

PHILIP. What kind of incentive is that? I may be quitting school.

SONNY. Now, Philly, don't be bitchy.

PHILIP. Oh, okay, all right. I don't care.

SONNY. Billie Mae?

BILLIE MAE. Well, I really want to know what you're planning for us.

SONNY. It's more fun than a barrel of grits.

BILLIE MAE. Yes, but what is it?

SONNY. If you don't sign up, you'll never know.

BILLIE MAE. Well, I'm really not that eager.

SONNY. If you don't honestly enjoy this game, Billie, I'll see to it that Cassy donates a thousand bucks to your old man's Sunday school, okay?

CASSY. Yeah . . . okay, it's a deal.

BILLIE MAE. It's a deal.

SONNY. Phil is in, Billie is in, Frieda is in— Luke?

JACK. You haven't asked me yet?

SONNY. All right, I'll ask you. Jack, are you in?

JACK. Sure, sight unseen.

SONNY. Very brave of you.

CASSY. You're so delighted to be included you'd volunteer for a suicide squad.

JACK. Yeah, a lot of people are like that. I just happen to know it about myself, that's all.

SONNY. Luke?

LUKE. Well, I would like to know a lot more about it.

SONNY. It's amusing.

LUKE. Very amusing?

SONNY. Most, most amusing.

LUKE. More Stepin Fetchit, I suppose?

BILLIE MAE. Oh, come on, Lukie, be a *mensch* for once in your *leben*.

LUKE. Oh all right. . . .

SONNY. Fine, now. . . . [SONNY *has been lighting his cigarettes with the long Japanese matches* PHILIP *used for drawing straws in the Hamlet game. Secretly he has saved six burned ones and placed them in the tube which he now hands to* CASSY *while whispering some inaudible instructions.*] Now, Mary Lou, if you will just come up here and get the lucky-draw match tube. [*Whispers in* CASSY's *ear.*]

JACK [*imitating an owl*]. Whoooooooooooo? Whoooooooooooo will the winner be?

SONNY. Our game can begin.

CASSY [*going first to* LUKE]. There now, kiddies, choose well. You first, Luke.

JACK. I never get to go first.

CASSY [*as* LUKE *draws*]. Maybe next time . . .

LUKE [*slight tremor of shock*]. Look, I——

CASSY. Yes, look, you won.

PHILIP. Well, I must say that was rapid.

CASSY *gives the tube back to* SONNY.

SONNY. Good then, the first winner has won, our game has begun . . . There now, friends. [*Points to cage.*] That is the locus of our entertainment.

BILLIE MAE. Well, what is that?

SONNY. A cage.

PHILIP. I didn't know your daddy did animal experiments.

SONNY. A couple of years ago a colleague of my father's got a monkey to observe—he kept it at home—but the poor thing suffered horribly from loneliness whenever he and his wife went out. . . . Well, they could hardly hire a monkey sitter . . . so they hit on something else. . . . They discovered that the monkey would be perfectly happy if they just turned on the TV. He'd sit and watch the images and masturbate . . . watch some more and masturbate some more . . . like that for hours on end—the perfect life. . . . Where do you think my Doctor Daddy got the idea of getting his own monkey? He kept it right here in the living room. He regards his life as his laboratory. He's got stuff spread out all over the place. He wanted to try the TV bit to see if his friend wasn't putting him on, and then he also thought that prolonged observation of the monkey would give him some insight into basic human needs—and then, I don't know—he got bored with the whole thing and sent the monkey off to a kiddie zoo.

BILLIE MAE. And kept the cage?

CASSY. Maybe he's got plans for Sonny's mummy we don't know about.

PHILIP. And our game? Are we going to perform an experiment in the noble name of science?

SONNY. No, in the nobler name of amusement. If monkeys act like people, I thought it might be fascinating to see if people act like monkeys?

CASSY. I think I see now.

BILLIE MAE. I do, too.

PHILIP [bringing the cage downstage left]. So do I.

JACK. Yeah.

SONNY. All right, Luke, let's begin.

LUKE. No.

SONNY. Why don't you want to be a monkey, Lukie? Don't you trust your fellow human beings? We're all civilized here.

JACK. Hah!

SONNY. Well educated. Some of us even study Latin.

LUKE. Why don't we play another round of Hamlet, maybe. I'll pick a partner and go out and prepare a scene.

SONNY. No, Lukie, we're going to play *this* game now. We all agreed to play before we began and now we are going to stick by our word. So begin by taking off your clothes.

LUKE. Nobody said anything about taking any clothes off!

SONNY [*dictator*]. Rule of the game, Lukie.

LUKE. No, I refuse.

SONNY. Oh, now, Lukie, we've just got to do this thing right.

PHILIP. Who ever heard of a monkey wearing clothes?

LUKE [*signs of hysteria, forced laugh*]. I've heard of monkey suits, haven't you, Billie?

BILLIE MAE. Are they like birthday suits, darling?

LUKE. I've seen chimpanzees dressed up in newsreels.

CASSY. That was before our time, sweetie. Besides, this is no newsreel.

BILLIE MAE. No, not to me it certainly won't be.

PHILIP [*intense*]. Oh come now, Luke, get out of your clothes and into your cage like a good monkey should.

SONNY. We're going to play this game, aren't we, group?

ALL. *Yes.*

They all close in on LUKE, *except* SONNY *who stays on his couch directing the operation.* LUKE *is stripped of his clothes to his underdrawers.*

PHILIP [*ad-libbing*]. Look at those shoulders. Heaven! Take his pants off. He looks like a camp counselor I once had.

BILLIE MAE. Put him in his cage.

PHILIP *and* JACK *put* LUKE *in cage and lock it.* BILLIE MAE *starts to sing "Oh, the monkey wrapped his tail around the flagpole."* PHILIP *keeps key on string.*

SONNY. Lukie wanna peanut?

JACK *throws peanuts at* LUKE.

LUKE [*shuddering*]. No.

SONNY. Now, Lukie-Monkey, that is not a proper monkey noise. Monkeys chirp . . . like birds.

CASSY. Cheep-cheep, cheep-cheep, chirp-chirp—like Sonny's mummy.

CASSY *and* JACK *and* PHILIP *rip balls off the Christmas tree and hurl them against the cage.*

BILLIE MAE. Now is your chance, Lukie-Monkey, to call upon the God you believe in for others. Try him now.

PHILIP. No atheists in monkey holes so they say.

SONNY. Phil, I'll take the key. [PHILIP *throws* SONNY *the key.*] Thanks, it would be awful to lose it. Not even monkeys want to be monkeys forever.

LUKE [*to* SONNY, *recovering a little*]. Wait till your father comes home. He'll punish you and he'll pay, too. My parents will sue him for everything he's got.

CASSY. Which is not a lot, I don't think. . . .

SONNY. Fact is, dear speakie-monkey, my daddy is not coming home this evening at all. He is up in old New England looking for a suitable nut club in which to enroll Mummie-Birdie. And he's got his latest greatest R.N. with him and they are probably right now bundled up in some Howard Johnson's lodge, tasting all twenty-eight flavors.

JACK. Twenty-eight. [*Strikes cage with* LUKE'S *belt.*]

CASSY. True, Lukie, true. The good doctor called not long ago from some place near Boston.

JACK. And if you think Sonny's Mummie-Birdie will be of any help, just erase it from your monkey mind. She's been out for hours . . . her world is all pills and pillows.

CASSY. And dear old Ernestine whom I so movingly portrayed a while back is safely sawing wood in her room by now.

PHILIP. Zzzzz.

SONNY. Maybe now, groupee, he'd like to see a little television.

JACK. Want to see television?

BILLIE MAE. Maybe *it* would like to see a little television.

LUKE [*bangs against cage*]. Let me out of here!

CASSY. Quiet, baby.

PHILIP. Now stop that, Monk. You'll only hurt your little monkey paws.

LUKE. Let me out. Oh, Christ!

PHILIP. He's not going to help you, dear, any more than His Father helped Him. I mean a daddy's power only goes so far!

BILLIE MAE. Yeah, even if He is a white daddy.

SONNY. Jack, bring over the television and we'll see how my daddy's buddy's baby sitter works on people.

PHILIP. Yeah, let's try it. It might even be more fun than the steam room at the Arabian Nights.

JACK. Arabian Nights?

PHILIP. You never mind, Jack.

CASSY. You know what?

ALL. What?

CASSY. Isn't it a shame Penny and Patch aren't on TV. Wouldn't that be a gas? Daddy Monkey and Momma Monkey doing the Monkey for their Baby Monkey's private pleasures.

SONNY. Okay, Jack, turn on something stimulating.

JACK. Do we need sound?

SONNY. No. Let's try movement only to start . . . that'll make the experiment more scientific. [JACK *snaps set on. All wait a moment*] It seems we have a very sophisticated anthropoid on our hands. This particular prime-time spectacular doesn't seem to arouse him.

PHILIP. You're right, Pithecanthropus non-erectus, as far as I can see, which is not very far in this light.

JACK. Perhaps we should try sound. [*Snaps on sound. Thundering-driving Scrugg's style country music, perhaps "Ballad of Jed Clampett."*]

BILLIE MAE. Oh, I hate that hillbilly crap.

PHILIP. Yes, dear, besides it's not the sort of thing you play on his banjo, is it?

All wait, a much shorter period this time.

CASSY. No, no, not working.

SONNY [*shouting*]. Shut it off! Shut it off! I've got a much better idea.

JACK shuts off the set.

CASSY. Well, what's your much better idea, Sonny, honey?

SONNY [*British explorer*]. Well, what we have learned so far is that pictures alone do not stimulate it. And that pictures with the aid of sound are no better.

BILLIE MAE. What is the reason for that?

SONNY. It seems that our monkey, much like those primitives who can make no sense at all out of photographs that explorers show them——

JACK. Aborigines.

SONNY. —that our monkey has a low response to things in two dimensions.

CASSY. How ever do we continue the experiment?

SONNY. I'm so glad you asked. By giving him a stimulus in three dimensions. [*Flips out fingers: 1, 2, 3!*] Count 'em!

BILLIE MAE. Oh no you don't! That cage is too small. Much too small to mate in nohow.

PHILIP. Yes, I'm afraid she's right, and besides that boy-girl stuff is pretty dull for some of us.

The phone rings.

SONNY [*commanding*]. You're on, Rose.

CASSY [*picking up phone*]. Hello. Happy New Year! Oh hi, Doctor Bo. Yes. . . . Yes, everything's fine. . . . Yes, Mrs. Boynton's sleeping now. . . . She's had a rather full day. . . . Yes, we read her stories and played records . . . she seemed a bit calmer, actually. . . .

LUKE [*screaming*]. Help! Doctor Boynton. Help. They've put me in the monkey cage!

CASSY [*covering phone with her hand*]. Shut him up! [LUKE's *shouts are muffled by the zebra cover that* PHILIP *puts over the cage.* JACK *throws peanuts.* CASSY *huddles over the phone to block out the sounds.*] There. Sorry, Doctor. . . . No, it was nothing. We turned it down. Just a rather thick slice of life on the trauma tube.

LUKE. Help! Let me out of here.

CASSY [*loud, in case* LUKE *should shout again*]. It's about this guy see, who wakes up sane in a psycho ward and they won't let him out. . . . Huh? Oh? Oh, sure. Yeah, I will. Sure. All right, you too, 'bye.

SONNY. You were superb, Rose.

CASSY. Thank you, o Monkey master.

SONNY. Now, Lukie-Monkey, as you can see, your yelling isn't going to get you anywhere. We'll let you out when you have satisfied yourself—and us—and not before. We have lots of liquor—and lots of time—although we'd appreciate your coming . . . coming through before midnight. . . . Say, maybe we can even dig out some of Daddy's champagne.

PHILIP. I have a much better idea. Maybe we should read him some of his own poetry.

JACK. Ugh.

PHILIP. That might just do the trick. Too bad I didn't pick up a copy at Doubleday's on the way over.

BILLIE MAE. Maybe a selection from the *Reader's Digest*.

SONNY. Sorry, we don't subscribe.

JACK. Maybe in the kitchen, maybe Ernestine——

CASSY. Naaaaah, she reads the Bible.

SONNY. It's like I said, we need a little live three-dimensional stimulation. Ladies, any volunteers?

BILLIE MAE. Not me, darling, I never perform in public. Never.

PHILIP. Oh, Cassandra, looks like you star again.

SONNY. Jack, put on some music— [*Points with match tube.*] —whatever's there, and our little girl will grind good to that.

JACK [*fumbling with the record player*]. I don't know how to work this damn thing.

SONNY. Now, now, we can't have talk like that from the staff. [*Puts match tube on top of sofa back.*]

BILLIE MAE. Oh, I'll shed a little light on the subject. [*Grabs tube of Japanese matches and tries to light one.*] Hey! They're all burned out.

Music up. BILLIE *is confused about the matches, but she gets interested in the dance as she returns match tube to* SONNY's *couch. Later the realization of the trick* SONNY *worked at the beginning of the game hits her.*

SONNY. Go, Rose, go!

CASSY *dances in front of the cage, beckons* PHILIP *to join her. Then* JACK *joins in. After a while* BILLIE MAE *starts to dance and the trio clears the floor for her.*

BILLIE MAE [*frenzy*]. Lawsie, Lawsie, we is going to see the great White Monkey from America, chil'un. [*Trio applauds.*] In person at the Sutton Point South tonight. [*Trio applauds.*] Lawsie, Lawsie, dats mo' excitin' dan de time my mothuh tuk us to see dee great Albino Rhino from Africa down in Birmin'ham when we wuz jus' tar babies.

CASSY, PHILIP, *and* JACK. Lawsie, Lawsie!

LUKE [*to* BILLIE MAE]. So you don't care either?

BILLIE MAE. Sure I does, honey, but it's like the man said. Rules is rules.

JACK. She's got a point there.

CASSY. Rules is rules.

PHILIP. That's the law, honey.

BILLIE MAE. Now you won't get nowhere if you don't play the game law-abidin' and peaceful-like.

CASSY. Hear, hear!

JACK *and* PHILIP. Hear, hear!

BILLIE MAE. Let's legislate this thing.

JACK. Hear what the lady said?

CASSY *and* PHILIP. Leg-is-late!

BILLIE MAE. Ain't that what they is forever tellin' us?

JACK. Always and forever.

CASSY. Leg-is-late.

PHILIP. Amen.

LUKE. But, Billie, I thought——

BILLIE MAE. Thought that I cared? No! Since birth you and your fair-skinned friends have deprived me of my humanity and now it's going to be a distinct pleasure to see you do without yours.

LUKE. The mob could turn on you next.

BILLIE MAE. Could turn, could turn? It already has.

CASSY *starts to whistle,* PHILIP *joins in.* JACK *begins to feel uneasy and starts for the front door.*

SONNY. Jack, you going? Why are you going? Because now that you've had all the kicks your feeble circuits can stand you've started to feel guilty, right? Feels so good to pray after a lynching . . . repentance prolongs the sensation.

JACK. Maybe he'll get sick in there . . . catch pneumonia or something. Perhaps we should let him out. . . .

LUKE [*almost a voice from the dead*]. Perhaps you should. And then again perhaps you shouldn't.

SONNY. Hark, our beast hath found tongue.

LUKE. I've been thinking . . . maybe I'm the luckiest person here. . . .

SONNY. Oooops, what are we in for? . . . An orgy of Christian resignation?

LUKE. No, but my case is simple. Either I get out of this cage or I don't. . . . But it's *not* so simple for any of *you* out there. . . . Jack, do you think that they'll ever in your whole life let you forget that you're a scapegoat? Do you?

JACK. Oh, they don't mean anything by it. They're just kidding.

LUKE. And now, ladies and gentlemen, after our long, hard, train journey, nice hot showers and nice warm lunches await you, now that we have arrived at Auschwitz. But, first to the showers. They didn't mean anything by that either, did they, Jackie? You don't think Sonny and Cassy are your friends, do you? This is their private concentration camp and you're their guinea *schwein*. [JACK *is silent and moves away*.] And you, Philip, when the police grab you out of a fruit bar and take you down to the station house and make you play host to half the force in your cell, how do you feel?

PHILIP. I feel like going to another party, that's how I feel. [*Starts to go*.]

BILLIE MAE [*gives* PHILIP *a shove that sends him to the floor by the sofa*]. No you don't, my little pansy pal, you're seeing this thing through with the rest of us.

PHILIP *crawls up on the sofa and whimpers on* CASSY's *shoulder*.

SONNY. Calm down, Philip.

LUKE. And you, Billie Mae, you were born conveniently colored so they don't even need a tattooed number to know you from the white ones—the right ones. You came into the world through the service entrance and without me that's just the way you'll go out. [BILLIE MAE *puts hand over her face*.] And you, Cassy . . . you . . . [*Scornful laugh*.]

CASSY [*to* LUKE]. You jerk!

SONNY. Phil, why don't you dig out a few bottles of champagne in the bottom of the bar there. You'll find glasses, too, I think. Let's all drink a toast to liberty—[*Gives* PHILIP *a slap on the shoulder*.]

CASSY. What's with you?

SONNY. —as we give our dear Luke his. Because I assume that's what you all want. You seem to have lost your sporting spirit all of a sudden. [*Holds the key above the back of his couch.*] Here's the key. [*Shakes it about.*] Well, who wants the honor? [*Nobody moves to take the key.*] What's wrong? Do you think our monkey might perhaps bite you? Hey, Billie Mae, don't you want to let him out? Aren't you his special pal? [BILLIE MAE *is silent.*] Surely, Phil. [*No response.*] Maybe, Jackie? [JACK *is silent.*] Mary Lou? [CASSY *gives* SONNY *a "not-me-honey" look.*] Sorry, Luke, looks like not even your closest pals want to let you out. I guess once you're up the creek no one wants to paddle for you. And you know I can't move because it would hurt my back.

LUKE [*shifting his approach*]. Well, perhaps they need more motivation than just pity. . . . I think I have a solution to this whole ugly mess.

SONNY. What ugly mess?

LUKE. The ugly mess you're going to be in when I tell people you put me in this cage.

SONNY. Because you're going to broadcast it on the *Penny and Patch Show*, I suppose?

LUKE. No, no, on police short wave.

SONNY [*suddenly serious*]. Well, just what is your solution? I mean if you were in our boots, what would you do?

LUKE. Well, besides trembling, you might try putting one of the ladies in here for a short tour of indecency.

PHILIP *uncorks the champagne, fills glasses.*

SONNY. Interesting, but I don't quite see.

LUKE. Well, if I came out and then helped you put somebody else in here I would be in on the game, and I wouldn't ever be able to tell anybody about it, now would I? If you see what I mean?

CASSY [*moving off a few steps with* BILLIE MAE]. No, I don't think Billie and I see what you mean, do we, Billie?

BILLIE MAE [*calm, brutal*]. No, Cassy, not at all.

SONNY. Hey, goddamn it, where's my champagne?

PHILIP [*serving* SONNY]. Here.

SONNY. Nice of you to think of me.

PHILIP *serves* BILLIE MAE, *intentionally spilling champagne on her dress.*

LUKE. Hey, Phil, don't I get a glass? I don't see any "Don't Feed the Animal" signs.

SONNY. Sure, why not give old Luke a glass?

PHILIP [*pours a glass of champagne for* JACK]. Here, Jack, you give it to him. You're the one who started feeling so sorry for him.

JACK. All right, I will. [*Takes glass to cage.*]

LUKE [*heavy whisper to* JACK]. Look, Jack, you can get me out of here. All you have to do is go out to the kitchen and——

CASSY [*who has been watching and guessed the drift of* LUKE'*s words*]. Don't count on it, Monkey-man. No. No. No. Whatever it is you're trying to cook up. Jack is very sure of his position here with us. You wouldn't be willing to take him on. No. You're much too busy with your poetry and your theology. Very happy here, huh, Jackie? All right, everybody, I want to have a toast to our monkey-man. Right. [*Takes glass from top of cage and sings; others join drunkenly.*]

> For he's a Jolly Good Monkey,
> For he's a Jolly Good Monkey,
> For he's a Jolly Good Monkey,
> That nobody can deny . . .

[CASSY *alone.*] Cheers.

PHILIP. Maybe we should let him out of there.

SONNY. A minute ago I offered the key—no one wanted it.

BILLIE MAE. Well, I think you should be the one to let him out, Sonny, it was your idea to put him in there.

SONNY. Careful, Billie, it was my idea to play this game, but if you will remember we picked our monkey by drawing straws.

BILLIE MAE. Yes, and you gimmicked the draw—with Cassy's help.

SONNY. Now how could I do that? There were six matches in all, right? Five good ones and one burned one. Can I help it if Luke picked the burned one first crack out of the tube?

BILLIE MAE. They were all burned matches . . . all of them and you put them in that tube and told Cassy to pass it to Luke first . . . he couldn't have gotten anything but a burned match. . . .

CASSY. Oh, now, Billie——

BILLIE MAE. Shut up! You're a part of it. You helped him. Where are those matches? Where are they?

SONNY [holds up tube over the back of his couch]. Here it is, Billie. Take a look for yourself.

BILLIE MAE grabs tube, pulls the top off, pulls out five good matches.

BILLIE MAE. You've switched them again.

SONNY. Nonsense, I never switched anything, dear. You're just trying now to duck your fair share of the responsibility for putting him in there. . . . Now that he may be getting out you want to be his buddy again. You may even fear that he won't see the humor of this whole thing. That's all there is to it. But you enjoyed it, Billie. And if you discovered those dead matches as you say you did, why didn't you shout foul right then and there? Why did you wait until now?

PHILIP. Fine, but who's going to let him out?

There is a moment of silence.

SONNY. Well, since there are no volunteers he had better let himself out. [Holds up key.] Here, Jack, take the key over and drop it into the cage. He can work his fingers through the bars and get at the padlock. . . . Daddy's monkey used to play with it all the time.

JACK *drops key into cage and stands near the door.*

PHILIP [*grabs his coat*]. Well, since this party is over I think I *will* go to another one. [*Sudden inspiration.*] Perhaps a private one. . . . Jack, hadn't you better get your coat and come with me?

JACK. Well, I——

PHILIP. You're so young and innocent and such a natural victim, you're sure to be next. Come on, get your coat and let's go.

JACK [*decides*]. Night. . . .

PHILIP. Good night all. . . .

CASSY. The little bastard!

BILLIE MAE. Oh, who cares?

LUKE *gets the key and in a few moments he has unlocked the cage door. He comes out slowly on all fours. The clock tolls twelve, with the sound of a Times Square New Year's Eve crowd after midnight stroke. He stands up, stretches, dresses quickly, and then, controlling his voice, trying to sound as if nothing had happened:*

LUKE. Come on, Billie, let's go.

BILLIE MAE [*fearful*]. But Luke, can't we stay here and see the New Year in with our friends?

LUKE. Remember, I've got some champagne at the house for us.

BILLIE MAE. Please, Luke . . .

LUKE [*decisive*]. We're going!

BILLIE *approaches* LUKE *cautiously, and begins buttoning his shirt.*

BILLIE MAE. Happy New Year, darling. [*She tries to kiss* LUKE. *He accepts her kiss and then shoves her away violently.*] Luke . . . Luke . . . what's the matter with you . . . Luke . . .

BILLIE MAE *falls hard on the floor.* LUKE *looks back for a moment at* SONNY *and* CASSY *on the couch, steps over* BILLIE MAE, *and goes out.*

CASSY. Idiot!

SONNY *gives* CASSY *a jab. She gets up, stumbles to bar for
ice and a towel.*

SONNY. Oh, she's only banged her brain on the broadloom,
that's all. Probably a bit of a concussion . . . but, if that
bump on her skull should turn out to be something more
serious, we'd have a lot of bother to bother with, huh.
Not to mention the smudge on our good clean kiddie
record. Feel her pulse! Rule One—Victims must have
victims, right? That explains the "accident."

CASSY. I can't find her pulse.

SONNY. Well, her heart then? Rule Two—Those who wish
to remain innocent must have solutions! [*Glances at*
CASSY *who has an ear to* BILLIE MAE's *chest.*] A faint
thumping, I suppose.

CASSY. Yes. Throw me a pillow.

SONNY *tosses her a small pillow from her couch.*

SONNY. I have a solution, Rose. Dress her in the maid's
uniform you wore during your touching little playlet . . .
load her into the service elevator, and send the elevator
down to the basement——

CASSY. Sonny, please, cut it out, we've got to get her some
help!

SONNY. Uh, uh . . . and when she wakes up down there
she'll be just another spade maid who's gotten a little
tipsy nipping at the punch at somebody's New Year's
bash, right?

CASSY. Sonny. Knock it off. I'm going to call an ambu-
lance. [*Trots to phone.*]

SONNY. All right. I've got it. Slip her into bed beside
Mummie-Birdie for the night, and then, when Mummie
comes to tomorrow morning, she'll think at first glance
that good black Ernestine has decided to share her
bed . . . as well as her board and master. . . . Won't
that be a gas?

CASSY *picks up phone and dials.* SONNY *gets off couch and
grabs phone away.*

CASSY. What are you doing, Sonny?

SONNY. You don't like that solution either, huh? The window—from the ledge it's a sheer drop into the drink, isn't it? Yes, and if the current is right it will float her home to Harlem.

CASSY. Sonny, stop it. Stop it!

SONNY. Yes, it will float her home to Harlem, and all this dreadful inconvenience will be washed away. Shut off the lights! [CASSY *does not move.* SONNY *pushes her out of the way, and snaps off the lights.*] Some old voyeur out there might just have his snooperscope focused on us.

CASSY. Sonny, stop it. We are not going to do anything silly. . . . I can't . . . I just can't.

SONNY [*snaps open curtains*]. Silly, Rose? It's such a beautiful, clear, crisp night.

CASSY [*heading for light switch*]. Sonny, I'm going to put the lights on.

SONNY. Yes, put the lights on, dear, and then put your coat on and go out of this room and never never return because I'll never never let you back into this room. Never, never, never.

CASSY. Sonny, please. Please, Sonny. Don't say that . . . please—

SONNY. Put the lights on, Rose, and take your junk-toothed, dyke-shaped self out of my living room and out of my life forever and ever. [CASSY *falters and knocks over some glasses.*] Be calm, Margaret. [SONNY *hooks* CASSY *brutally in one arm, then walks her toward* BILLIE MAE.] Just be calm. You'll take a sleeping pill and snooze a little . . . yes . . . and someday we'll look back on that as an unfortunate adolescent mishap . . . like a back street abortion . . . or a hit-and-run accident . . . not really our fault at all . . . maybe it will even be the subject of one of our parlor games. . . . [*Shakes* CASSY, *who is sobbing quietly.*] So come on, dear, get into action! Hey, you know what? If you promise to help me do this dandy little deed, and never, never, never breathe a word of it to anyone in the whole wide, wide, wide world . . . I'll promise forever and ever and ever to

call you by your very own name. Won't that be nice?
[SONNY *moves from* CASSY, *smiling.*]

CASSY [*clinging to* SONNY]. Cassy? . . . Cassy . . .
Cassy . . .

Curtain.

A MESSAGE FROM COUGAR

A *One-Act Comedy*

by

JEAN RAYMOND MALJEAN

To My Wife
Virginia

OSBORNE
COUGAR
TRACY

THE PLACE: COUGAR's bedroom
THE TIME: Now

A *Message From Cougar* was first presented by Bro Herrod's Playwright's Opportunity Theatre at the Thirteenth Street Theatre, New York City, on March 13, 1967. The cast was:

OSBORNE	Daniel MacRae
COUGAR	Harry E. Miller
TRACY	Marguerite McNeil

The play was directed by James Doolan, stage manager Ingrid Pelenus, lighting by Carl Kooring, production by Marcia Weston's Lyric Players, Inc.

A MESSAGE FROM COUGAR

As the scene opens we see a deathbed-type scene with COUGAR: *tall, husky, sweaty, and bearded, lying still on his bed while his brother,* OSBORNE, *prays over him.* OSBORNE *is tall and awkward. The words that* OSBORNE *utters are not real words but inarticulate prayer mumblings read breathlessly.*

OSBORNE [*a meek, humble, shy, naïve type of man*]. Mbncvxdsxz sdswq asder lkjuyrtcvfdswe xcvn mnjhy gfdresdzx sweqwa fghytiu noiumnb——

COUGAR [*he-man type—ladies man, swaggering fellow— but at the moment helpless*]. Do you think I'm going to die right away? This morning?

OSBORNE. Loiuyt vbgf cxdswe zxc bv nmjhytg vgfders xzaswq cvfgtre vcfd cfds——

COUGAR [*louder*]. I said do you think I am going to die? Before breakfast?

OSBORNE. I don't know. That's why I'm praying. Jkjhyt gfdre xcxzsaqw vcfd——

COUGAR. Who are you praying to?

OSBORNE. God. Jyutreds xcdsf gfhytg vbnmkj jhyutg fdser cxsawqe dfredse——

COUGAR. Are you allowed to do that? I mean, aren't you going over somebody's head?

OSBORNE. No. Jkjhg vbfdres xcxzsaw sder fgtrewqas xcdsdasred vcgfd nhjuyt——

COUGAR. Stop mumbling! How the hell do you expect God to hear you?

OSBORNE. Please don't always shout at me. It upsets me. Jhgfd cvfdswe fred——

COUGAR. When you were praying just now did I hear you say something about—rain?

OSBORNE. I was praying for your soul and I got to thinking about how the weather has turned so dry lately, so I included some prayers for rain. Nbvgfd cvfds xcdsderf vghgfrt bnjhuygf vcfdse cxdsewasdfg.

COUGAR. That's great! I'm on my deathbed and my own brother is worried about his flowers!

OSBORNE. Asdewq zxsder vfgfd cxsawqe xcdsawq zxdfred cvgfbhgyt bnhgfre zxc——

COUGAR. You listen to me! Stop praying for rain on *my* time.

OSBORNE. I'm sorry, Cougar.

COUGAR. My own flesh and blood. The only reason you came here is because I'm dying. You haven't come to visit me or write a card in two years. Why didn't you come to visit me last year?

OSBORNE. You weren't dying then.

COUGAR. I was so.

OSBORNE. No, Cougar. It was the year before.

COUGAR. I think you're wrong.

OSBORNE. If you were dying last year I would have visited you. I have always come to you when you're on your deathbed. It's traditional.

COUGAR. Are you going to stay overnight?

OSBORNE. No. I'm going home, Cougar.

COUGAR. Can't you stay at least one day?

OSBORNE. No. I have to feed the cat.

COUGAR. But you can't go home. The elevator's broken, Osborne.

OSBORNE. That doesn't matter. I only live three flights down.

COUGAR. Leave me when I need you the most.

OSBORNE. But I have already taken one day off work for this. And I'll lose a day with the funeral, too.

COUGAR. Then, at least let me make a deathbed request of you.

OSBORNE. Of course, Cougar. Anything you want I'll do for you. Anything at all. Anything.

COUGAR. Promise me that you'll carry on my life's work when I am gone.

OSBORNE. Anything. Anything except that. Hjhgfd cxds xcvfdsew xcdsfdcgf——

COUGAR. Osborne, you're a coward.

OSBORNE. I know. I know. Xsdsaw xzcxdsew zxcdfdsghytr cvfgfds xcvbn mkjh——

COUGAR. Why are you afraid to do it? You've seen me do it a hundred times.

OSBORNE. I'm afraid to talk to people on the telephone. I'm not as confident and self-assured as you are.

COUGAR. A brilliant man like you? A man who guards the health of our city!

OSBORNE. That has nothing to do with talking to people.

COUGAR. You must talk to *somebody* at work.

OSBORNE. Nobody. I just stand in a dark little cubicle and candle eggs all day. When I'm finished I go home.

COUGAR. Then I'll put the telephone in a closet and you can make the calls from there.

OSBORNE. No, Cougar. I'm afraid.

COUGAR. To think my own flesh and blood——

OSBORNE. Why don't you use the new machine you've been talking about. The one with the recorded messages?

COUGAR. It's a poor substitute. I'm going to send it back. For the last time—will you make the calls?

OSBORNE. No, Cougar.

COUGAR. Very well. Then I have but one alternative. [COUGAR *rises, covers himself with his sheet like a Roman, and crosses to phone.*]

OSBORNE. What are you up to? You shouldn't be out of bed.

COUGAR. What do *you* care!

OSBORNE. Why don't you stay in bed and finish your new novel. You said the publishers are after you for it.

COUGAR. If you won't make the telephone calls, I will.

OSBORNE. But not in your condition. You——

COUGAR. I'll die with my boots on.

OSBORNE. Please, Cougar. Don't pick up the phone or——

COUGAR. Don't concern yourself with my feelings. Since I've been ill for a week I've fallen so far behind in my calls that I'll *never* catch up.

OSBORNE. Please go back to bed. You're not strong enough to spend your whole day on the telephone.

COUGAR [*starting to dial*]. It doesn't matter anymore. Besides, it's only me.

OSBORNE. Wait a minute, Cougar. I'll—I'll—help you.

COUGAR [*slams down the receiver and dances over to OSBORNE with chair. OSBORNE is resigned*]. Osborne, you've reaffirmed my faith in you. Sit down. I have the numbers right here on the table.

OSBORNE. You don't look as if you're about to die. Are you sure that you're not just playing on my sympathy?

COUGAR [*falling into a fit of pain*]. Ohhhhhh . . . no . . . Osborne . . . Ohhhhhhhhhh. It's just that . . . I keep . . . forgetting that . . . I'm dying . . . and I start to . . . become active . . . ohhhhh . . . and it brings . . . back the pain.

OSBORNE [*picking up the phone*]. I'm sorry to have doubted your intentions. But don't be too hopeful or elated about this. I'll probably fail.

COUGAR. Not that phone, Osborne. That's for incoming calls. *You*—fail? *You?* Who has created all of these magnificent paintings in oil? [COUGAR *picks up a pile of canvasses.*] This is not the work of a failure!

OSBORNE. But you've always hated my paintings. You said they were vapid.

COUGAR. But that's the art of it. It is their vapidity that is arresting and compelling! *All* paintings should be vapid. Like yours.

OSBORNE. That still won't help me on the telephone.

COUGAR. As I told you before—a brilliant man like you needn't worry.

OSBORNE. I'm not brilliant.

COUGAR [*washing his beard in a bowl*]. Oh, yes, you are! Only the other day Mr. Brugelhoffer said to me, "Your brother, Osborne, is brilliant."

OSBORNE. Mr. Brugelhoffer said that?

COUGAR. IIc said it right out.

OSBORNE. That was nice of him. Who is Mr. Brugelhoffer?

COUGAR. A very brilliant man.

OSBORNE. Oh, that's a compliment, coming from him.

COUGAR. All right. Sit down.

OSBORNE [*picks up phone. Starts to dial*]. Here gocs.

COUGAR. You'll have to wait a minute.

OSBORNE. Why?

COUGAR. I never phone anyone before nine A.M. Once I did and I got hell from a woman.

OSBORNE. All right. I'll wait. But that will only make me more nervous.

COUGAR. I have a little mark on the left next to each name. When the call is completed you make a mark on the right. If the number has been changed make a note of it in the margin.

OSBORNE. In the margin.

COUGAR. Most of the time if the number has been changed it is an unlisted number as a result.

OSBORNE. I hope I don't sound too nervous when they answer.

COUGAR. Nonsense. They get more nervous than you do. I guess you can start now. Get ready, get set, *go!*

OSBORNE [*dials*]. I'm very upset. I'm shaking!

COUGAR. You'll get over it.

OSBORNE. It's ringing.

COUGAR. Good. Keep a stiff upper lip, Osborne.

OSBORNE [*making a stiff upper lip*]. Stiff upper lip. [*Some difficulty speaking.*]

COUGAR. Clench your jaw.

OSBORNE [*now clenching jaw also*]. Stiff upper lip. Clenched jaw. [*More difficulty.*]

COUGAR. And grit your teeth.

OSBORNE [*stiff upper lip, clenched jaw, gritted teeth*]. And gritted teeth.

COUGAR. Atta boy!

OSBORNE [*barely understandable*]. But if I have a stiff upper lip, clenched jaw, and I grit my teeth I won't be able to talk. [*Slams receiver down.*]

COUGAR. What happened?

OSBORNE. She answered.

COUGAR. That one doesn't count. You also got her husband in trouble.

OSBORNE. I'll try again. I'm shaking from head to toe, Cougar.

COUGAR. Go ahead. But for Pete's sake, don't hang up again. It's rude!

OSBORNE. I'm sorry. It's ringing. . . . Hello. . . . Hello . . . errr . . . I—errrrrr——

COUGAR. Don't stutter. Go right on.

OSBORNE. Hello. Is this Alice Green? Well, I . . . I—I —errr . . . I called . . . to . . . to say . . . say . . . that——

COUGAR. Go ahead, Osborne.

OSBORNE. I just phoned to say that I'd like to go—to bed with you—and—make *love*—to you. [*After a pause, he looks at* COUGAR, *surprised.*] She *hung up!*

COUGAR [*exasperated*]. You are really stupid, Osborne!

OSBORNE. She hung up.

COUGAR. What kind of way was that to talk to someone on the telephone?

OSBORNE. Wasn't I good?

COUGAR. You're supposed to use *obscene* words.

OSBORNE. I'm sorry.

COUGAR. Here. [*Dials.*] Watch me. And try to learn from it.

OSBORNE. I told you I'd fail.

COUGAR. Shhhhhhhhhh.

OSBORNE. Why don't you use the recorded message machine?

COUGAR. Shhhh. . . . It's ringing. . . . Hello. . . . Is this Amy Green? . . . Well, how would you like to nitzell with me?

OSBORNE. Nitzell?

COUGAR. Shhhh. . . . Did anyone ever tell you that you have a beautiful mibly gleep? . . . Oh, baby, could we skeeble!

OSBORNE. Mibly gleep? Skeeble?

COUGAR. Shhhh. . . . Yes. . . . I know. . . . I'm sorry. . . . I couldn't phone last week. I was ill . . . I still am. . . . I know I usually phone you on the seventeenth but I'm all off schedule with this sickness. . . . I know. . . . I thought you might have . . . [*To* OSBORNE.] She had waited in all day for the phone call. She was worried about me. . . . [*To phone.*] No. Now that's silly! It would be ridiculous to phone you to say I couldn't phone because, then I'd be phoning you anyway and I might as well have just said the obscene words and be done with it. . . . I asked my brother to give me a hand but he refused me. . . . But, look, you're holding me up. . . . I've got a million obscene phone calls to make to catch up. . . . Yes. . . . All right. . . . I will. . . . Skeeble skeeble. Good-bye. [*Hangs up.*]

OSBORNE. I thought you were going to use obscene words. What is this "nitzell" and "mibly gleep" and "skeeble"?

COUGAR. Boy, are you a gumustable!

OSBORNE. I know.

COUGAR. I suppose you always use those ordinary four-letter words.

OSBORNE. I don't even know some of them.

COUGAR [*using a hair dryer on his beard*]. That's what makes the difference between an amateur and a pro. These words I used are far beyond obscene. They happen to be the dirtiest words in our language!

Osborne. I don't really get around much.

Cougar. I can see that you're going to be one of those run-of-the-mill obscene phone callers.

Osborne. I told you I'm a failure. Besides, I don't believe in sex.

Cougar. In order to be successful with these women one has to have command of the highest language of obscenity. Your problem is your strict puritanical background. It's made you neurotic.

Osborne. But you had the same background as I had.

Cougar. Yes. But it can be overcome. You must be determined to overcome it!

Osborne. I'll be determined. I shall overcome.

Cougar. You always let Mom and Pop beat you down. Why, they were so prudish that they thought *Snow White and the Seven Dwarfs* was a dirty movie.

Osborne. Yes, but I sneaked out and saw it anyway.

Cougar. It was like living in a religious institution.

Osborne. It was a religious institution. Daddy was a preacher.

Cougar. That explains it.

Osborne. Cougar, there's nothing wrong with religion.

Cougar. Until it starts interfering with your sex drives.

Osborne. I don't mean to criticize you, Cougar, but I think you're preoccupied with sex.

Cougar. What the hell makes you say that?

Osborne. Oh, I've noticed. There are signs.

Cougar. Like what?

Osborne. Little things. For instance, the way you make a living—writing those paperback books.

Cougar. Oh, so now it's an offense to write paperback books!

Osborne. Cougar, I didn't say it was an offense.

Cougar. What I write is perfectly within the law.

OSBORNE. I know. You've written six novels and every one of them has been dismissed of lewd charges brought about by the post office.

COUGAR. You're skeebly well right.

OSBORNE. Watch your language.

COUGAR. I'll say what I mibly well like. So don't start in again about all this nonsense about my being preoccupied with sex.

OSBORNE. I'm sorry.

COUGAR. Especially when you spend your spare time painting dirty pictures.

OSBORNE. Dirty pictures? My flowers?

COUGAR. Everybody knows that flowers are the sex organs of plants.

OSBORNE. I've never thought of it that way before. I'm embarrassed!

COUGAR. And what's more, you spend your whole day examining the sex products of chickens.

OSBORNE. Oh, dear! It seems to me that sex is everywhere nowadays.

COUGAR. Now make the next call. We're late.

OSBORNE. Couldn't you try the recorded message machine just once?

COUGAR. It's not personal enough.

OSBORNE. Do it just once—so I can judge. How does it work?

COUGAR. Very well. Just to shut you up. You attach this to the phone and it automatically dials the numbers and a tape plays when the call is completed. [*Sets it up.*]

OSBORNE. Does it have your voice on it?

COUGAR. Yes. Here it goes.

VOICE OF THE OBSCENE MACHINE. This is a recorded obscene phone call. You and I could make such a skeeble together, baby. Listen, you mibly gleep, I'm going to go right over there and make nitzell with you. Do you hear?

When you hear the beep tone you may start talking and finish by the sound of the second beep. [*There is a beep.*]

OSBORNE. This could revolutionize the industry!

COUGAR. Now whomever the machine has called is answering and I can play it back later on tape.

OSBORNE. It's amazing.

COUGAR. But impersonal. No. I'm sending it back. There were too many complaints. [*Dials phone.*] Now enough of this nonsense. Get on with the show, Osborne.

OSBORNE [*taking receiver*]. Which one is this?

COUGAR. Her name is Ava Green.

OSBORNE. I just don't have it. I'm a failure with girls.

COUGAR. Be a man. Accept failure once in a while. Grow up, Osborne.

OSBORNE. Hello . . . hello. . . . Is this Ava Green? . . . Oh, *no!*

COUGAR. What's the matter?

OSBORNE. Are you A—Are *you—Ava Green?*

COUGAR. What is it?

OSBORNE. It—Ava Green is—a——man!

COUGAR. He's lying. Demand to speak to Ava Green.

OSBORNE. See here, sir. Ava is a girl's name and—— Yes . . . yes. . . . I. . . . [*To* COUGAR.] He says he always has this trouble. . . . [*To phone.*] Yes . . . I can see that. . . . Oh, dear. . . . [*To* COUGAR.] Once he applied for a job and they thought he was a girl and——

COUGAR. Who the hell cares? Why must you listen to his problems? Get rid of him. Get him off!

OSBORNE [*to* COUGAR]. All right. [*To phone.*] Yes. . . . Why don't you change it legally?

COUGAR. Osborne, hang up!

OSBORNE. That's my brother. . . . He wants me to hang up and make more obscene phone calls. . . . Yes. That's right. . . . Try phoning a lawyer.

COUGAR. This is not the legal aid society. Get him off.

OSBORNE. I've got to go now. . . . [*To* COUGAR.] Cougar, do I say anything obscene to him anyway? Just for the record?

COUGAR. What are you? Some kind of a pervert?

OSBORNE. Hello? . . . Yes . . . yes. . . . I must be going. Ava . . . yes. . . . 'Bye. [*Hangs up.*]

COUGAR [*dialing phone*]. You are a mooblcr.

OSBORNE. I'm sorry. I'm no good at this sort of thing.

COUGAR [*hands phone to him*]. Here, take this. It's Barbara Green.

OSBORNE. Hello. . . . It's still ringing. . . . Nobody's home. [*Tries to hang up.*]

COUGAR [*prevents him*]. Wait a bit longer.

OSBORNE. Hello. . . . Is this Barbara Green? Did anyone ever tell you that you have a beautiful mibly gleep? [*A look of shock on his face as he slams receiver down.*]

COUGAR. What's wrong? Why are you so upset? [COUGAR *dials phone.*]

OSBORNE. She shouted something lewd at me.

COUGAR. Do you see what I have to put up with? It isn't easy to do what I do. Everybody thinks it's fun until they have to put in a typical day of it. [*Hands receiver to* OS-BORNE.] This one is Bertha Green.

OSBORNE. I can't go on with this. I'm not a man of the world like you. [*To phone.*] No, I wasn't talking to you. . . . Is this Bertha Green? . . . How would you like to skeeble with me? . . . Did anyone ever tell you that you're a borfer claub?

COUGAR. A borfer claub?

OSBORNE [*to* COUGAR]. I picked that up in the gutter. [*To phone.*] Hello. . . . [*To* COUGAR.] She's giggling. . . . [*To phone.*] Thank you. [*To* COUGAR.] Gee! [*To phone.*] Thank you. I've never been told that before. . . .

COUGAR. What did she say?

OSBORNE. She said I have a nice voice.

COUGAR. Say something dirty, Osborne. We haven't got all day.

OSBORNE. My brother wants me to finish and hang up. . . . Yes, we're late with our dirty phone calls.

COUGAR. Say something obscene.

OSBORNE. Mibly gleep . . . skeeble. . . . What? . . . I said mibly gleep. . . . My brother told me to. . . . Yes, he is. . . . We're late, Bertha. . . . Listen, I've got to hang up. . . . Yes. . . . I'll call again, Bertha. . . . 'Bye. [*Hangs up, pleased with himself.*]

COUGAR. Are you getting the hang of it now?

OSBORNE. Yes. I'm surprising myself. I've never talked to girls before and now I don't seem so scared of them.

On stage left a spot picks up TRACY *on other side of wall. She is beautiful, has a sexy walk, and is dressed in a diaphanous gown. She comes on strong.*

TRACY [*on phone, as if there were no wall at all, loud and clear, causing* OSBORNE *and* COUGAR *to jump*]. Mong zum Tracy Booch chong hung ving dung owaaaaa how mug Bohemian Quarterly for Enlightened Contemporary Non-Materialistic Masses. Vin vong zin gong Bowwwww-wwwwwwwwwwwwwwwwww. [*Pause. Angry.*] Mug hung bom nitzell zin yow bung mibly gleep vom. [*Slams down receiver.*]

OSBORNE [*as* TRACY *dials another number*]. What was that?

COUGAR. The girl next door.

OSBORNE. The walls of this building are terribly thin—like paper.

TRACY [*on phone*]. Nobski bleep Tracy Booch ooskie morshka bornya poon yaska horski zeeb obska jorma snipski Bohemian Quarterly for Enlightened Contemporary Non-Materialistic Masses. . . . *Pushla beepski?* [*Pause. Angry.*] *Mishka zeeski sobla boobla nitzell hoch!*

OSBORNE. Is she French? [TRACY *dials another number.*]

COUGAR. I don't know. Shhhhhh   I'm trying to make it out.

TRACY [*on phone*]. Gleich nibz Tracy Booch zeitingzie klei-
ner schoopenzeebler und mousker zeeten ober hopen-
skopeldouser brownbuskel breeble zeit und klein zeist
Bohemian Quarterly for Enlightened Contemporary Non-
Materialistic Masses? [*Pause. Angry.*] Arowz mit deina
schnitzengeesker!

COUGAR [*light on her goes out. As* TRACY *slams receiver
down*]. She's a real skeeble. I saw her once.

OSBORNE. Did you ever phone her?

COUGAR [*looking in phone book*]. I was tempted to. I
should have. It's the neighborly thing to do.

OSBORNE. Maybe you'd better not, Cougar.

COUGAR [*dialing*]. Here it is. This will probably slow us up
again, but I feel an obligation. [*Phone rings at* TRACY's.
She answers.] Hello.

TRACY. Hello.

COUGAR. Hello, baby. This is sexpot speaking.

TRACY. Hello, sexpot. What's brewing?

COUGAR. How would you like to nitzell with me, you mibly
gleep?

TRACY. I'd love to.

COUGAR. You're a real glusker, baby.

OSBORNE. Glusker? Did you say glusker?

TRACY. Yes. He said glusker.

OSBORNE. Thank you, Miss.

COUGAR. Yes, sweetie. You're a real glusker.

TRACY. You're no slouch, yourself.

COUGAR. I can see we're going to hit it off real well, sugar.
Good-bye. [*Hangs up.*]

TRACY [*hanging up but still talking as if on the phone*]. 'Bye,
stud. Don't forget to phone again, lover boy.

COUGAR [*as if still on phone*]. I sure won't forget you, baby
doll.

TRACY. See you around.

COUGAR. Good-bye, sugar.

OSBORNE. Tell me what she said.

COUGAR. Well, I phoned her and she answered and I said, "Hello, sexpot——" Stupid! You heard it all—through the wall!

OSBORNE. That's true.

COUGAR. Wait a minute. If we could hear her through the wall—then—she—she—could—she could hear——

OSBORNE. She probably knows where the call came from.

COUGAR. Ooooooooohhhhhh! Do you think she heard?

OSBORNE. Maybe.

COUGAR. She might call the police. [*There is a knock on the door.*]

OSBORNE [*they stare at each other for a moment*]. Nmnbvf cvfds xcds xzsaqwe vbg nbvc fdsaz xcxzx. [OSBORNE *prays and* COUGAR *jumps into bed.*]

COUGAR. Who is it?

TRACY. The girl next door!

COUGAR. I'm not at home!

TRACY. Open the door, lover boy! [*The knocking grows more intense. Now it is like a pile driver.*] Open up!

COUGAR. No. I'm on my deathbed.

OSBORNE [*throughout, praying*]. Nmjhg vbvcfd xcxzsaqwe dfdsaret hgjuyhgfd. . . .

TRACY. Let me in! [*Bangbangbang.*]

COUGAR. Go away!

TRACY. Open up!

OSBORNE. Bnbvc fdssa cxdsa zxsdf bvhgbn mnbvcxzsawert-fdsd cxdsawqasdfdszxsd vc. . . .

COUGAR. Go back to your apartment!

TRACY. All right! I'll go back to my apartment.

COUGAR [*as they both fall silent, the knocking stops and there is a long quiet pause as they listen for her. At length* COUGAR *whispers*]. She did go back to her apartment.

TRACY [*whispers*]. Yes, I did.

COUGAR. Thank goodness!

The silence is broken and so is the wall when TRACY *comes crashing through the paper thin wall, leaving a big gaping hole between apartments.* COUGAR *and* OSBORNE *leap in fear.*

TRACY. These damn paper thin walls! [*Sizes up* COUGAR. *She touches his sheet-toga as both men cringe in fear.*] What time is the next chariot race, Daddy-o?

COUGAR. I beg your pardon?

TRACY. You're pardoned.

COUGAR. I don't understand.

TRACY. Like here I am.

COUGAR. Yes.

TRACY [*fussing with him*]. So you're Cougar.

COUGAR. Yes. I'm Cougar.

TRACY. You Cougar, me Jane. [*She thinks this is very funny.*] Hahahahahaha. [OSBORNE *breaks out in a fit of laughter but catches himself.* TRACY *approaches* OSBORNE.] Well, well. What do we have here? [OSBORNE *runs away.*]

COUGAR. That's m-my b-brother, Os-Osborne.

TRACY. How do you do, Osborne. My name is Tracy.

OSBORNE. I see.

TRACY [*to* COUGAR]. I've always been afraid of cougars.

COUGAR. I see.

TRACY [*all over him*]. Well, do your worst.

COUGAR. I don't understand.

TRACY. When do we start, Buster?

COUGAR. Start what?

TRACY. Oh, you're really something else. The *action*, baby —the *action*!

OSBORNE. You're sitting on his deathbed.

TRACY [*reclines on bed*]. Yeah . . . how *about* that?

COUGAR. See here, now . . . errrr . . . you can't . . . errrr . . . I . . . errrr. . . .

TRACY. I've been hoping to meet a masterful cat like you for a long time. With all that brillo on your chinny chin you look like Ernest Hemingway.

COUGAR. Please leave.

TRACY. Are you for real? Let's get on with it.

COUGAR. With . . . what?

TRACY. The nitzell . . . the mibly gleep. The glusker, sugar. . . . Well, say something.

COUGAR. D-d-d-don't t-t-t-touch m-me!

TRACY. Well, that's *something!* [*Kisses him. He is in a cold sweat.*] Oh, you mad impulsive animal person!

COUGAR. Please leave me alone!

OSBORNE. Lkjhgfv bnbvcx dfdsaw ered xcfdfghytuiopk mnjhgfre cxdsa zxdsew. . . .

TRACY. Who turned you on?

OSBORNE. I'm praying.

TRACY. For what?

OSBORNE. For Cougar's virtue.

TRACY. Bully for you, you mibly gleep.

OSBORNE. Watch your language. Lkjhnb vbgfd xcdsaz xdsew cfdsew xcfdfgtytre. . . .

COUGAR. Keep praying. And leave out the part about the rain.

OSBORNE. But it's been so—dry.

COUGAR. Shut up and pray.

OSBORNE. Lkjhnb bvgfdc xcdsaz xsdwew sdsaqwe cxdsew cxdse vcgfrtred xcdsaz. . . .

TRACY [*chasing after* COUGAR]. What luck I have! I must have really stepped in something!

COUGAR [*running away*]. Please go away!

OSBORNE. Kjhuytg vbgfd xcdsazsaw xzsds vcbnmnb vbghyt vfdsxcxzs dswwetrfd. . . .

TRACY. Is that any way for a cougar to act?

COUGAR. Why bother with me? You're a pretty girl. There must be——

TRACY. There must be two million men in this town and *eight million girls.*

COUGAR. Go away!

TRACY. I've been listening to you in here for a long time—phoning all those girls—every day hoping I would be next. Well, now I hit bingo—and you act like *queersville!*

COUGAR. Please! Go away! Go back through the wall!

TRACY. So when I get a phone call from a cougar suggesting a mibly gleep I *mibly gleep,* Cougie! Now let's get this show on the road! [*She overpowers him.*] Now what do you say to a little glusker? How does that grab you, baby? How about we have a gasser?

COUGAR. Ohhhh . . . the pains! The pains are here!

TRACY [*looking around*]. Where? What? What?

COUGAR. The pains! I have migraine headache, watery eyes, runny nose, chapped lips, sore throat, clogged lungs. . . . [*Falling onto bed.*] Ohhhhh Osborne! [*Writhing.*] I have abdominal pains! Ohhhhhhhhhhh . . .

OSBORNE [*running over to him*]. Cougar. . . . [*Examining him.*] I think you have intestinal flu . . . and . . . bad breath.

COUGAR [*rising for a moment*]. Bad breath?

OSBORNE. Yes, I said bad breath! *Bad breath!*

COUGAR [*collapsing again*]. Ohhhhhhh. . . . That woman! She's the cause of all of this! Make her go away!

OSBORNE. He looks ill. Mnbhg vcfd cxsdwe xcdsz xcdse ghgbgfred xcdsasdfg. . . .

TRACY. Boy, do I draw the prizes! [*Shakes him but he is out like a light.*]

OSBORNE. He did say that he was going to die. I thought he was faking.

TRACY. This is par for the course. Are you sure that this cat is not turned on?

OSBORNE. I think he's turned off.

TRACY [*sitting on bed. Head in hands*]. Mibly gleep.

OSBORNE [*shocked*]. Oh, dear. You're a libertine woman.

TRACY [*looks at him*]. ?????

OSBORNE. You ought to repent your sins and lead a clean life.

TRACY. What sins? This is the first cat I've kissed in eight months and it's fatal, yet!

OSBORNE. What kind of woman would burst into a man's apartment and offer herself to him?

TRACY. A desperate woman. Look. I used to play hard to get and a fat lot of good it did me. [*Starts to cry.*] I did everything but stand on my head. I'm hip—attractive—I'm a kind person and all that jazz. Maybe I need Micrin or something.

OSBORNE. I'm very sorry. Have you tried meeting a man in your church?

TRACY. Sure. I met married men and single men who obey eleven commandments. I tried the church first because I was brought up very strictly.

OSBORNE. You should not have tried to seduce my brother.

TRACY. Look, mister, I wasn't the one who made the phone calls. You——

OSBORNE. Don't come any closer. It was my brother. Not me. Cvfds xcxzsaw. . . .

TRACY. You know I like you even better than Cougie. Take away his fuller brush and what have you got? C'mere, lover.

OSBORNE [*terrified*]. Nbvgfd cxdsawer cxdfdsazwew xcdawe vbnmkjhuytgf vcfdsx. . . . D-d-d-don't touch m-me!

TRACY [*reaches through hole in wall and comes up with a bottle of Scotch*]. Osborne, baby, we're going to have a gas and you'd better believe it. Look what I've got, baby-o.

OSBORNE. Is that—a bottle of—liquor?

TRACY. It ain't egg cream.

OSBORNE. Oh, dear!

TRACY. Have a slug.

OSBORNE. No, thank you. I have no use for it.

TRACY [*slams the bottle on the table*]. I said have a drink!

OSBORNE. I'll drink it against my will, but I won't like it, I assure you. [*Drinks it, chokingly.*] Oh, dear.

TRACY. Do you like my gown, Ozzie?

OSBORNE. Girls like you are out after one thing.

TRACY [*fussing with him*]. You're really something else.

OSBORNE. Ooooooooooooooohhhhhh. . . . Leave me alone. [*Runs away.*]

TRACY [*grabbing him*]. My mother warned me about going into strange men's apartments. And these are strange men.

OSBORNE. You will be punished for your loose ways.

TRACY [*catches him. Embraces him*]. Ozzie, you really turn me on.

OSBORNE. It won't do you any good. I'm pure! [*She mauls him.*] Leave me alone! [*All of this has been too much for* OSBORNE *who now falls into a stupor—stone cold stiff.*]

TRACY [*shaking him to no avail. After a pause she knocks on his head*]. Hey! Are you in there? Osborne? Osborne? [*She has a slug of Scotch.*] He's closed up shop. [*Has another slug.*] Osborne, whatever the hell your brother's got—you've got it, too. . . . I think I must be some kind of carrier. [*Turns on radio for music.*] Well, Osborne, baby, I'm not going to let this bug me. You may not be here now but I *am*. So let's dance. [*She dances him around the room. His body is rigid.*] Just like the church social. [*As they dance.*] You know, Osborne, you're just too much. Like sexville.

OSBORNE [*in response to "sexville"—in a monotone as if he is reading it*]. Sex is a very bad thing. My mother warned me about it. It is a sin. Sex is evil.

TRACY. Why is sex evil?

OSBORNE. It is bad for digestion and creates warts.

TRACY. That ain't all.

OSBORNE. It is likely to drive a person insane.

TRACY. You'd better believe it.

OSBORNE. My mother told me that sex can give you migraine headaches, watery eyes, runny nose, chapped lips, sore throat, clogged lungs, abdominal pains, intestinal flu, and bad breath.

TRACY. You dance divinely. So light on your feet. But you always talk about sex.

OSBORNE. Dancing is evil.

TRACY. I get the feeling you're trying to tell me something. [*Shakes him.*] Wake up, Osborne!

OSBORNE [*wakes up*]. Aaaagggghhhh! What are you doing to me? Bvgfd cxds xzsa. . . .

TRACY. Don't flip your wig. We're dancing, Ozzie, baby.

Even though he has awakened he is stiff as they continue to "dance." She pushes his rigid body about the room.

OSBORNE. Dancing is——

TRACY. I know. Evil. We went through all that jazz.

OSBORNE. But I don't know how to dance.

TRACY [*hugging him closer*]. No, really? That's hard to believe. You're putting me on.

OSBORNE. No. It's the truth. This is the first time I ever danced with a girl.

TRACY. I guess it just comes naturally. Some have it. Some don't.

OSBORNE. Put me down.

TRACY. No. [*They dance for a while without speaking.*]

OSBORNE. Do you really think I dance well?

TRACY. You were born to it. How could I describe your style? Do you know the meaning of the word klutz?

OSBORNE. No. I don't.

TRACY. Well, you dance like a klutz.

OSBORNE. Thank you.

TRACY. Now, you see, I haven't hurt you so far, have I?

OSBORNE. Not yet.

TRACY. Sugar, you've got to maintain your cool. Like—relax. I'm not so bad.

OSBORNE. You're evil.

TRACY. Tell the truth. You do feel a little safer with me now, don't you? [*Pause.*] Answer me, Ozzie.

OSBORNE. A little. But not—very. I'd feel safer if you would put me down. [*He is trembling.*]

TRACY. Okay. You win. [*Puts him down.*] Don't be frightened of me. I shouldn't have treated you this way when it was he who caused all of this.

OSBORNE. I don't think you're a bad woman. I just don't know how to act with girls.

TRACY. If this goes on much longer I won't know how to act with boys.

OSBORNE. I never knew girls had such problems.

TRACY. There are a lot of things about girls that you don't know.

OSBORNE. That's for sure.

TRACY. Perhaps I can put you at ease if you tell me about yourself.

OSBORNE. There's not much to tell.

TRACY. Surely there must be more to you than eating, sleeping, egg-candling, and church.

OSBORNE. Well, sometimes I write poetry.

TRACY. Would you recite some of it for me?

OSBORNE. I'm too shy.

TRACY. But I'd love to hear some of it. Just a little. I really dig verse.

OSBORNE. You don't seem to be the type for poetry.

TRACY. I'll have you know I'm the poet laureate of *The Bohemian Quarterly for Enlightened Contemporary Non-Materialistic Masses.*

OSBORNE. What is *that?*

TRACY. It is a magazine of protest.

OSBORNE. What does it protest?

TRACY. Everything. Mostly its own subscribers. It's translated into seventeen different languages.

OSBORNE. What is the circulation?

TRACY. Seventeen.

OSBORNE. Could you read me one of the poems you wrote for the magazine?

TRACY. No.

OSBORNE. Why not?

TRACY. Because it's written in a language I can't speak.

OSBORNE. Oh. What is it about?

TRACY. About two pages long.

OSBORNE. You must make a lot of money writing.

TRACY. No. In fact, they charge me for printing it.

OSBORNE. But how do you make a living?

TRACY. Just recently I started telephone canvassing for them. Selling subscriptions.

OSBORNE. Oh, then you're like my brother—on the phone all day.

TRACY. Yes. Except I don't use obscenity as he does.

OSBORNE. That's nice.

TRACY. Yes. The obscenity is in the magazine.

OSBORNE. I see.

TRACY. Of course, if they don't take a subscription I start in with the mibly gleep, nitzell, and glusker, and all that.

OSBORNE. I see.

TRACY. Perhaps we could use your poem in our quarterly. Read it to me.

OSBORNE. I really shouldn't. I'm sorry. You'd laugh at me.

TRACY [*giving him a big sloppy kiss*]. Oh, Ozzie, baby, I'd never laugh at you, you little nitzell!

OSBORNE. I wish you wouldn't do that.

TRACY. I'll stop kissing you if you read it to me.

OSBORNE. I d-don't t-think I s-should.

TRACY [*kissing him*]. Have it your way.

OSBORNE. I—I think I should.

TRACY. Good. Recite it.

OSBORNE. You'll laugh at me.

TRACY. No. I won't.

OSBORNE. You won't like it.

TRACY. I'm sure it's very cool.

OSBORNE. Oh, my. All right.

"An egg is by a chicken laid
Inside are yolk and white
And all around it is a shell
Through which I shine a light.

"And inside the egg I see
If it is dark or pale
Or if there is a spot of blood
And whether it is stale

"Or not."

TRACY [*after a long pause*]. I'm all choked up. You didn't write that, did you?

OSBORNE [*proudly*]. Yes, I did.

TRACY. You're putting me on. You have got to be kidding.

OSBORNE. No. I wrote it all by myself.

TRACY. Sounds like Allen Ginsberg to me. No. More like Keats.

OSBORNE. Keats? What are they?

TRACY. What are Keats? They are to poetry what Brahms are to music.

OSBORNE. Nobody ever told me that before.

TRACY. Told you what?

OSBORNE. That my poetry was like Keats.

TRACY. Well, I've got news for you. You're not about to hear it again in a hurry.

OSBORNE. Would you like to hear more?

TRACY. No. Here, lover. Have a blast. [*Gives him a drink.*]

OSBORNE. I've had one already.

TRACY. Have another. [*He does, chokingly.*] Tell me, what other talents have you? I mean [*Fondles him.*] besides all this.

OSBORNE. I paint pictures.

TRACY. May I see some of your work?

OSBORNE. You won't like it.

TRACY. Is it anything like your poetry?

OSBORNE. Not as good.

TRACY [*pause*]. Let's see it, anyway. [*He shows her canvasses.*] Say, these are groovy, Daddy-o. You're a real hippie!

OSBORNE. Thank you.

TRACY. These are even *better* than your poetry.

OSBORNE. Very much better?

TRACY. Bubbie, you'll never know *how* much better. I think you could sell a few of them for some bread. They're charismatic.

OSBORNE. Really?

TRACY. Have another drinky.

OSBORNE. I really shouldn't. [*Does without a twist of the arm.*]

TRACY. Why didn't you become a professional artist?

OSBORNE. I wanted to but my parents said that an artist's life is immoral.

TRACY. What did they want you to be?

OSBORNE. A notary public.

TRACY. Look, sweetie, maybe my magazine could publish your pictures. They're dirty pictures, you know, of course.

OSBORNE. Yes. My brother told me. I had no idea——

TRACY. Good! It's as good as done!

OSBORNE. But why should you go through so much trouble for me?

TRACY. Because I like you.

OSBORNE. I . . . err . . . I like . . . you, too. You're not so evil.

TRACY. Thank you. I'm sorry I was so forward with you.

OSBORNE. I'm glad you were. Otherwise I would never have known I could dance so well.

TRACY. Yeah . . . you're really out of sight.

OSBORNE. Would you like to have another dance?

TRACY [*grabs him*]. Crazy. [*She pushes him around the room again—rigid.*]

OSBORNE [*as they dance he melts*]. You know, you dance like a klutz.

TRACY. You know it, Ozzie, baby. [*They dance for a while without speaking.*]

OSBORNE [*as they approach the hole in wall*]. I think I'd better stop dancing.

TRACY. Why, Osborne?

OSBORNE. Because I feel strange. I have a migraine headache, watery eyes, runny nose, chapped lips, sore throat, clogged lungs, abdominal pains, intestinal flu, and—bad breath.

TRACY. I've noticed. It must be the gown I'm wearing.

OSBORNE. You're right. It disturbs me. In fact, *you* disturb me.

TRACY. I'm sorry. I don't want to bug you. Why should you suffer for what lover boy over there started. I'll split the scene, Ozzie. [*Starts to exit.*]

OSBORNE. Good-bye. I hope I haven't hurt your feelings.

TRACY. No. I dig you the most. I like you. Would you do me a favor? Would you kiss me good night?

OSBORNE [*trembling*]. Well . . . uhhh . . . errr . . . I——

She kisses him.

COUGAR [*praying*]. Cxcda zxsdewq vbnmjhgtyrf cdfdsa zxdsawerewq xdsawecxv. . . .

TRACY. Now that we're acquainted, perhaps you can stop by my pad sometime to borrow a cup of sugar—or—something? [*Exits.*]

OSBORNE. Yes. I will. I will. [*Walks around the room in a daze. He is in a state of ecstasy.*] Wake up, Cougar.

COUGAR [*rising*]. Is she gone, Osborne?

OSBORNE. Yes, Cougar. She's a very nice lady.

COUGAR. We've wasted enough time today. Let's get back to the phone. I'm going to train you to be the best damn obscene phone caller in the whole mibly country.

OSBORNE. No, Cougar. I'm afraid that——

COUGAR. Don't be chicken! Be a man! There's nothing to——

TRACY [*popping her head in*]. Oh, Osborne . . . I left my bottle in your apartment. [COUGAR *dashes under the bed*.]

COUGAR. Xcvbghgfds cxcffderwszxcvbnmkjh bhgytr cdfds xsdewq zasdf cvgf. . . .

TRACY. Will you give it to me, please?

OSBORNE [*handing it to her, trembling*]. Y-yes. H-h-here it is.

TRACY. Would you like to have a nightcap at my place before going to bed?

OSBORNE. Well, err . . . perhaps——

COUGAR. Don't do it! Mnbhg vcfd xcsdawqe xcdszxse cvfgty bnjhuiytred xcd. . . .

TRACY. Tell me, do you ever do any painting from life?

OSBORNE. I never have.

TRACY. Perhaps I could be your model.

OSBORNE. Well, I——

TRACY. Would you like to do your painting at my place?

OSBORNE. You mean you'd like me to paint your apartment?

TRACY. No, silly . . . *me!* I'll get into something—more—comfortable. [*Exits*.]

OSBORNE. Excuse me. I'll be right there. . . . I have to set something up. [*He sets up the obscene machine, runs and grabs easel and canvasses and climbs through the hole*.] Dig you later, Cougie, baby!

VOICE OF THE OBSCENE MACHINE. This is a recorded obscene phone call. You and I could make such a skeeble together, baby. Listen, you mibly gleep, I'm going to go right over there and make nitzell with you, you hear? When you hear the beep you may start talking and finish by the sound of the second beep.

There is a beep.

Curtain.

FRENCH GRAY

A *Play in One Act*
by
JOSEF BUSH

Dedicated to W. H.

French Gray was first presented at The Playwrights Workshop Club, Inc., New York City, on November 28, 1966. It starred Phoebe Wray and was directed by Roberta Sklar.

FRENCH GRAY

As the curtain slowly parts, we see a dim room, windowless, and unrealistically designed to represent a stony cell. It is furnished with a heavy wooden table, a chair with a broken back, which stands against the wall, and a heap of straw and some soiled quilts that make a bed. Straw and debris litter the floor. There are crusts of bread and some rinds of cheese in or near a broken dish by the bed. There is an unemptied chamber pot under the table, and on the table are scraps of food, a bowl, and a spoon.

A heavy, slotted prison door is directly against the rear wall.

A rat appears out of the heap of straw bedding, and after sniffing a bit, scurries across the floor, crossing behind the table, center left, and disappearing into the gloom of the wings. Rats chirrup to one another, and one rat, larger and darker than the first, crosses directly across the stage, brushing the foot of THE WOMAN.

THE WOMAN *sits on a stool, hunched over, or rather, sprawled across the table, her prie-dieu. The light from one thick candle stub is falling over her head and particularly over her two clenched, bony hands. Her head is bowed low over her arms, and we see these hands clearly, though her face, for a few seconds, is obscured. They are fine slender hands, aristocratic, tapering, and nervous, streaked with grime and stained. They might be the hands of a witch. She is clutching an improvised cross made of a piece of the lyre back of the broken chair and a piece of untrimmed wood. The two pieces, upright and crossbar, are tied with a strip of pink cloth —probably lingerie silk.*

The light of the solitary candle does not quite penetrate the shadow of her cell, but makes an island of the table top. It is only with difficulty that we can identify the various objects in the room.

The reason for this is more than atmospheric: in this darkness, the many hiding places for the pieces of costumery she will don, must be invisible. As she takes them, one by one, she must appear to do so by pulling them out of the air or out of the vapors of her mind— a kind of magician's act—until the conclusion of the play.

When the rat brushes against her foot, THE WOMAN *rises with a start, as though having kept a difficult vigil, during which she slept for only a second, or an hour that seemed a second, opening wild, haggard eyes—eyes drunk with sleeplessness and fatigue far beyond endurance. In a second she is up, swinging her cross like a club or a hockey stick after the rat, slashing into the shadows, clubbing with it, striking the floor; muttering, grunting. And it seems an old game. Then, breathing heavily and wiping her face with her sleeves, she stumbles toward the table and collapses upon it, her elbows thrusting down, making vulture steeples of her shoulders. The cross is still in her hand, and under the cap, her face has the look of a whipped beast. And it is not, in repose, a pleasant face. It needs illumination from within, to make it "work."* THE WOMAN *is thin and exhausted. All the points of her body that touch the garment she wears are projections, blades; and the garment itself is like a shroud, colorless, shapeless; it screams prison. Her feet are bare, rat-scarred, scratched and bleeding from the constant action of her nails, warring on lice. She speaks without focusing her eyes.*

Sometimes you miss, that's all——

Then she returns to her prayer at the table and the position in which we found her, under the shadow of the cane-tall cross. She raises her eyes.

—Father which art in heaven; hallowed be thy name. Amen. Hallowed and most holy be thy blessèd name. *Thy* kingdom come. Sweet Jesus, oh, Suffering Holy Prince, let me learn to say it as You said it— Thy will be done. Thy will be done—

She sighs, letting the cross fall to the table, but still holding it with one hand, rests her cheek on the table.

—on earth— Thy will? On earth as it is in heaven. And

forgive us our trespasses as we forgive our trespassers.
And lead us not into temptation, but deliver us from
evil— I know Thou canst deliver me, Jesus. Oh, God,
let me not be in the dust. I forgive me—You—our trespassers. I do. I forgive them all. I forgive them all. The
judges and everybody, I forgive 'em. Deliver me this cup
which runneth over with— Oil? As I walk through the
valley of the shadow—of shadows— *Nell mezzo del
camin de nostra vita, me retrovai per una serv oscura,
che la diretta via era smarita. Ave Maria gratia plena.*
. . . Eh? Eh? Holy Mother full of grace, pray for us
sinners now and at the hour of our deaths, *che la diretta
via era smarita.* I am not afraid to die, I am only afraid
to die without honor. And I want to make some kind of
peace. I don't even remember all my prayers, though it
seems to me I once knew how to pray. Somebody
taught me, that I know. But I get it confused with
poetry. Dante isn't a prayer. A comedy's a comedy, no
matter where it takes place. Hail Mary, Marie, full of
grace. The Lord is with thee. Blessèd art thou amongst
women, and blessèd is the fruit of thy womb—

              Jesus

——I'll wait. Let me be the last. The very last. Only let
me be a Magi queen, and travel behind black Balthazar,
to lay my worthless riches at Your feet, and enter at the
gate behind the poor, the poorest of the poor, my knees
blistered with repentance, as indeed they are now—
Ah! I think I will scratch myself to bits in heaven! My
bed, that straw, is alive with lice. How can one pray and
hunt vermin?

She is sitting up now, vigorously scratching and writhing.

Deliver me! Ha! Holy Mother, can you kill lice? Great
unspotted Virgin, Mother of God, I am a mother too.
Grant me a little peace, a tiny space of time before I
die, in which to beg, with dignity, for mercy. Make me
a human being again for a minute, and I will offer you
my soul—unless my soul has become one great itch. I'm
trying. I want to hope. What does the poet say? "Death
does not frighten the unhappy." But a little hope can

be built upon. Give me just a little. Let me make a graceful exit.

A rat, noisily squeaking, has entered, stage left.

Forgive me for laughing, saints and angels, but is this a sign? Is this my prison annunciation? Has this dainty quadruped come to tell me, his whiskers metamorphosed out of wings, that instead of one pure life to nestle under my heart, I will bear a thousand of God's appointed on my skin—?

Rising and shrieking hysterically.

In my hair? I'll kill you, you twitching, miserable fiend. You hairy piece of filth.

She has risen, and runs about the room madly, weeping and striking at the rat, which by now is no longer visible to us.

Disgusting thing! Filth! Stand and let me dash your brains straight to hell, where you belong. Fight! Fight! You always wait till I'm asleep. Why can't you try it now, eh? Why can't you bite me now? You and your friends. Eh? Your dinner is fighting back, you little vampire rat bastards all of you, your food is fighting you back!

She sinks, sobbing, to her stool.

We must not be humiliated. We must not permit ourselves to be . . . to be ruined in our own eyes. We must try to take a little pride with us into our graves, no matter where they may be. Hope is, after all, only hope. What good is it? And despair? Another caprice. We do only what we can. We resign ourselves to ourselves. The grave settles it all. And then . . . good night. Unless we live again . . . like this. Confined in solitude. Will this candle, once extinguished, relight itself in an empty room? Confined in solitude? Dawn and my trip through the streets is almost here; though the window tells me there's an hour. Tonight is short. Tomorrow night? I can't pray. Let me think, while I can, and defend myself against calumny. Let me be eloquent, though there's nobody but myself to hear, and convincing, though

these barriers make all thought of contact absurd. Now,
since I am a woman and dislike to be alone, let me speak
to women.

She removes her cap, revealing a fine head of hair.

Women of my mind and of this night, give me your attention before I die. Be introspection. Be me aware of me,
until the dawn. Let us have only the truth between us
now. You cannot refuse any more than can the shadows
thrown on my cell's wall by this low flame that's doomed
to sputter out in half an hour. It trembles toward the
last, a shivering blaze of will that gives, in one brief
space, more light than ever it had in all its life. This
tiny gasp of fire illuminates the corners of my soul. . . .
A good start. A defending lawyer should be eloquent.
And now what, women? My fortune? It's bad. I have
been rich, and now I'm in prison. They *are* going to kill
me. The butchers! That I'm an aristocrat there can be no
doubt. Where my grave will be—who knows? But
there are worse things. Listen. It would freeze your blood
to know— And I am watched. Night and day I have no
privacy. None. Women, do you hear me? There are no
women in this place. . . . Although the soldiers bring
prostitutes from time to time. I hear laughter, sometimes, when I press my ear against the door. But I may
be wrong. *I HAVE NO PRIVACY!* I must beg, beg, for
everything. For these flint-faced peasants, these "citizens"
of the "new order," I must grovel for a piece of soap.
There are eyes behind the chinks in these walls. I hear
them breathe, or cough, sometimes as I move about the
room . . . women . . . when my time of the month
comes—the "Widow Capet" has to beg for a piece of
soap with which to wash. Yes! Yes! I, who never slept
but on silk, who used to see myself reflected in the eyes
of hundreds of amorous men and envious women, whose
mirrors were cheerful witnesses to the style, beauty, and
sumptuousness of my clothing, I used to think it a
crime, but now I'm glad to be without a mirror. I had
certain gestures which—how can I describe them?—
gestures which the Baroness des Moulins—

She has slipped on a glove—black, fantastic, transparent, and spangled with jewels.

—used to call, "moving and simple." That's the way it was. People loved me. Simplicity in great people is a crowning grace. That is what nobility means. And now! The things they say! Apparently I'm some kind of bogey. Mothers frighten their children to bed with—

Suddenly she has slipped on another transparent jeweled glove.

—"Be careful, little Jean-Pierre, Hercule," whatever the little beast's name is, "or the Austrian woman will get you." Where do these superstitious riffraff get their ideas? One day Monsieur What's-his-name came to me and said, "The children are starving in the streets." Well, what is one to do? I give to charity every penny I can spare. My dear, everybody knows I'm tireless when it comes to charity. "The people must be cared for," he says. Then let them work, and let them save for hard times. Thrift, Monsieur! Think of thrift! "There are no jobs." Then let them join the army. "We are at peace." Then let them take holy orders. "It is very difficult to tax the church." Farms? "Famine." Indeed, indeed. "As a mother, Madame, think of the women—" And that is precisely what I *am* thinking of. Don't you realize, I said, that this constant flow of charity is turning these women into whores? Haven't we enough whores? Enough bastards? You think that just because you give these people money that they should be—grateful? Eh? Don't you? You poor naïve bourgeois. They aren't. They think it's their due, and that we, that *we* are to blame. Let me tell you, there are certain parts of the city I do not dare to enter. Why *do* people live in such squalor? And if they choose to do so, why can't they leave the rest of us alone? Such hostility! Heavens!

Here she falls, decorously, upon her mattress of straw, much as though it were a mossy hillock and she were about to spread picnic cloths. A magnificent fan appears in her hand.

I distinctly heard a sharp intake of breath. What? There's
a prude somewhere about. A bluestocking. What was it?
"Whore?" Faugh! We can say anything we like here.
This is not, after all, freedom—the street. This is disci-
pline and, perhaps, punishment. Obscenity forbidden in
solitary confinement? Fancy that. Well— Better die al-
fresco. I shall have to be genteel at the gibbet. God-a-
mercy.

She rises, laughing, and we see that she now has on a
skirt and panniers. On the back wall, to the right and left,
we seem to see candles burning in sconces on paneled walls,
curious carvings, and the glimmer of ormolu. The light
has come up so gradually that we can't say when it began
or where it comes from. These magnificent and beautiful
furnishings are projections from some kind of phantas-
magoria: lantern-slide images. And THE WOMAN *has begun*
to sparkle in her transparent rococo garments.

Yes, yes. It's funny now, of course. Quite funny. Memories
have a way of coming back. But the joke is on somebody
else. On me? I don't think so. No. What I've done, I've
done without shame. On the contrary. I have a great deal
of pride about it. Indeed, I am proud. But Zozie. Oh!
Oh! There was a proud woman. My sides are fairly splitting as I remember it. Even here, here in this black
mirror of my condemnation, I can feel the prick of my
triumph in her utter humiliation. Mind you, I don't say
she was without her points. Many— Well, some say she
had perfect arms, that her shoulders and breasts were
unsurpassable. Yes—believe it if you can—I laugh. She
looked like a boiled chicken to me. Her bosom was positively unwholesome, caked with stale powder. Ugh! And
she thought herself a woman of birth and position. Imagine!

A bell, heavy and solemn, rings four times, beginning as
she says the word, "Imagine," and ending as she finishes
her sentence with "all this time."

One talks to oneself. I would have died a thousand times
before I had to face this moment, but I didn't. And isn't

it sad that my, my what—my sense of humor—if that's
what it is called?—kept me alive all this time. I wanted
to die. I wanted to exile myself, to pass a decree against
myself for permitting this ghastly misfortune to happen,
and pass my remaining days in some gracious old château
on the Loire. But—

Laughing again.

—Zozie. Zenobia Irene Sofia de Charnloup. What a
name! Oh, I could burst into a volley of evil smells for
laughing at the presumption of it. That a creature like
that should have the nerve to affect such a diminutive
— And to broadcast it about. Why, before she was in
the palace half a day she was sending pages about to
announce her as "Zozie." Straight out of a compost heap
into a corset. The bitch. I pretended not to notice her.
I'd simply not let my eyes rest upon her whey face. I
hadn't any idea of where she came from, but I knew I'd
find out. I did. The divine de Polignac, my own, my
most beautiful of friends, that goddess, my persuasive
friend de Polignac— Ah! Ah! She happened to mention
to me that certain family friends were sending a girl
to be with her at court. A girl! She was thirty and had
disgusting breath. Her looks were invitations to debauch.
A girl— The flower of an old feudal family, one of the
oldest in France. And she, de Polignac, was wondering
if—the child might one day be presented to her majesty?
Presented to the not-very-merry-widow Capet. Ah! Do
you hear that, Citizens? The lesbian with a face like something the dog did on the carpet, wanted to be presented
to me. Anything is possible in France, and none of it good.
They specialize in killing women in this country, and
wearing too much perfume. It takes a woman to show
them how to die. What was it? Mischief? Or the thirst
for annihilation? We were sitting at cards—the usual
game, the usual people—and poor Pipo began to lose
quite a considerable sum. He was white as milk under
his rouge. After all, he owed the *comtesse* and myself
eleven or twelve hundred louis d'or already. The ambassador dealt. Two or three cards, and I took the trick with

the brutality of an archangel. With icy hands he congratulated me on my fortune and begged me to accept this magnificent emerald. I slipped it on, and dimpling, so, waved him away. They say he went back to the archbishop. Then, by chance, into my field of vision sailed this Zenobia of the provinces. Under the sunbeams of my smile she billowed over the shining surface of the floor, her bow dangerously close to the now-empty chair. We arranged ourselves into an armada of open faces, ready, perhaps, to smile. I arranged my armaments and lit my jewels. Polished my pikes. With consummate aplomb she gained the armchair on my left and sat, rocking slightly, dizzy with self-approval. In an instant the room was silent, the only sound the surfbeat of our blood. I rose, a sister ship on either side, and lit the silent cannon of my eyes. "There's some mistake," the ambassador said. The first broadside was his. "What have you done, my poor dear child?" That was the Baroness whose aim is never anything but superb, tearing her rigging and shattering her masts. Magnificent! With wounded looks she took a parting shot that sent the rustic hulk up in flames. "This cannot be." And now I threw my gentle broadsides into her. Mine the *coup de grâce*. "The queen is not permitted, Mademoiselle, to sit with whomsoever she pleases. We do not know you." She rose, and shuddering into a bow, drifted off into oblivion. We saw her sink on the horizon, a flight of jeering gulls trailing her wake. An incident. One has to pass the time.

By now she is afire with jewels. Several great rings flash on her fingers and in her ears. Two beauty marks, mouches, have appeared on her face.

Then Louis said to me one day, "My dear, we can't afford to keep the fountains going. The cost is ruinous." Ridiculous! There's water everywhere, and who ever heard of water costing anything? Besides, Versailles is hideous without fountains. One has to pass the time. I'd had other triumphs. The old king had kept the place full of his whores. I, daughter of the queen of Austria, dauphine of France, bowing and scraping to one lowborn tramp

after another. Du Barry was a fool, a thoroughgoing spend-
thrift, irresponsible and vain. Oh, the luxury and pre-
tension of the woman! As soon as I got my crown she got
her walking papers. What a blessing that was. And they
call me extravagant. I saved thousands pitching out
doxies. Naturally I wanted a trinket or two for myself.
This necklace, for instance——

*She is putting on a giant phantom diamond necklace as
the bell tolls again.*

How will they know that the shabby figure in the cart on
her way to the knife is their queen? They will see me—
yes—and the children will point and scream, "Mama,
is that the Austrian woman? Is she taking the bread out of
our mouths?" Ridiculous. Dynasties do not fall because
of a diamond necklace. People don't eat diamonds. One
has responsibilities. Style, in a monarch, is a heavy responsibility, and magnificence costs money. The cause of the
monarchy is, of course, the cause of France. You see
that, don't you? How can a queen conspire against herself? Her state is herself. And I am accused of treason.
Why should I want to ruin France? Absurd. Obscene.
Then why these entertainments? These diversions?
Games? Why this obsession to fill in the minutes with—
with anything—with pleasure, whenever possible? With
whatever and whoever came to hand? You could not
call me— I—— As queen I have a public life. I am to be
seen smiling and waving from my carriage window, but I
never could be happy in life, or believe in—love, the
power of life. I glittered and was cold when all about me
glowed with heat, enthusiasm. A kind of joy I was never
able to feel— I came to this country a happy, perhaps a
silly girl, and for seven years after that, my life was hell,
a nightmare. I dreaded the setting of the sun more than
I dread its rising today. My marriage? My marriage, which
took place at the great palace of Versailles, on May the
sixteenth, seventeen-seventy, was a triumph of diplomacy.
It was to have confirmed the *alliance* between France and
Austria. I suppose it did. But then, the court was so cor-
rupt. It would be difficult for anyone to adequately de-

scribe the corruption, the decay of generations of luxury, the stench of privilege, and to describe what it did to mine. My husband was a shambling, shuffling oaf. A beast in bed, a boor at table, a blockhead in the council chamber. My mother's policies tied me under this stale lump of Bourbon flesh. My wedding night was ghastly beyond dreams. The lout had never—fucked— before he came to me. They taught my Prince Charming, with pictures. Pictures! His idea, poor idiot, of connubial bliss, was a series of *tableaux vivants* in which he, fat, beetle-browed and duty-bound satyr, twisted my body into a series of postures that were supposed to excite him and satisfy me. I could write volumes on one word. Disgust. This sweaty fumbler, the dauphin of France, was my loving husband. I am a woman, women, and I say virginity in a groom is as useful as hair on an oyster. A Catholic? Yes. And a queen. Yes. But the truth is, nobody wears a crown to bed, and seven years is a long time to be married and yet without a husband—without even children. I went to bed every night for seven years hoping, hoping he might be too tired out from hunting—he hunts incessantly—or fixing clocks, to fulfill his duties as husband. That's the way he said it, his "Duties as husband." But he never was. Never. He made me do everything. Things I— Oh, the stamina of him! He would find— ways—to excite me, to raise me to a pitch, and then leave me, gasping and screaming, to find my own way as best I could, to the ground. Sleep? Never in seven years. I would lie silently, nerves like violin strings till morning, and then run to any diversion, any pleasure that might divert my mind from our nocturnal games. They said the dauphine is driven from gaiety to gaiety, to late hours, revels, parties, gambling, plays, and balls; to friendships of a peculiar nature; to liaisons—and to debauch. Debauch. The word is music to my ears. I say it again and my skin prickles. I was indeed driven.

A man's voice cries out indistinctly a command, and the amplified sound of the guillotine is heard making its track down to the block. The sound and the terrible offstage reality of the sound that is unmistakable nearly shatter this

*rococo decor of dreams. The lights flicker, fade; the entire
stage seems about to dissolve into a few bitter sparks. The
voice might be heard saying, "Prepare! Hut!" But the mil-
itary drawl of the shout and its distance offstage blur the
sound into just a voice. Once again the command is given.
THE WOMAN stands transfixed in an agony of fright, her
heart pounding, her eyes bulging from their sockets, her lips
dry as ribbons. After the knife strikes the block a second
time, there is a silence. A deep pause. We hear her draw, with
a force of great will, a breath, and then another. She seems
to be massing every atom of her being into her last moment,
and as she does, she grows to her full specter glory. In the
interim, she has slipped on clothurni, and now, upright,
stands taller than before, as regal as an ascending Christ,
with the stage in full phantom light.*

No! I will be alive until the end. No cross, no rack, no trial,
no inquisition, will rob me of my glory. I was born to glory.
Thirty-eight years. This is not long to live. Thirty-eight
years, but it is long enough. There have been kings and
queens of France ever since the beginning, and this is
as it should be. Indeed, the church—all the porticoes
of all the great cathedrals advertise the fact—gives me
my charter and my scepter. France belongs to me. It was
a wedding present, and I am in no position to bequeath
it to a pack of howling bloodthirsty dogs that put themselves above their country's anointed sovereign. This
"estate" is to be passed on to my children. Intact. Their
rights— My little son's rights—must be preserved.
What am I saying? They will kill him. They will find
a way to kill that helpless child—

She is singing the Marseillaise.

Come, come my children of the fatherland,
The day of triumph is at hand.
Let us stand against tyranny.

No! This is a blood republic! The constitution. Faugh!
What a tissue of absurdities. Who would think that in
the enlightenment of the eighteenth century such adolescent drivel could be set to paper. My noble attitude, even

in the face of the atrocious accusations of Fouquier-Tin-
ville, commands—or, perhaps I should say, commanded—
the admiration of the crowd. Everyone told me that this
was absolutely so. To hell with my enemies. And weren't
my answers skillful? A mockery of a trial! Listen. Monsieur
de Dum-de-dum-dum rises, postures, stretches forth a finger, and screams— "Is it established that maneuvers and
communications have existed with foreign powers and
other external enemies of the republic, the said maneuvers,
etcetera, tending to furnish them with assistance in
money, give them an entry into French territory, and
facilitate the progress of their armies?" You see? This
is intended to make me look like a traitor. I'm supposed
to have invited foreign intervention. "Is Marie Antoinette
of Austria—" The swine. Marie Antoinette of France!
—"convicted of having co-operated in these maneuvers
and maintained these communications?" The eunuch!
Of course I did. What else was I to do? And who was he,
after all? Some twopenny little fly-by-night provincial of
a notary. Well, probably. "Is it established that a plot and
conspiracy has existed tending to kindle civil war within
the republic by arming the citizens against one another?"
Now tell me, have you ever heard anything more ridiculous? Why these people were my very children. I cared
for them as I cared for the sacred land itself that had been
given to me by God in the holy oil with which I was
anointed. As for my soul—! I'm not permitted my *own*
confessor. Some simpering sadist, recruited from the
rabble, comes to gloat over his "fallen queen." He thinks
me a Jezebel and quotes biblical platitudes. "You go this
morning to meet your Maker, Widow Capet, a just and
terrible God. Are you prepared, my child?" Am I prepared? Are you listening to me? Then hear me pronounce
a curse on this rattling, wheezing, vicious old hypocrite
in the sky. This drinker of the blood of armies. "Protect
us, O Lord of Hosts, and aid us in our holy slaughter." I,
the humiliated, I, the anguished and abused queen of
France, I swear, that should I see this stuffed and bloody
fetish, I will spit, like a common woman, into his face:
three times, good Catholic that I am— One for each. In

the name of the Father! And of the Son! And of the Holy Ghost! Amen. I stand alone, as do we all, at the last moment, in my own frantic radiance, against God, the world, and public opinion. Free!

A terrible roll of drums and the light vanishes. The drums throb for a couple of seconds, the candle sputters out. The stage is totally dark. The rear door is thrown open and a beam of yellow light falls diagonally across the floor. A VOICE *calls out: "Widow Capet. Are you ready?" The miserable figure, dressed as she was in the beginning, walks quickly to the threshold, stops, turns slightly, and with the grandeur of a marble pylon, speaks:*

The queen is ready.

The door slams behind her. The stage is black. The drums continue for a second or two more, then the dreadful thump of the guillotine, and the roar of a crowd of thousands, which fades, gradually, as the lights go up on the empty stage as it was. A pause. Then:

Curtain.

THE ABSTRACT WIFE

A Play in One Act

by

URSULE MOLINARO

For Lawrence Wunderlich

CHARACTERS

THE WIFE. *A frail woman in her thirties. Pale. Thin-boned. Long black hair (asbestos flash-paper wig) twisted into a bun on top of her head.*

HER HUSBAND. *Any husband in his thirties. Business suit.*

HIS (former) MISTRESS. *In her thirties. Large-featured and solid. Helmet of thick red hair. Loud green velvet dress or suit. Eager laugh.*

The Abstract Wife was first produced by Theatre 1961 at the York Theatre on April 17, 1961, with the following cast:

WIFE	Mary Hara
HUSBAND	Roberts Blossom
MISTRESS	Peggy Pope

The play was directed by Roberts Blossom.

THE ABSTRACT WIFE

THE SET

An old-fashioned bathtub on feet stands lengthwise down the center of the stage. At left head end, a chair with one red and one black towel thrown over back. On chair seat, a package of cigarettes, matches, an ash tray. In front of tub and chair, a black bath mat. On it, a pair of high-heeled glass slippers.

Behind head end of tub, a full-length mirror in a thick gold frame. Ideally, the mirror frame should remain in its place while the pane can be moved backward and forward; usually the whole mirror moves back leaving a space behind the tub wide enough for HUSBAND *and* MISTRESS *to stand behind the* WIFE, *who does not see them.* HUSBAND *and* MISTRESS *act out whatever the* WIFE *imagines they did together, gestures the* HUSBAND *made toward the* WIFE *and which she remembers.*

HUSBAND *and* MISTRESS *do not speak. Their mouths are taped with a large red cross. When the* WIFE *imagines their conversations, or repeats what her* HUSBAND *said to her, quotations of what his* MISTRESS *said to him, banalities made deep by his desire, brought home to his* WIFE *as so many gems of wit, a tape recorder plays back their speeches: speeded up; slowed down; normal; echo-chamber effect; hollow drone; loud; whispers, etc., changing with the* WIFE's *emotions.*

As the curtain rises, the WIFE *sits in the tub, looking at her hands.*

WIFE [*slowly, imitating someone else's—her husband's— voice*]. . . . Cool, sensitive hands. . . . Like ivory flowers. . . . Like the pictures they paint. . . . So delicate. . . . [*She kisses her ten finger tips; she makes a fist. Her own voice; very loud.*] Abstract! [*Less loud.*] like the pictures they paint. Cool sensitive delicate stillborn abstractions, painted by the hands of a ghost. . . . [*Very loud.*]

I'm a ghost! A ghost! [*Less loud.*] My body died when his desire deserted it. [*Pause. Softly.*] He used to light my cigarette with the sun. Through a magnifying glass. Before . . . when he loved me. [*Pause.*] How *could* he have loved me, if it's solid flesh he likes? . . . [*Loud.*] The hands of a ghost painting ghost pictures—[*Beating a fist against the rim of the tub.*]—so cool and sensitive and abstract, they can't hold onto their husband. I hate you! I hate you! I hate you! [*She stops beating her fist.*] Ouch! [*She dips hand into bath water. Holds it up. Strokes it with other hand.*] Poor hand. I didn't mean to hurt you. I thought you were dead. Too dead to feel. Hasn't he hurt us enough? [*Pause. She shrugs.*] Now I hurt. When it's over. When he wants me again. . . . [*Pause. Little laugh.*] He wants me again. . . . [*Pause.*] I wish I could want *him* again. But ghosts don't want. They remember. And remember. And remember. [*Imitating* HUSBAND's *voice.*] Can't you forget? Let me forget her? It's *over*, I told you. I told you I told her it's over. . . . [*She turns to look at herself in the mirror behind her. Normal voice.*] He's right: I *am* getting thin. [*She feels her jaw and neck.*] Too thin. An old bag full of bones. Do I rattle when I walk? When he touches me? [*She turns away. The mirror slowly withdraws.*] Because he touches me again . . . [*Pause. Self-mockery.*] . . . My "elegant bones." . . . My "porcelain skeleton." . . .

HUSBAND *steps out from behind the mirror. Looking down on* WIFE's *head. His recorded voice is deep and low, a faraway echo.*

HUSBAND.   Let—me—touch—your—porcelain—skeleton— your—elegant—bones. . . .

WIFE [*viciously unhappy*]. Now he prefers the flesh on them. The red-haired woman's flesh. Pink bouncy tires that toss his hand high up into the air—for a comeback —when he whacks her one on the bottom.

HUSBAND [*sigh; less loud*]. Whacked. Whacked. Not whacks. A gesture of the past. I'm sorry I made it. I was sorry the minute I made it. My hand made it. All by itself. I don't know what possessed me. But it's over

now. All over. I told you I told her it had to be all over.
. . . Do you want me to fire her to convince you?

WIFE. No. No. That wouldn't be fair. Why should *she*
be made to pay? Always the woman. . . . She must be
unhappy enough now, if it's *really* over between you. . . .

HUSBAND. It *is* over. [*Echo.*] O——ver. Please let me touch
you again. . . . [*He tries to touch* WIFE's *shoulder, but
his arm is too short.*]

WIFE. She probably hates me now, if it's *really* over. . . .

HUSBAND [*sigh*]. Really over. [*Echo.*] O——ver! Please!
Can't-you-let-me-forget—let-me-forget-her? [*He tries to
touch* WIFE's *hair; his arm is too short.*]

WIFE. Does she hate me then? [*Pause.*] I don't hate *her.* I
never hated her. Not even while this thing was going on
between them. I didn't know this thing was going on
between them. I knew, but I didn't know. Not before
he told me it was over. [*Pause.*] I don't hate her. She has
no reason to be loyal to me, when my own husband—
She doesn't even know me. [*Pause.*] No, no, you mustn't
fire her. . . . [*Pause.*] Maybe you should quit. . . .

HUSBAND [*loud; echo-chamber effect*]. Quit my job?! And
what are we to live on? She's got a husband to take care
of her!

WIFE. I know she's got a husband—[*Intent whisper.*]—and
red hair! I know. I know all about her. Everything. She
doesn't know me, but I know everything about *her.* Her
thick red hair. Her tight green dresses. She always wears
green—and she can't spell. . . . [*Pause.*] I know, because he told me. He couldn't stop telling me about her,
at first, when she first came to work for him. How big and
solid she was. The way her hair would fall all over the
pages when he showed her a spelling mistake she'd made.
. . . Every night he rehearsed his desire for her. With
me. . . . How could he desire *me, ever,* if it's red hair
he likes? Until he touched her. . . .

HUSBAND [*gradually increasing speed*]. They gave me a new
secretary today. Real amazon. Makes the office look small
to have that—that lady wrestler enthroned behind the

typewriter. Huge mop of red hair. Can't spell to save her life. You wonder where they go to dig up these girls. . . . Well, at least she's introduced a little color to the place. . . . Somehow you can't get angry at hair like that. It looks so misplaced in an office. . . . I didn't know you had called. I'm sorry. Was it important? Big Red Riding Hood forgot to tell me. Too busy thinking about a new green velvet suit she bought for herself during lunch hour, I imagine. . . . What a relief, a woman who doesn't feel overqualified all the time. Doesn't penalize you for her unfulfilled ambitions——

WIFE [*cutting him off*]. Until he started to have meetings at night.

A *telephone rings on tape.* WIFE *holds her hand to her ear, as if holding a receiver.*

HUSBAND. Would you mind very much eating dinner without me for once, dear? I have a distributors' meeting tonight. Tried to squeeze out of it, but you know how it is. . . .

WIFE *drops her hand into the water. The phone rings. She puts her hand to her ear.*

HUSBAND. Another distributors' meeting tonight. Don't wait up for me, dear. . . . [WIFE *drops her hand into the water. The phone rings. She puts her hand to her ear.*] Another meeting tonight. Sorry.

WIFE *drops her hand into the water. The phone rings. She puts her hand to her ear. These gestures, and the ringing of the telephone, are repeated eight more times, while the* HUSBAND *says:*

HUSBAND. Meeting tonight. Meeting tonight. Meeting tonight. Meeting tonight. Meeting tonight. Meeting tonight. Meeting tonight. Meeting tonight.

WIFE [*puts both hands to her ears*]. Meeting tonight meeting tonight meeting tonight meeting tonight meeting tonight meeting tonight meeting tonight——[*She drops both hands into water with loud splash.*] Perhaps you should quit?

HUSBAND [*loud*]. Quit my job? And what are we to live on? Your painting? [*Less loud.*] I'm sorry. I didn't mean it to sound that way. You're a fine painter. A very fine painter. So delicate and sensitive. Just not very commercial. Too abstract, let's face it. She's got a prosperous husband to take care of her!!!

WIFE [*pointed smile*]. Are you still jealous of him?

HUSBAND [*loud*]. I? Jealous? Of that balding clown of a husband of hers! When was I ever jealous of her husband? I feel sorry for him. . . . Even if he makes more money than I'll ever make. . . . That's why she married him. For his money. She told me. [*Fast.*] I slapped her face when she told me. Hard. That's how "jealous" I was of her husband.

WIFE [*intent whisper*]. He loves to slap her. Her face. Her behind. Everywhere. On her breasts maybe? . . . [*Pause.*] That's how it started between them: with a slap on her behind. He told me. He said he found her bending over a filing cabinet, and his hand went out all by itself, and whacked her one on the bottom.

HUSBAND [*gradually speeding up in embarrassment*]. It always took her forever to find anything—[MISTRESS *steps out from behind the mirror and bends over an imaginary filing cabinet. Muzak.*]—so I got up to find the thing myself. And there she was, practically doubled over, red hair hanging into the contracts, and those green amazon buttocks staring up at me. . . . My hand went out all by itself, before I knew what it was doing. . . . [*His hand reaches out, but does not touch* MISTRESS.] I don't know what came over me. I don't approve of animal instincts in an office—[*He pulls back his hand.*]—except, long ago, as a boy, I used to enjoy driving my grandfather's buggy, on summer vacations. The whole landscape blotted out by an enormous pair of brown velvet buttocks—[*Slow and tender.*]—green velvet buttocks. . . . [*He whacks* MISTRESS *on the bottom.*]

MISTRESS [*straightens up, laughing in surprise*]. Oh, Mr.
Biedermeier—

HUSBAND [*to* MISTRESS]. Yes. Mr. Biedermeier. Bud Biedermeier. Who did you think it was? [*He slaps her
again, harder this time, and once or twice more, keep-
ing his hand on her bottom, rubbing it between slaps.
To* WIFE.] I felt like a fool, standing there at the end
of my hand. My hand had committed me. I couldn't cut
it off, could I?

MISTRESS [*lifts his hand from her behind and returns it to
him as though it were an object*]. Now, now, Mr. Biedermeier. What would your wife say to a thing like
that?

WIFE. It was easier to cut *me* off.

HUSBAND. I *didn't* cut you off. Never. I never stopped loving you. In spite of appearances. . . . Please. Let me
touch you again. [*He tries to touch* WIFE's *hair, but
cannot reach it.*]

WIFE. Red-haired appearances. . . .

HUSBAND. And she knew it too. She was very jealous of my
respect for you.

WIFE. His respect! As though I were his mother, when
he's three and a half months older than I am. . . .

HUSBAND [*to* MISTRESS]. My wife? What my wife would
say to a thing like this? [*Short laugh.*] She's hardly the
type one taps on the fanny. [*He slaps her again, lightly.*]
I'd be scared to break her bones. . . . She's too abstract for this sort of thing. . . . [*He turns* MISTRESS
*to him. Long kiss of two taped mouths. A telephone
rings several times and is not answered.* WIFE *soaps her
neck.*] Let me touch your helmet . . . your halo. . . .
[*He runs his fingers through* MISTRESS's *hair. Pause.*]
And your husband? What would your husband say?

MISTRESS. My husband? [*Laugh.*] He'd say nothing. He'd
hit me.

HUSBAND. Where? Where would he hit you?

MISTRESS [*laughing*]. I don't know, Mr. Biedermeier.
[*Shrug.*] In the face, I guess.

HUSBAND [*slaps* MISTRESS's *face*]. I don't want him to hit you! [*Slap.*] I don't want anybody to hit you! [*Slap. Changed tone.*] The hazards of office life. He shouldn't let you go to work, if he's so jealous.

MISTRESS. Your wife doesn't work?

HUSBAND [*sigh*]. My wife paints. . . . [*Pause; mussing* MISTRESS's *hair.*] Nooooooooooo. Don't worry. My wife won't notice when I come home. I told you: she *paints*. . . . [*To* WIFE.] You always complained about cooking dinner. That it didn't leave you enough time to paint. . . . You don't imagine I *enjoy* distributors' meetings. . . . [*To* MISTRESS, *kissing her hair with taped mouth.*] Beautiful, beautiful hair . . . flames. . . .

WIFE [*drops the soap; shakes her head*]. And the woman has a husband. What does her husband say when she comes home so late? Does he know?

HUSBAND [*to* WIFE]. *Did!* since it's over. If he *did* know, he also knows that it's over. [*Echo.*] O——ver. O——ver. . . .

WIFE [*resolutely*]. It's over! [HUSBAND *and* MISTRESS *disappear behind the mirror, which slowly moves back to its initial position.*] He wants me again. [*She reaches for a towel and dries her face and arms. She stands up in the tub, draping the towel around her. She takes a cigarette from the package on the chair. Puts it in her mouth. Takes the matches. Looks at herself in the mirror.*] How *can* he want me, if it's red hair he likes? [*Encouraging smile, with the unlit cigarette between her lips.*] But he does. He does want me again. . . .

She continues to smile at herself. Strikes a match. Brings the flame close to the cigarette. Does not light it. Lights her hair instead. Stands smiling, looking at her burning hair for as long as possible, while lights black out.

PASSACAGLIA

A Play in Two Acts

by

JAMES PAUL DEY

For Jean-Pierre Voos

CHARACTERS

John Jones
Mary Jones
Johnmary Jones, *their son*
Maid Jones, *a very black person*

John Smith
Mary Smith
Maryjohn Smith, *their daughter*
Maid Smith, *an albino transvestite*

Scene: The U.S.&A.
Time: Mid-twentieth century

Passacaglia was first presented by the International Theatre Club at the Mercury Theatre, London, in 1965.

PASSACAGLIA

ACT ONE

SCENE I

A row of telephone booths resembling human dwellings. The only factor that distinguishes one house from another is the degree of "cleverness" its inhabitants have used to frost its façade. These inhabitants are identified by "suitable" name plates or signs. Extending from left to right, they read: "John & Mary," "Mary & John," "John & Mary," etcetera.

Enter the Joneses from their house on the right. They form a line across the front of the stage and speak directly to the audience.

JOHNMARY JONES. Her name is John. His name is Mary.

MARY JONES. No, no, dear! *My* name is Mary. *His* name is John!

JOHN JONES. Our last name is. . . . What is our last name, Mary, dear?

MARY. Why . . . it's . . . Well, really, John Jones. . . . Don't you know?

JOHN. Jones! That's it! Jones!

MARY. Of course, you silly thing! [*She laughs.*]

JOHNMARY. My name is Little Annie Rooney.

MARY. Oh no, no, darling! Your name is Johnmary.

JOHN. Johnmary Q. Jones the Eighth, dammit!

MARY. He's our little boy.

JOHN. And damn lucky to be, I say! Hell, when I was thirteen-and-a-half years old, I knew which end was up! You bet your sweet life I did!

JOHNMARY. I've tried to compensate by helping save the nation from spontaneous assumption.

157

MARY. He can do the cutest imitation of Shirley Temple you ever saw.

JOHN. Hell, when I was thirteen-and-a-half years old, I could drink four quarts of booze without going to the——

MARY. *John!* Please! Watch your language in front of the child!

JOHN. Strong will power, you know what I mean? They don't make kids like they used to.

MARY [*to* JOHNMARY]. That's true, darling. And that's one reason those damn Russians are getting ahead of us.

JOHN. Hell, yes! You never hear of them Commies having to stop in space to take a leak! Nevertheless, in all other respects, my boy's a true-blue-jewel-of-a-Joe!

MARY. A true-blue-jewel-of-a-John! Johnmary, that's his name.

JOHN. Okay . . . Okay! So I guess we've spoiled him. But you know how it is with us upper-lower-middle-class rich-lovers-of-liberty. We like our constitutional conveniences . . . and, by God, we'll blast hell out'a any son-of-a-bitch who tries to interfere with God-fearin' folks' right to freedom!

MARY. Tell 'em, John! We want our boy to grow up in a world of plenty of peace and tranquillity . . . and all sorts of nice things like that. After all, he is our only child.

JOHN. You really love to rub that "only child" bit in, don't you?

MARY. Please, John! Not here!

JOHN. You know damn well that——

MARY. Please, John! Please, John! Please, John! *Please!*

JOHN. You know goddamned well you've flushed at least three down the——

MARY. John! Please! We made lamps out of two of them, and you know it! [*To* JOHNMARY.] Quick, darling! Say something pithy before your father shows his crudity and shatters your concepts!

JOHNMARY. I'm going to be an idiot when I grow up.

MARY. You see, John? You see? You see how honest and egregious his little ego is? Say something else, darling. Say something wholesome and stimulating about this age we live in.

JOHNMARY. In a clinical study, made over the past seven years by a group of impartial observers, our group had fifty per cent fewer brains than less fortunate groups.

MARY. You see, John? You see? Isn't it wonderful and encouraging and heart-warming to see such overt manifestations of sincerity?

JOHN. I'd rather see a little hair on his tongue once in a while!

MARY. I know, John. . . . I know.

JOHN. By God, when I was thirteen-and-a-half years old, I'd already made half the sheep on a five-thousand-acre farm.

MARY. I know, John. . . . I know. But don't forget, your mother was half-French.

JOHNMARY. What'd he say? What'd he say?

MARY. He says he's going to run for President as soon as we can get rid of this one.

JOHNMARY. Oh goody! I could have a White House wedding.

JOHN. "Goody"! What kind'a faggot talk is that? Can't he ever say: "hell" or "goddamn"? Doesn't he know *any* dirty words?

MARY. Say, "pee-pee" for Daddy, Son.

JOHN. Oh shit!

JOHNMARY. What'd he say? What'd he say?

MARY. He said you were Daddy's little pride and joy.

JOHNMARY. Oh, that's lovely.

JOHN [*mimicking* JOHNMARY]. "Oh, that's lovely"! Jesus!

JOHNMARY. I've just finished reading *The Journals of John Birch* and redrafting the U.S. Constitution . . . and he says, "Jesus"! Jesus!

JOHN. I swear, Mary . . . that kid's goin'a grow up to be a fairy! I can see it all over him.

MARY [*taking* JOHNMARY *in her arms and kissing him profusely*]. Ohhh, darling. . . . You wouldn't do a mean nasty old thing like that to Mummy, would you? Of course you wouldn't. Shame on you, John, for putting ideas like that in his precious little head!

JOHN. I gave him a life-size machine gun for his birthday. So what does he do? Takes one look at it and tries to shoot me!

MARY. Now, John, I'm sure he meant it affectionately. Anyway, you know very well, he's asked you time and time again to shoot yourself.

JOHNMARY. I say, I do wish some modern theatrical device such as the doorbell would ring, and relieve this strained domestic situation.

JOHN. You see! You see! There he goes again! Always trying to degrade me! He wanted an unlisted doorbell, so I got him an unlisted doorbell! Now the little bastard wants to hear it ring!

MARY. Now you know that's true, dear. Daddy-John did it for no other purpose than to save us from the public clamor and the onslaught of creeping Socialism.

JOHNMARY. Yes, Mummy, I know. But both you and your husband seem to ignore the fact that I, as a human being, a fluke of divine miscalculation, am therefore and nevertheless acquainted with the process of activated acquiescence.

JOHN. Well I should hope so.

JOHNMARY. However, I'm afraid I am forced once again to remind you that the phylogenetic physiognomy of neo-physostigmine is *still* a colorless and/or pinkish crystalline alkaloid, extracted from the far-from-being-extinct calabar bean.

MARY. Oh, my God, John! Wasn't that gorgeous?

JOHN. Sounds to me like he's been reading them Commie comic books again!

MARY. Oh shut up! Don't you even recognize culture when you hear it? Rave on, darling.

JOHNMARY. I'm glad you brought out that point, Mary. And let me make myself absolutely clear. I do realize how difficult this may be for you people of the older generation to understand. However, I want you to know that it is only because I love, honor, and cherish you that such paradoxes necessitate a somewhat cloudy view of that which would be no doubt totally opaque to less sensitive free spirits roaming at random in a world dominated by so terribly many ineffectual and obviously fraudulent Homo sapiens.

MARY. O, my God, John! Did you hear that?

JOHN. I heard it! "*Homo*," what?

MARY. Knock it off, John!

JOHNMARY. Therefore, I must say with my traditional candor and honesty that there are moments when I feel it would be to all our advantage if we could adopt a somewhat less conservative policy toward conception and constipation.

JOHN. You see? You see? There he goes again!

MARY. Please, John! Please, John! Please, John! *Please!* You have no right to condemn our only child, simply because he makes you feel stupid!

JOHNMARY. Tell him, Momma! Tell him!

MARY. Just don't forget, John. . . . You were as common as dirt until I helped you rid the D.A.R. of subversives!

JOHNMARY. Tell him! Tell him! And don't forget the Rainbow girls!

MARY. They were *my* friends, not yours, John!

JOHNMARY. Yeah! Put that in your pipe and smoke it!

MARY. You've climbed on me socially, John, and don't you forget it!

JOHNMARY. Oh . . . you've got a lot to be thankful for, John Jones! And don't you ever forget it!

MARY. But truthfully, John, your inadequacies never seem to bother me much, except when you're at home. And even though you are my mother's ex-husband, and I'll never be able to forgive you completely for what you did to me as a child, you are my husband now, and I'll never let you down.

JOHN. I know, Mary, I know. You're always so understanding. I know I have my faults. But try not to forget that I was a great war hero. Name one other man who stayed on without pay in his foxhole in New Guinea for twelve years after the war was "officially" over. Name one! Just one!

MARY. I know, John . . . I know. . . . You must get terribly homesick sometimes. But I do the best I can.

JOHN. What greater love could a man show for his family and country? I didn't trust them Chinks then any more than I do now. And if they'd listened to me there wouldn't be any Chink problem today!

MARY. I know, John, I know. You needn't rub it in. [*She is in tears.*] Your theories have always been far too advanced for educated people.

JOHN. And just don't forget all those medals and badges and scrolls and citations and souvenirs and shrunken heads I brought home to lay at your feet.

MARY. I know, John, I know. And how fortunate for us all that they were full of gold teeth. We'd never have been able to buy Westchester County without them.

JOHN. And besides all that, I did give the child a respectable name.

JOHNMARY. Ha! Calvin Coolidge!

JOHN. Jones, you little bastard! Jones!

JOHNMARY. All my friends call me Annie Rooney.

JOHN. Oh, Christ!

MARY. There, there, John. We all have our cross to bear. Your first wife had her faults too, you know. So classical. Socially, she was at least two weeks ahead of her time. But in our scorn, let us never forget that even though she was a midget, Mother had enormous dignity.

JOHNMARY. Yes, but even so, Mummy, I'm afraid I'll have to agree with John. From the very beginning, Granny should have confided in him and told him right out that she was a Liberal, as well as a Lesbian.

MARY. Poor Mother, she was always so afraid she'd hurt someone.

JOHN. I know, Mary, I know. But still, if things hadn't been as they were, things might not be nearly as modern as they are today.

JOHNMARY. That's deep thinking, John.

MARY. Oh, Daddy, did you hear what our darling thirteen-and-a-half-year-old son just said?

JOHN. Speak up, Son! Mumbling is a sign of impotence!

MARY. Don't be neurotic, precious. Tell Daddy what you said. He said you were the most wonderful John a boy could ever hope to have.

JOHN. You see? You see? There he goes again! Why can't he ever call me "Daddy" like you?

MARY. He said you were dynamic and clever as all hell, John.

JOHN. You see? You see?

MARY. He said you were A number one in his book!

JOHN. You see? You see!

JOHNMARY. Oh, piss!

MARY. Darling!

JOHN. Oh golly Moses, Mary! Did my boy really say what he just said? I mean, did my boy really say what I'm sure he just said?

MARY. Indeed not, John! But he did say you were as sweet as sugar and unquestionably the world's foremost authority on obligatory bureaucratic necessitarianism.

JOHN. What the hell does that mean?

JOHNMARY. It means you've screwed some of the best people in the country, "Daddy."

JOHN. Gee-whiz, godamity, Son! Is that what you really said?

JOHNMARY. I wouldn't shoot you, Dad.

JOHN. Maybe I've misjudged you, Son. Say something else. Try something in the layman's language.

MARY. Go on, darling. Shock the hell out of him!

JOHNMARY. I think I'm going to have a baby.

MARY [*ecstatic*]. Oh, darling!

JOHN. What'd he say, Mary? What'd he say?

MARY. He said that as soon as we get the Coke machine installed in the fallout shelter, he thinks we'll have everything in the world to be happy for. And then *you* said, "I just love my family and life in general and togetherness and prosperity in particular." And then he said, "It's really a big, wide, wonderful world!" And then we all gaily laughed.

They all laugh "gaily."

JOHN. We really do have wonderful times when the family is all together, don't we?

JOHNMARY. The family that bangs together, hangs together.

MARY. Why doesn't anybody ever ask me what I said?

JOHNMARY. What do you say, Mary?

JOHN. Yes, Momma, what do you say?

MARY [*surprised and self-conscious*]. Well . . . when you put it that way, I . . . I . . . don't really know. I've really never thought very much about it. However, I will say this: When it comes right down to it, John, as an adult person you really . . . sort of make me sick. I mean, I find you rather excessively revolting, John. You know what I mean?

JOHN. I think so, dear. Go on.

MARY. I mean, well . . . as a stepfather, I suppose you possessed a certain sensual charm. But as a husband, well, truthfully, John, and I wouldn't want to hurt your feelings, but you do leave a great deal to be desired. I mean particularly in the social, mental, and lower physiological regions.

JOHNMARY. From this, one might definitely conclude that Mary's chronic halitosis is caused by nothing more than a psychosomatic defense mechanic.

JOHN. Well, I don't give a damn what you or anybody else thinks! I like you, Momma. You're my kind of Mary. So you go ahead and stink if it makes you happy!

MARY. I suppose some extremist groups might not consider us very religious, but we're very strong on righteousness and the King James Version of the Bible.

JOHN. You bet your sweet ass we are! God bless godamity!

MARY. I was a card-carrying Catholic until John told me that nuns shave their heads. Disgusting, isn't it? I mean. . . . Well, really! I just don't think good Christians should do that.

JOHNMARY. I've reconciled myself to becoming an important moral influence. That is, if I turn out to be an idiot as planned.

JOHN. By God, I say what this country needs is a conservative policy with a little hair on it!

MARY. I've always said that John would be a very smart man, if he had any sense.

JOHNMARY. I think we should invade Canada!

MARY [embarrassed]. Oh, for heaven's sake, dear! You don't think any such thing! At least not until we get things cleaned up in Asia.

JOHN. I say Napoleon can take his gold standard and shove it up that Carmen Market!

MARY. You know, it's a little-known fact, but we have it on expert authority that the Statue of Liberty has never become a naturalized citizen.

JOHN. And the U.N. is nothing but a mealy-mouthed plot to unite nations!

MARY. I say, keep the ecumenical movement out of religion!

JOHN. We want God put back in school!

MARY. They've taken in all the niggers, but they've thrown God out!

JOHN. I say if they don't like it here, then let 'em go back to Israel!

MARY. Who ever heard of a *black* angel? Now really!

JOHN. Fluoridation is an insidious Communist plot to sterilize American studs!

MARY. And just ask yourself: What's it going to do to the flavor of Coke?

JOHNMARY. We love the minority of all white Protestant majorities, regardless of race, creed, or color.

MARY. Don't exaggerate, darling. Remember the golden ruler. Mummy would hate to spank you for bigotry.

JOHNMARY. God helps those who help themselves to God.

MARY. Yes, I suppose that's true, dear. However, we do feel that our government could, and should, be considerably more selective in our immigration and deportation program, don't we?

JOHN. You bet your big boobs we do! I put fifty thousand dollars in the pot at election time, so I've got a right to help wipe out corruption!

MARY. Tell 'em, John! Tell 'em!

JOHN. No, you tell 'em, Momma! You can talk louder than I can.

MARY. But you carry a lot more weight than I do, John. You're a war hero *and* a tycoon, so you've got a right to say what you've got to say! Tell 'em!

JOHNMARY. Tell 'em, John!

MARY. Go on, John! Let 'em have it with both barrels! Tell 'em!

JOHN. Well, by God, I still like Dick!

MARY [*to* JOHNMARY]. He means tricky Dicky Nixon, darling. Go on, John! Go on!

JOHN. And I say we'd better blast hell out'a them Russians, before they blast hell out'a us!

JOHNMARY. Give 'em hell, John! Give 'em hell!

JOHN. And then we'd better blast hell out'a China before they beat us at blastin' hell out'a any place else we want'a blast hell out of!

MARY. You're doin' good, John! You're doin' real good!

JOHN. And then we'd better blast hell out'a Vietnam and Cuba and Egypt and France and all them other Dominican Republics that don't have no respect for Wall Street and God-fearin' folks' right to. . . .

MAID JONES *has entered from the Jones house. She carries a long whip, which she now lashes across the floor.*

MAID JONES [*at the top of her voice*]. Quiet!!! Tha's what I say! Befo' ah blas' hell out'a all'a you's!

The JONESES *stand petrified.*

JOHNMARY. It's so important to be serious these days.

MAID JONES. That means you too, Snow White! When ah says shet up ah means *shet up!* Now, get on in there in your pearly palace and eat your soup! Ten-hut! [*The* JONESES *come to rigid attention.*] Hup, tue, three, fo! Hup, tue, three, fo! [*The* JONESES *march off into their house.* MAID JONES *now comes down center and speaks directly to the audience.*] I'm a Black Muslim, disguised as a so-called Negro. When I'm not engaged in militant nonviolence, I work here as a domestic spy for that bunch o' pinko-weirdos next door. But I say, comes the revolution and all you honkey bastards will be the slaves! Right? Right! Hell yes, I got jis as much right to be queen as anybody! Right? Right! Hell yes . . . why not! Allah be praised!

The lights black out.

SCENE II

The same.

Enter the SMITHS *in exactly the same manner as the* JONESES.

JOHN SMITH. My name is John.

MARY SMITH. My name is Mary. Oh yes, we know who we are.

JOHN. Our last name is Smith. It's hyphenated.

MARY. We spell it: W-(hyphen)-P-S-double M-I-T-(hyphen)-double H.

JOHN. The "P" is silent.

MARY. It used to be spelled quite differently. But because of so much prejudice and bigotry in this country, we have been forced to Americanize it.

MARYJOHN SMITH. My name is Bertrand Russell.

JOHN. No, no, darling. It's Fidela. Fidela Marxella X.

MARY. No, no, no, no. It's Maryjohn. Just plain, folksy Maryjohn Smith, Jr.

MARYJOHN. I'm almost sure I'm somebody else's child . . . so my parents have naturally tried to instill a strong sense of not belonging.

MARY. We think that's the way whoever she really belongs to would want it.

JOHN. Mary has always claimed she found her in a box of Cracker Jack, floating down the Harlem River.

MARYJOHN. I was the prize.

MARY. We find it a less confusing explanation of John's sterility until she is old enough to really understand the subtleties and pleasures of infidelity.

MARYJOHN. I have therefore tried to compensate for my inherent depravity by advocating the violent overthrow of capitalistic imperialism.

MARY. Oh, John! Did you ever hear such poetry flow from the mouth of a three-and-a-half-year-old child?

JOHN. Groovy! Real groovy.

MARYJOHN. Look, man, when will you ever get it through your thick head that I was at least twenty-seven when I made this scene!

JOHN. Now don't talk back to your mother, darling, unless it releases pent-up hostilities.

MARYJOHN. I *knew* I should have stayed in Appalachia!

MARY. She has such a marvelous little horny imagination.

JOHN. Give Daddy a big wet kiss and say you're sorry.

MARYJOHN. What's a girl to do? That's all he ever thinks about! Day after day after day after day after day!

MARY. She's going through that marvelous awkward period of discovery.

JOHN. However, she's already burned her draft card, started twelve race riots, and been arrested eighty-three times for antidefamation.

MARY. It's not much, I suppose, but we feel that any sign of potential martyrdom is worth a little euphonious escalation.

MARYJOHN. I've just finished reading Mao Tse-tung's poems about gorillas and found them absolutely delicious.

JOHN. I guess we've spoiled her. But we're very strong on early absolutism.

MARYJOHN. I've always felt at home among the apes.

MARY. We believe in surrounding a child with provocative and stimulating stimulants.

JOHN. For example, we have a set of book ends which are authentic reproductions of Karl Marx's testicles.

MARY. They serve as a constant reminder to us all, of just how much weight he really carried.

MARYJOHN. I got a perfectly adorable little free-form—form for my birthday.

MARY. John made it himself out of some old swords and plowshares.

MARYJOHN. Truthfully, I found it a trifle *mauvais goût*, but nevertheless useful for cracking organic walnuts and policemen's skulls.

JOHN. Police brutality is nothing short of shocking when you really get them cornered.

MARY. I suppose we're what you might call, way—way-down-to-earth-folks.

MARYJOHN. We grow all our own marijuana and opium from seed.

MARY. It's really amazing what you can do in a flowerpot, if you're seriously interested in politics.

JOHN. We're not completely opposed to free enterprise, as long as it is collectively lucrative for liberators.

MARY. John is completely heterosexual, but he's not nearly as dumb as he looks.

MARYJOHN. We're opposed to being opposed by people opposed to our being opposed to opposition.

MARY. Down with all white Anglo-Saxon bigots! Down with war and intolerant, prejudiced, ignorant, wrong, red-neck sons-o-bitches!

JOHN. Tell 'em, Mary!

MARYJOHN. We're so progressive, it almost makes us feel productive.

MARY. But don't you just love controversial things?

JOHN. Mary's foster mother had a second cousin who's girl friend was the childhood sweetheart of her uncle's brother who was hanged for high treason.

MARY. I'm in charge of a fund-and-hell-raising committee to erect a monument for him in Arlington National Cemetery.

MARYJOHN. Although we have all converted to atheism, John is able to trace his ancestry straight back to God Almighty.

MARY. That's how he got his first antipoverty grant.

MARYJOHN. John is much more intelligent than Mary, even though she was a high school dropout, spent three years in the Women's House of Detention, and audited a course in labor relations at the New School.

JOHN. It was while on field trip to Mississippi that Mary and I first met and decided to nonviolently co-ordinate.

MARYJOHN. You see, John, who was there for the Ford Foundation, making a survey of Southern latrine graffiti, had infiltrated the white ladies' toilet at the local bus station disguised as Billy Graham. And Mary, who also likes folk music, was in the same compartment, secretly engaged in collecting specimens for the Fair Play for Cuba Committee. When all of a sudden——

MARY. Oh really, darling! When will you ever learn not to romanticize! It's a disgusting capitalistic malignancy!

JOHN. The child has no concept or appreciation of real, basic, honest, uninhibited, spontaneous vulgarity!

MARY. I know, John, I know. What's happening to youth? Where have we failed? Darling, you are an utter beast!

MARYJOHN. Thank you. May I go into the house and play with matches now?

MARY. I don't know, I just don't know! You have exhausted my hate! Take her in the house and do an improvisation, John.

MARYJOHN. Oh no! Please! Not that! Not again! At least not before dinner!

JOHN. Don't take that hypocritical attitude with me, young lady! As long as you live in this pad, you'll improvise when I'm ready to improvise!

MARYJOHN. But Daddy! I'm your darling daughter!

MARY. How dare you say such a thing to your father!

JOHN. Are you calling me a dirty old man?

MARY. I think so, John! I think so! Anyway, that's the way I interpret it!

JOHN. Where is she picking up these back-lash concepts, Mary? Has that little creep next door been giving her those capitalistic comic books again?

MARY. I think so, John. I think so! I caught them playing whorehouse in the outhouse again yesterday!

JOHN. Ah-ha! Ungrateful bitch!

MARYJOHN. It's not true! It's not true! We were playing outhouse in the whorehouse! I swear!

MARY. Oh God, John! Bang her with your banjo!

MARYJOHN. Please! Please! Allow me to redeem myself! I'll run back in the ghetto and picket my nose!

MARY. Oh God, John! She makes me sick! She truly makes me want to puke!

MARYJOHN. Happiness is a thing called Little Annie Rooney.

JOHN. You bang her, Mary! Bang her with your guitar!

MARY. *Little . . . Annie . . . who?*

MARYJOHN. I hate Uncle Claus and Santa Sam!

JOHN. Oh for Christ's sake! Don't you know any real people?!

MARYJOHN. Down with all the ups!

MARY. Stop it!

MARYJOHN. Up with all the downs!

MARY. Stop it! Stop it this instant! Now, I demand to know just who this Little Annie Looney person is!

MARYJOHN. Rooney! Rooney! Little Annie Rooney!

MARY. She said "Looney" the first time, John! I know she did! Her syntax was disgracefully articulate, but I understood her! Admit it, you little slut!

MARYJOHN. Okay, okay, I admit it! It's the boy next door who is the girl of my dreams!

MARY *screams.*

JOHN. "Looney" sounds Irish to me, Mary!

MARY. Oh bang her, John! Bang her with our uncommon can of Campbell's continental cadaver consommé!

MARYJOHN. I hate leprechauns!

JOHN. This is no time for prejudice, child. This could be Freudian. Now, tell Mummy and Daddy just where it was that you met this "Looney" person.

MARYJOHN. It was at a Valentine's Day anti-ism screw-in in the Washington Square fountain. He's married to a dog.

MARY. You didn't by chance get *his* name?

MARYJOHN. I think it was Rover. He has a neon dildo.

MARY *and* JOHN. *Rover?!!*

MARYJOHN. Or, Spot. Maybe it was Spot!

MARY *and* JOHN, *Spot?!!*

MARYJOHN. Or, Speck . . . or Spook. . . . Christ, I don't know!

MARY. She doesn't know! She doesn't know!

MARYJOHN. Well, he didn't talk much! Just banged the bongs and sang "Old Black Joe" in Yiddish! Over and over and over and over and over and——

MARY. And *she* didn't get his name! *She* didn't get his name!

JOHN. Darling, do you have any idea who you were talking to?

MARYJOHN. I told you I didn't say a word to him! It's Little Annie Rooney who's my sweetheart!

MARY [*in tears*]. She didn't say a word to him! She didn't say a word to him! At the same anti-ism screw-in with Speck Spook the Pithy Poet, and *she* didn't say a word to him!

MARYJOHN. I bit him!

MARY *and* JOHN [*shouting*]. *You* . . . *what???!!!*

MARYJOHN. You heard me. I bit him.

JOHN. Oh, bang her, Mary! Bang her with your handmade Mexican shoulder bag!

MARY [*banging her*]. You mean to tell me there wasn't one innocent bystander you could have bitten?

MARYJOHN. Well, everybody was biting everybody. And besides, he'd lifted his leg on my shoe.

MARY. Oh, bang her, John! Bang her with your three-dimensional Bhagavad-Gita!

MARYJOHN. He later proposed to me.

MARY *and* JOHN [*shouting*]. *Proposed to you???*

JOHN. Darling, you mean *propositioned*, don't you?

MARY. Oh, John, it's simply too revolting not to be revolutionary!

JOHN. Our little girl! Our little girl! Selected from all the others.

MARY. What a glorious thrill it must have been for you.

What did you do? Tell Mummy and Daddy all the vital, graphic details. What you said . . . how you felt. . . .

MARYJOHN. *Very* wet!

MARY. But philosophically, darling. Mummy means, was that groovy neon dildo spiritually and physically satisfying?

JOHN. And what of your plans? Tell us of your plans. Your hopes and fixations.

MARY. The strategy! That's what I want to know! What was your strategy?

JOHN. Oh the hell with the strategy! Did you accept? That's what I want to know.

MARYJOHN. I lifted *my leg* on *his shoe!* [MARY *and* JOHN *scream.*] I think I may have drowned him.

MARY. But you did say "yes," didn't you, darling? You did say, "Yes! Oh yes, yes, yes, yes indeedy-do!" Didn't you, darling. *Didn't you?*

MARYJOHN. He just ruined my suede boots!

MARY. But you did say "yes"! Please tell Mummy you did say "yes"! Oh, John . . . choke her with your love beads! Goose her with your rosewood recorder! Take away her peacock feathers! But make her say she did say "yes"!

MARYJOHN. My fiancé's father got his brain shot off during the war, and then wiped out four hundred Japs with a lead pipe, single-handed! [MARY *screams.*] He has a whole basement filled with medals, badges, scrolls, citations and dynamite. [JOHN *screams.*] My fiancé's mother is one of the original Pilgrims!

JOHN. But they're *normal,* darling! Don't you understand?

MARYJOHN. Nevertheless, we've both decided to become astronaughts.

MARY [*screaming and collapsing on the floor*]. Oh please, John! Please, John! Please, John, *please!* Chop off her head! Pull out her tongue! Plug up her twat! Or at least change the subject!

JOHN. I think you've upset your mother, darling.

MARYJOHN. Tough tit! I'm sorry, John, but I've always felt it the personal responsibility of each and every citizen to find his own hole, large enough to jump in.

MARY. Listen to her! Just listen to her! How dare you say such a thing after what they did to Fatty Arbuckle!

JOHN. If I really gave a damn about Mary, I might be able to disagree with her. But what I have is simply too big to be satisfied by social security.

MARY. Mercy! Mercy!

JOHN [*taking* MARYJOHN *by the arm*]. Come, darling, it's time for your improvisation.

MARYJOHN. Why not. A dog's a dog, I always say. [*As they exit.*] Day after day after day after day after day.

MARY. Mercy! Mercy! Mercy!

Enter MAID SMITH *with a large hypodermic needle.*

MAID SMITH [*curtsying*]. Madam called?

MARY. Fix me! Fix me!

MAID SMITH [*mimicking*]. "Fix me! Fix me!" That's all I hear! Okay, stick your ass up here, I'll fix you! [*She administers the injection then moves to the edge of the proscenium and speaks directly to the audience.*] My name is Mercy, the Mongoloid Maid. However, in real life, I am a simple albino transvestite of Indo-Cuban stock. My present disguise as a Red Chinese cultural revolutionary exchange student became necessary in seeking employment here as a domestic spy for that bunch of gringo blue bloods next door. But I say, comes the bloody revolution, and *all* you blue-eyed bastards will be the spics and chinks! Right? Right! I've got just as much right to be better than everybody else as you have! Or at least generalissimo! Right? Right! Hell yes. Why not? Screw all of you! Viva Fidel! Viva Mao! And Ho, Ho, Ho!

The lights black out.

SCENE III

The same, enter JOHNMARY *from his house.*

JOHNMARY. *Thank* God, dinner is over! At the risk of
sounding superior, which in all humility is true . . . I
must say that we *do* eat well. It seems to be a common
misconception among less fortunate nations of the world
that American children are wasteful, as well as revolting.
This, however . . . judging from my own personal experience, is a despicable case of mealy-mouth continental intervention. For your information and edifica-
tion, I would like to put an end to this "wasteful"
stigma once and for all by announcing that I ate *everything* that was on my plate. I also ate the plate . . .
two spoons . . . the butter knife . . . and a small
vase of imported plastic peach blossoms. So there! After
a good meal, there is nothing I like better than to
recline on our ceiling-to-floor carpet and gnaw on the
table leg for a couple of hours. However, since my
parents feel this to be somewhat detrimental to our late
imitation Early American furniture, they have tried to
instill in me the more artful and less noisy pastime of
picking my nose and watching television. Being an ex-
ceptionally gifted example of thwarted brilliance, I have
therefore been forced to compensate by becoming an
authority. Although there is really very little in this
field at which I am not extremely clever . . . in an
effort to co-operate with the government, I have decided to devote my life to the creative arts. Although I
find that I am able to express myself more profoundly
by the removal of dog ticks from our cat, this evening
I'm afraid I shall have to be content with the writing of
literature. You see, our dear old cat died yesterday from
eating a baked apple filled with particles of a broken
Steuben glass spittoon. Particles that I, myself, had

placed there in order to conceal the evidence of a small
indiscretion. You might find it interesting to know
that the cat's name was Rover. This quite naturally
indicates a childhood trauma of no small significance,
but nevertheless serves as a moral fortification against
any charge of stupidity from ignorant folk. Since I have
already written Rover's epitaph, I shall now attempt
to eulogize. With the present world situation, I feel
it would be a case of overt selfish folly to deprive posterity of my productivity. Please do not disturb me.

He sits on the ground and begins to write. Enter MARYJOHN
from her house.

MARYJOHN. Thank God, dinner is over! I suppose we
  eat as well as anybody. . . . Although I must say I do
  find it a shocking waste of time. I didn't eat a thing
  that was on my plate. In fact, I was so hooched up
  I couldn't even find the table. However, I understand
  from the latest statistics released by General Crock-
  water, that American children rarely eat anything. And
  less than one out of five hundred is fit for the U.S.
  Marine Corps. So, you see, we're really not as bad off
  as you might think. After a good meal, there's nothing
  I like better than doing nothing. However, I sometimes
  do amuse myself by righting wrongs and wronging
  rights and all sorts of modern, fun things like that that
  keep children in the streets. But, of course, after an
  improvisation and a few drags of pot, even love and
  goodness becomes a bit of a chore. So what else is there
  left to do besides cultivate one's brain . . . or blow
  it out? Oh well, Justice will just have to do without
  me for a while tonight. I've decided to devote the next
  few minutes to the literary works of my boy friend . . .
  who also happens to be my bitterest enemy and confi-
  dant. That's him squatting there with the serious look
  on his memorandum. The one and only, Johnmary
  Q. Jones the Eighth . . . who of course in real life, as
  you should all know by now, is none other than the
  fabulous Little Annie Rooney, the girl of my dreams.
  To be perfectly frank, I enjoy looking at dirty pictures

much more than reading. But to be perfectly franker,
I must confess, some of his political speeches, closet
dramas, editorials, and epitaphs are better than an enema
any day. Just listen to this epitaph he has written for
that damn cat I always thought was a dog.

> "Here lies an otherwise . . .
> A sacrifice for some idle lies."

Doesn't it just almost tear you in two? But don't let the
simplicity fool you. As any simpleton can plainly see,
it's much too neurotic-symbolic to be nonsense. Now
of course most of us cotton pickers would have just said
something gutsy and to the point . . . like:

> "Here lies Rover in the clover . . .
> With glass in his ass."

But you can plainly see how a simple statement of fact
in anything as serious as an epitaph has a tendency
to completely medicinalize the mystery. Oh well, that's
the way the cookie flops. I am also reading the unex-
purgated version of his essay on Political Tedium. Although I find the work insufferably dull and monotonous, one cannot help but be caught up in the
universality of its controversial theme. I think I shall
now tippy-toe over and ask him for his autograph . . .
then, progressively, but subtly put the make on him.
If there's any time a girl should be with the thing she
loves, it's at bedtime. Yoohoo! Yoohoo! Johnmary Q.
Rooney! Hello! Hello! Hello! How's every little thing?
How's every big thing? How's the world treating you?
How's your pater and mater and your pet alligator? How's
your fairy maid and all your Dixie cups? How's the
world situation? How's your sore ear? How's the outlook
from the lookout? How's your darlin' dead dog? And,
incidentally. . . . How's about it?

JOHNMARY. Don't bother me! You repulsive, insensitive
teeny-bopper bully!

MARYJOHN. Oh, just fine, thanks. And how's yourself?
I'm awfully sorry about your dead bird.

JOHNMARY. Can't you see that I'm in the middle of the creative process? When will you ever understand that my fascination for you necessitates my complete denial of your very existence?

MARYJOHN. Oh Johnmary, you always say the sweetest things. Why can't you see that I'm so full of love . . . so pure and holy . . . so sparkling and delicious . . . that even you, radiant as you are, are reduced to ashes by my burning desire to help you find the "real" you. The "new" you . . . which couldn't possibly be the "old" you, since after all, you're only thirteen-and-a-half years young.

JOHNMARY. Please! You're making me lose my train of throbbing truths! Begone!

MARYJOHN.

"I dreamt I was born with crystal balls
That the earth was mine between four walls
That the sun rose only for my delight
And I would always be one who's right."

JOHNMARY. How dare you take such liberties with my poetry?

MARYJOHN. Because I love you so much, Johnmary. If you could only love me . . . then perhaps we could learn to like each other.

JOHNMARY. Dammit! Now you've made me lose my prodigious premise!

MARYJOHN. Shall we play, Premise, premise, who's got the premise?

JOHNMARY. And let you win again? Never!

MARYJOHN. Oh what does it all mean, Johnmary? I mean, what is the meaning of it all?

JOHNMARY. You shouldn't wonder about things you don't understand, unless you're prepared to accept them.

MARYJOHN. But I was referring to "This Mad World We Live In." Tra-la.

JOHNMARY. Volume four, verse thirty-seven, I've clearly explained it in the parable about the maggot and the chicken.

MARYJOHN. Oh yes . . . yes. I remember. It was so beautiful. I cried and screamed for three weeks after reading it.

JOHNMARY. You're much too emotional about animals.

MARYJOHN. My parents thought I was dying.

JOHNMARY. What a disappointment it must have been for them.

MARYJOHN. Well naturally, at first. But then they decided it was a wonderful display of self-expression.

JOHNMARY. Please go away. You know how I loathe mingling with the substructure.

MARYJOHN. But you shouldn't isolate yourself so much, Johnmary. It's likely to warp your sense of insecurity.

JOHNMARY. Sometimes I think you are deliberately engaged in a diabolic conspiracy to shatter my dreams.

MARYJOHN. In a million pieces!

JOHNMARY. I thought so.

MARYJOHN. But it's decadent and greedy to keep one's dream in one piece, Johnmary.

JOHNMARY. And I suppose in return, you would be equally willing to share your nightmare?

MARYJOHN. Only if it would make you semantically happy.

JOHNMARY. No, I'm afraid that would be what we guardians of the virtue refer to as the paradoxical peculiarity in the pointlessness of polemics.

MARYJOHN. Then marry me, Johnmary. Please marry me. I only want to help balance your profits.

JOHNMARY. That would accomplish nothing but throw our parents into a state of shock.

MARYJOHN. But what more could you want? Some day when you're older, you're going to need someone to be unfaithful to.

JOHNMARY. I know . . . I've thought about that. But to be perfectly blunt, you don't excite me sociologically.

MARYJOHN. But I promise you, I can more than make up for that in bed.

JOHNMARY. Don't be vulgar!

MARYJOHN. All right! But if I can't live with you in shame, I refuse to live without you nobly. Unless you tell me why I'm so revolting?

JOHNMARY. You don't shave under your arms. And I simply can't stand that!

MARYJOHN. But Johnny, neither does your father! And he's always chasing me.

JOHNMARY. Yes, but he was raised on a farm.

MARYJOHN. But . . . oh, Johnny, I get hot flashes every time I see you naked.

JOHNMARY. Love is a silly, imaginary state of controllable extravagance.

MARYJOHN. My father thinks I'm the dearest girl in all the world.

JOHNMARY. That doesn't say much for him, does it?

MARYJOHN. I once swallowed a firecracker . . . but it didn't go off.

JOHNMARY. Pity.

MARYJOHN. I think I'll drink a bottle of nitroglycerin then go play football with that old gang of mine.

JOHNMARY. Be my guest.

MARYJOHN. Or maybe I'll just stick an ice pick in my ear.

JOHNMARY. Excellent. Try this one. [*He hands her an ice-pick.*]

MARYJOHN. You haven't by chance in your travels ever come across a . . . roughly, three by five foot box of Cracker Jack, have you?

JOHNMARY. No . . . but believe me, if I could spare the time, I'd build you one.

MARYJOHN. You're certainly not very sensitive or sympathetic to bewildered reformers.

JOHNMARY. I've got problems of my own. Of what possible use could you be to someone who has everything?

MARYJOHN. Well, I can say my ABC's to D and count to ten. I can dress up in funny costumes and make people extremely nervous. I can wail and moan and groan and whine and yelp and howl and bawl and scream and bang on the guitar louder than almost anybody! I can fret and fume and murmur and mutter and growl and grumble and clamor and croak and grunt and gripe and spit through my teeth and make love in broad daylight! I can make wry faces, gnash my incisors, wring my hands, tear out my hair, beat my breast, throw myself under buses, bang my head against walls, chain myself to pillars and posts, roll on the floor, show signs of prostration, tell fortunes, *and*, with a little co-operation . . . even have a baby.

JOHNMARY. All right, tell my fortune.

MARYJOHN. I'd rather have a baby.

JOHNMARY. I said, tell my fortune!

MARYJOHN. You are a colossal moron!

JOHNMARY. Look, you fool . . . I'm giving you an opportunity to hold my hand!

MARYJOHN. I'm going to have a baby, Johnmary.

JOHNMARY. All right, *don't tell my fortune!*

MARYJOHN. Okay, okay, okay! [*She takes his hand and looks closely at his palm.*] You're going to become a father.

JOHNMARY. Don't be ridiculous! I don't know how.

MARYJOHN. Marry me, Johnmary . . . before people start to mumble.

JOHNMARY. Our political ends can never entwine.

MARYJOHN. But there are far too many bastards in the world as it is.

JOHNMARY. That's your opinion. Now go on with my fortune before I withdraw the offer.

MARYJOHN [*quickly drawing out a deck of cards*]. Okay . . . pick a card . . . any card. [JOHNMARY *takes a card,* MARYJOHN *immediately retrieves it.*] Hmmmmmm. . . .

JOHNMARY. What does it say?

MARYJOHN. You're going on a very short trip.

JOHNMARY. Really? Where? Does it say where and when?

MARYJOHN. *Now!* Right over there in the bushes. Come on!

JOHNMARY. And just what will I find there? A treasure, no doubt?

MARYJOHN. Some people think so.

JOHNMARY. Be serious, will you?

MARYJOHN. Serious!? I am serious! Come on! It's free.

JOHNMARY. No. I don't trust you or the cards. Use my palm. There are things I really need to know.

MARYJOHN. Oh, Christ! I'm gonna have a baby, dammit!

JOHNMARY. Not until you've told my fortune. Now, go on . . . what do you really see?

MARYJOHN [*again taking his hand*]. Water.

JOHNMARY. Ah . . . an ocean trip!

MARYJOHN [*smelling his palm*]. Cat piss.

JOHNMARY. Stop it! I'll bet it's the River Jordan.

MARYJOHN. Well, that's possible . . . but I think I'd tend to favor the Old Mill Stream. Oh-oh! The boat is sinking! But have no fear . . . I see right here in lower-case type it says that at the very last moment, you'll decide to walk across.

JOHNMARY. Really? And it's the Jordan . . . you say?

MARYJOHN. Shhhhhh! You're approaching the shore now. Oh my God! Oh my. . . . Oh Lord! Oh no. . . . Oh my God! No . . . no! . . . Oh Lord. . . .

JOHNMARY. What is it?

MARYJOHN. Oh Lord! . . . Oh my God! No! Not that! Oh Lord! . . . Oh no! . . .

JOHNMARY. For God's sake, what is it? What is it?

MARYJOHN. Oh my God! Oh Lord! . . . How revolting! Oh. . . .

JOHNMARY. Please! Please. . . . Tell me what it is!

MARYJOHN. Nothing. It was nothing. Absolutely nothing. Everything is going to be all right. You have absolutely nothing to fear. However, I do think it would be extremely wise for you to lock yourself away from the world for fifteen or twenty years.

JOHNMARY. No! Please!

MARYJOHN. Have I told you I'm going to have a baby?

JOHNMARY. I must know what you saw! Please don't do this to me!

MARYJOHN. In case you're interested, an angel seduced me.

JOHNMARY. Tell me what you saw, or I'll kill you!

MARYJOHN. I said, *an angel seduced me!* Don't you give a damn about angelic experiences?

JOHNMARY [*in tears*]. I hate you! I hate you!

MARYJOHN. They'll have my picture on calendars within a week!

JOHNMARY. How you've changed, Maryjohn. . . . How you've changed. . . .

MARYJOHN. Ed Sullivan has made me a terrific offer.

JOHNMARY. How could you stoop so low? How? . . .

MARYJOHN. I'm an exhibitionist! Besides, they've had a helluva lot worse things than babies on TV!

JOHNMARY. You don't suppose Mr. Sullivan would give me a few minutes to speak directly to the people, do you?

MARYJOHN. Oh Christ! How do you like that?! I switch to the psychological approach and he wants to become a movie star! What a fool I've been.

JOHNMARY. I know, I know . . . but we can't all be perfect.

MARYJOHN. Oh God. . . . What does it all mean? I mean, what is the meaning of it all? Must we always ask the man who owns one?

JOHNMARY. Who is better qualified to answer?

MARYJOHN. Me! Me!

JOHNMARY. Ah, but in that case, what would be the outcome?

MARYJOHN. That would obviously depend on the income of the man who doesn't own one.

JOHNMARY. Do you really think God is dead, or simply playing hard to get?

MARYJOHN. That would depend on the assimilation of his anachronistical anonymity.

JOHNMARY. Why must you always bring politics into it?

MARYJOHN. I'm deadly opposed to anabiosis. Why don't we go lie down and squeeze each other and try to forget we're people.

JOHNMARY. I'm sorry, but I really must finish revising my memoirs. Time is wasting.

MARYJOHN. Oh, screw posterity! If nobody gives a damn about you while you're living. . . . At least have the courage to become a public nuisance before you're dead!

JOHNMARY. The point is taken. Now, good-bye!

MARYJOHN. I don't suppose you've told about the time we ran amuck in Mecca?

JOHNMARY. Of course not.

MARYJOHN. And I'm sure you haven't mentioned a word about the time you raped me in the nasturtiums?

JOHNMARY. Mythological and inconsequential!

MARYJOHN. I was beautiful until I was disfigured.

JOHNMARY. Most things become fashionable, sooner or later.

MARYJOHN. Or was it a rosebush, Johnny? You said it was a bed of violets . . . but it was a brier patch, wasn't it? Wasn't it? Yes, I know that now. You lied to me. . . . You led me on with your worldly ways before I was even born.

JOHNMARY. We are all victims of tradition.

MARYJOHN. I was much too volatile to be violated . . . in a brier patch.

JOHNMARY. Those were trying years.

MARYJOHN. The nice soft grass would have been much more thoughtful. Incidentally, Johnmary, have I told you that I have a disease? I'm all eaten up with good.

JOHNMARY. Why must you constantly try to make me feel inferior?

MARYJOHN. My baby will be a monster. It will haunt us and torture us . . . and stick pins in your pelvis.

JOHNMARY. I am impervious to evil and armed for Armageddon.

MARYJOHN. Oh, what *does* it all mean, Johnmary? I mean, what really is the meaning of it all?

JOHNMARY. Stop asking such corn-ball questions and go kill yourself!

MARYJOHN. I believe the world is a mote in my eye.

JOHNMARY. Then why don't you gouge it out and shut up about it.

MARYJOHN [*picking up one of his manuscripts and assuming the roll of an interviewer*]. Excuse me, sir, I'm conducting a survey for the Galloping Pole. Do you really think a tycoon's whack can break a cotton picker's back?

JOHNMARY. Not if he has been carefully trained in the art of pragmatic servitude.

MARYJOHN. Do you feel that our country is going from bad to worse, worse to badder, good to gooder, or just simply gone?

JOHNMARY. I'm glad you ask that question. Now, I'd like to make myself absolutely clear. I don't know.

MARYJOHN. In our mechanized society, do you still feel that a stitch in time will save . . . oh, roughly around nine?

JOHNMARY. Enlightened persons would hope for three and rejoice at five.

MARYJOHN. Will a lovely jar of homemade apple jelly really fill a doctor's belly?

JOHNMARY. Only if he's a creeping socialist.

MARYJOHN. And now, sir, last but not least. Will the least never be last?

JOHNMARY. Not if *you* have anything to do with it . . . or unless he's first.

MARYJOHN. I was once first.

JOHNMARY. That doesn't count. You're an only child.

MARYJOHN. But that makes me first and last and least and largest. How do you account for that?

JOHNMARY. It's perfectly logical. You're a freak.

MARYJOHN. I see. Thank you so much for your co-operation. When we Flower Children take over the world, you'll be hearing from us.

JOHNMARY. Don't call us, we'll call you.

MARYJOHN. All right, if you refuse to spread my petals, would you consider telling *my* fortune?

JOHNMARY. You don't have any.

MARYJOHN. Please be serious. There must be something. Look closely. [*She extends her hand.*]

JOHNMARY [*taking her hand, looking at it a second, then dropping it*]. No . . . nothing. Just hair.

MARYJOHN. Hair?! Are you sure? [*She looks.*]

JOHNMARY. I only report what I see.

MARYJOHN. Oh, but I am an enigma! The *crux criticorum.* I'm almost sure I am! Otherwise, life would not be worth wallowing in! Why do you persist on persecuting me by constantly twiddling my *terra incognita*?

JOHNMARY. It pains me to admit it . . . but after all, I'm only human.

MARYJOHN. You should love, honor, and cherish me.

JOHNMARY. I suppose. . . . But it's *very* difficult.

MARYJOHN. You're very lucky to know me.

JOHNMARY. I feel exactly the same about you.

MARYJOHN. I know you're lying . . . but I believe you.

JOHNMARY. I am, but it's the truth.

MARYJOHN. Do you swear?

JOHNMARY. I swear.

MARYJOHN. Thank you. That was very kind of you.

JOHNMARY. I'm glad you agree with me.

MARYJOHN. You don't think it makes me dull?

JOHNMARY. Of course not. Don't be so vain. Now let's talk about me some more.

MARYJOHN. But you're so marvelous . . . it seems rather futile even to discuss you.

JOHNMARY. It's good for the soul to talk about wholesome things.

MARYJOHN. Well, as I think you already know: I first came to public attention at the age of twenty-seven. Life had been, what you might say, rather cramped for me. . . .

JOHNMARY. You've already told me that at least a thousand times! Tell my fortune again.

MARYJOHN. I know what! Let's play like people in the spring!

JOHNMARY. No. I must know more about the future. You may hold my other hand this time. I insist!

MARYJOHN [*taking his hand*]. Well . . . it does seem a little cleaner. But of course that doesn't necessarily mean it's clearer.

JOHNMARY. Look closely. Shall I be magnificent, brilliant, radiant, exalted, and nimbus-lit?

MARYJOHN. Oh yes . . . yes. Definitely nimbus-lit.

JOHNMARY. Shall I be courageous, brave, stouthearted, valorous, mettlesome, resolute, manful, and manly?

MARYJOHN. Absolutely. *Unless*, you are nipped in the bud . . . which seems highly probable.

JOHNMARY. What of fame and fortune?

MARYJOHN. Oh that's very exciting! It says that on your twenty-first birthday you will inherit a secondhand fishhook in a cigar box full of ancestral fingernail clippings.

JOHNMARY. But will I be happy?

MARYJOHN. It says that by the time you reach puberty you will have several uilited fronts in your rear. But you will be very susceptible to nationalistic nasal drips and in grave danger of drowning in your own dribble.

JOHNMARY. But will I be respected?

MARYJOHN. Oh yes! You will receive thousands of get-well cards.

JOHNMARY. Then that would seem to indicate that I will also be loved and adored.

MARYJOHN. *Fervently!* However, there is an indication here that you may be hit in the mouth by a flying anvil at any minute.

JOHNMARY. What matter . . . if only I am adored.

MARYJOHN. In the event of direct contact with the afore-mentioned flying object . . . you might be interested to know that you will be reincarnated three days later as a cross-eyed doodlebug.

JOHNMARY. But remembered. . . . If only I am remembered.

MARYJOHN. Oh there's absolutely no question about that. It clearly says right here where there ought to be a callus . . . that you will *most definitely* be remembered.

JOHNMARY. Thank God! Then my life will not have been entirely in vain.

MARYJOHN. You will be well remembered. . . . *But*, for only one thing.

JOHNMARY. My philanthropic thoughts?

MARYJOHN. Oh no . . . *no.*

JOHNMARY. My anagrams and epitaphs and autobiographies?

MARYJOHN. No . . . no. None of them. I'm sorry.

JOHNMARY. My compassionate, semiprejudiced love for most of humanity?

MARYJOHN. No . . . no . . . no. . . .

JOHNMARY. My beauty? My charm and wit? My flair for conservation?

MARYJOHN. No . . . no . . . no. . . .

JOHNMARY. My long eyelashes? My dimples? My——

MARYJOHN. No . . . no, Johnmary! It has nothing to do with your civic achievements.

JOHNMARY. Then what, for God's sake? Tell me. Have I done something wonderful that I didn't intend or that I've forgotten?

MARYJOHN. Shameful and sacrilegious!

JOHNMARY. What? What?!

MARYJOHN. You once farted in Lenin's tomb!

JOHNMARY. You're insane!

MARYJOHN. The Albanians will never forget it! Nor indeed will the civilized world forgive you!

JOHNMARY. But that's impossible! I've never even been there!

MARYJOHN. You'll become known throughout the world as: "Labor's Laminated Litmus, Laureate"!

JOHNMARY. Why you hateful, obnoxious, odious, abominable, repulsive, invidious, malicious, repugnant, loathesome, revolting, venomous prophet of doom! How dare you?!

MARYJOHN. I only report what I see. But wait! There's more. . . . At exactly three forty-seven and one-half past the witching hour on the first spring day in May . . . an insipid incredulity will crawl up your schnozzola and suffocate you. And nobody will cry but me.

JOHNMARY. It's an evil, subversive, distasteful lie!

MARYJOHN. Wait and see. . . .

JOHNMARY. My life line runs from the tip of my thumb to my elbow! My head line completely encircles my hand! My heart line is infinite! Look!

MARYJOHN. Horrible warts and stains!

JOHNMARY. That's your finger!

MARYJOHN. You've been playing with frogs again, Johnmary. Frogs are evil omens. You are a toad in your own road!

JOHNMARY. I am a polyphonic pacifist! I sing a song of peace!

MARYJOHN. Ah . . . but the toad's croak is always dissonant!

JOHNMARY. It is surely the duty of all mankind to liquidate evil with the most lucrative expedience!

MARYJOHN. Ah, but one man's evil may be another man's empire! I am a saint, Johnmary. Did you know that I am *come* only to announce the august presence of aerosol ambrosia?

JOHNMARY. You're a moron in desperate need of anamorphosis!

MARYJOHN. Oh, Ananias! Ananias Anaphora! Hear me, and know that I speak only as a humble servant of Prophylactis Anachronosis! My true name is Aphrodisiola. I was born of the sea slime. The red sea! The seared-sea! The mud sea! The blood sea! The crud sea! Out of the muddy, cruddy, bloody sea, I spewed! The bride of doom . . . with a tomb for my womb. My father was the wind. . . . My mother a seed. And I am their union, confused as a weed. Oh harvest me now, my dear little Annie . . . and you'll be amazed at what pops from my cranny!

JOHNMARY. Oh for God's sake! Stop it! You'll frighten the neighbors! Mother! Mother!

MARYJOHN. Why must you always turn to people who don't understand you?

JOHNMARY. I love only my mother!

MARYJOHN. Then you love me! I am your real mother, Johnmary! You were stolen from me at the age of your father's folly!

JOHNMARY. That's a lie! My father never had any children!

MARYJOHN. Then we shall give him one. Listen, listen! It's starting to move. And I can almost hear it cry. Listen! Give me your hand. . . .

JOHNMARY. I hear nothing! You're totally insane! Go home!

MARYJOHN. It's coming, Johnmary! It's coming! The tide is in labor and it's roaring in! It's splashing and kicking. It's moaning and groaning! There *is* something alive in me! It's trying to wiggle out! It's clawing and gnawing at the walls of my womb, Johnny! It's gasping for breath, Johnny! It's kicking and screaming for birth, Johnny! Birth! Birth! [*Still clinging to his hand, she now falls to her knees.*]

JOHNMARY. Let me go! Let me go!

MARYJOHN. I feel it, Johnny! The pain is insufferable! Like a billion tiny feet! Tramping! Tramping! Tramping through my flesh! Help me!

JOHNMARY. Help! Police! Help!

MARYJOHN. The pain, Johnmary, the pain! The pain of a thousand million little booted feet! Marching! Marching through a sea of blood!

JOHNMARY. Stop it this instant! Have you no respect for human decency?

MARYJOHN. It's almost here, Johnmary! It's almost here! Please help me! In the name of God or man or beast . . . pull it out of me!

Enter MAID JONES *in a rage.*

MAID JONES. Whass goin' on here?!

JOHNMARY [*still struggling to free himself*]. She says she's having a baby!

MAID JONES. *Baby!!*

MARYJOHN. Help me . . . help me!

MAID JONES. Oh lawzy, Miss Scarlet, I don't no nussin' 'bout bursin' babies!

MARYJOHN *now gives out with a terrifying, earth-shaking scream. The opening sequence of* The Hallelujah Chorus *fills the air, as the lights black out.*

ACT TWO

PRELUDE

Seven chimes are heard, followed by a loud gong.

RADIO VOICE. Eight a.m. by the century-old gong in hysterical City Hall. . . . Where the mayor and his three million employees live and work in a very big piece of prosperity and ride around in the rest of it.

Singing, with piano and banjo accompaniment, now fills the air.

> Good morning, masturbators,
> It's time to bring you
> Another cheery greeting,
> To soothe you while you're eating.
>
> Ten billionth call to breakfast,
> Come have a ball at breakfast!

An alarm clock sounds. The curtain rises.

SCENE I

The same, next morning. MR. & MRS. SMITH *and* MR. & MRS. JONES *are seated at small tables in front of their respective houses. Both tables are piled high with food of all sizes, shapes, colors, and descriptions. Both* JOHNS *are hidden behind newspapers. The headline on* JOHN JONES'S *paper reads:* "How" *and the headline on* JOHN SMITH'S *paper reads:* "Why."

Both MARYS *sit slouched in their chairs, mechanically stirring their coffee. They are both dressed in very wilted housecoats.* MARY SMITH'S *hair is in a wild, tangled mess, while* MARY JONES'S *head is covered with enormous plastic curlers. Their faces are bleached and expressionless.*

Enter MAID JONES *and* MAID SMITH, *who take positions beside their respective families.* MAID JONES *now carries a fly swatter. At certain moments during* MAID SMITH'S *speech (indicated by an asterisk *) she swats flies on either of the* JONESES.

MAID SMITH. It is morning in the home of John and Mary Smith. That middle-aged Lolita they call their daughter is still tied firmly in Papa Bear's bed. She played "Show and Tell" with that revolting little bureaucrat next door until we finally overpowered her and escalated a policy of brass-knuck pacification. I would've killed her if these two creeps handn't stopped me! * Doctor says she is suffering from an acute case of vaginal hiccups and verbal diarrhea. Oh well, that's life on the lighter side. Anyway, here sit the original "fun couple," John and Mary Smith, gargling and gorging their traditional macroorganic breakfast, consisting of such taste-tempting tribulations as dried figs, prunes, apple cores, pumpkin rind, acorns, seaweed flakes, alfalfa blossoms, wormy raisins, turtle egg-rolls, pizza pie, instant hominy, Camembert doodles, salami croquettes, Cuban sugar tits, kosher mountain oysters, candied chicken gizzards, hot-cross matzoh balls, Salvation Army donuts, and polyunsaturated Pepsi Cola.* For the moment the sun is shining profusely and the smell of new-mown pharmaceuticals is perfuming the air. The buzzards are on the wing, and the espresso machine is sputtering like a spastic oracle. The *Daily Dirge* has been obtained, and the garbage tossed out the window. The transistor says that sales are up on clubs, cannons, bombs, napalm, blood, caskets, Sterno, and flowers. The weatherman predicts continued hacking and spitting, with a possibility of consumption by sundown. Blessed are they who sniff their glue with the morning dew. [*She moves to the edge of the proscenium and speaks confidentially.*] I went straight out last night and slugged seven policemen*, four taxi drivers*, two pregnant nuns*, a white Muslim, and a one-legged rabbi*! But I must hurry or I'll be late for my appointment to address the U.N. Security Council on the persecution of American Indians in Hollywood! *Sayonara.*

A gong sounds. Exit MAID SMITH.

MARY SMITH. Don't you love oriental music? . . .

MAID JONES *has gone a bit berserk with her fly swatting. Now realizing that she is "on," she moves forward to speak.*

MAID JONES. Lawzy! It is also morning in the home of John and Mary Jones. From all indications it is the same morning previously mentioned by Susie Wong. Johnmary Jones, or whatever his name is, is still nestled snugly in his wee little strait jacket. He played with the local beauty queen until the neighbors started to get aroused and throw money. Then we gave him an injection, shoved a wad of Juicy-Fruit in his mouth, and sent him off to dreamland. He was tired and nervous. In fact, one might even say he seemed a bit shook up. But I don't wonder, having to put up with these two mealy-mouthed mother intercoursers! Well, anyway, as you can see, Big John and the Great White Goddess are having their breakfast early so they can get in a coupla good hardy brunches before lunch. It consists of many lovely things that I prepared myself from old greasy Southern recipes. A good Black Muslim Aunt Jemima is hard to find these days. That is, one willing to accept the status quo of the existing state of affairs at any specified time . . . like for instance, now. Anyway, I am pleased to announce that the frost is on the honeysuckle and the magnolias are in a state of shock. The smart birds are twittering in the bushes and the chicory is churning in the Silex. The *Morning Mugger* has been delivered and the precious white milk put away. The Dow-Jones stockade average announces heavy trading on mutual admirations, with an eye for an eye and a tooth for a tit, still out front. But the weatherman, he say it'll be a perfect day for a blast-off. Blessed are they who arise with an erection and seek perfection. [*She curtsies and returns to the house singing "Do-da . . . do-da . . . do-da. . . ." Just before exiting, she turns back toward the* JONESES *and screeches:*] Black power!

The following dialogue is done as one continuous, monotonous speech. Movements and gestures should be identical and in unison when possible.

BOTH MARYS [*after a long slurp of coffee*]. The coffee's good this morning, isn't it? . . .

MARY SMITH. You really shouldn't put so much sugar in your coffee, John.

MARY JONES. Too much sugar's not good for you, John. You oughta watch that.

MARY SMITH. How were your eggs, John?

MARY JONES. You shouldn't put so much salt on your eggs, John.

MARY SMITH. Too much salt's not good for you, John.

MARY JONES. They say it causes high tension——

MARY SMITH. It's very bad for the complexion——

MARY JONES. They say that at least two per cent of all acne is caused by eating too much salt.

MARY SMITH. 'Course, they say pepper does the same thing.

MARY JONES. Wonder why people don't put sugar on their eggs?

MARY SMITH. Did you ever think about that, John?

MARY JONES. Hmmmm . . . I guess it would probably make 'em too sweet——

MARY SMITH. I imagine a person could get used to it, though——

MARY JONES. Don't you imagine a person could get used to it, John?

MARY SMITH. Sure . . . I imagine a person could get used to it.

MARY JONES. It's all a matter of what you're accustomed to . . . I guess.

MARY SMITH. People used to think it was terrible to put beer on corn flakes.

MARY JONES. Oh, I've been meaning to tell you, John—there's a loose step on the back porch.

MARY SMITH. Oh, by the way, John, that loose piece of plaster over the bathtub is getting looser every day. . . .

BOTH MARYS. My God . . . it makes me a nervous wreck just to think about it.

MARY SMITH. Probably come crashing down one of these days and kill you. Or what if it hit me?

MARY JONES. I knew a girl once who got her skull fractured that way. . . .

MARY SMITH. It's enough to drive a person crazy. I mean, just worrying about things like that.

MARY JONES. Name was Mary . . . I think.

MARY SMITH. I say, take care of hazards in the home, before you start supporting 'em abroad.

MARY JONES. You know we were real close chums in school. . . .

MARY SMITH. They say Mary what's-her-name got her neck broke that way.

MARY JONES. A darling girl. But a real creep. You know what I mean?

MARY SMITH. But if I know her, she made out all right with her bottom.

BOTH MARYS. Hmmmmmm . . . wonder what ever happened to Mary.

MARY SMITH. Well, looks like it's going to be another hot one, dudn't it?

MARY JONES. Seems like it's always too hot or too cold any more.

MARY SMITH. Looks to me like that's something the U.N. *could* do something about.

BOTH MARYS. Did you ever think of that, John?

MARY SMITH. 'Course you know they say it's not *really* the heat——

MARY JONES. I guess it's just this damn humidity——

MARY SMITH. Personally, I don't think that Tex Ritter knows his ass from a hole in the ground about the weather.

MARY JONES. Those damn Russians will stop at nothing to make you sweat. . . .

There is a short pause.

BOTH MARYS. Got that terrible pain in the back of my neck again this morning——

MARY JONES. Suffered all night——

MARY SMITH. Woke up with a splitting headache. . . . Suffered like a son-of-a-bitch all night. . . .

A slight pause.

BOTH MARYS. *I said I suffered all night!*

MARY SMITH. Oh well, it's probably just that old trouble with my ovaries again.

MARY JONES. I wouldn't want to upset you, John, but I think I've got a brain tumor.

MARY SMITH. Personally, I don't think it's my ovaries at all! I think it's my gall bladder!

MARY JONES. Have you ever noticed anything kind of peculiar about my head, John?

MARY SMITH. I haven't told you, John, but the doctor says I've got *syphilis!*

MARY JONES. Oh well, what the hell. It's probably just those damn Russians.

MARY SMITH. It's getting so you can't trust *anybody.*

BOTH MARYS. Did you ever think about that, John?

They both yawn, then begin to read the backs of their respective papers.

MARY JONES. Hmmmmmmm . . . looks like a good picture on at Loews tonight.

MARY SMITH. Oh, for God's sake, John! Did you know they've sent Susan Hayward to the gas chamber again?

MARY JONES. Says it's a "wonderful, family-type entertainment."

MARY SMITH. And they call this a free country!

MARY JONES. Says Wanda Hale gives it four-and-a-half stars.

MARY SMITH. They couldn't have taken that Julie Andrews, or Ronald Reagan! Oh, no! They had to take a Bronx girl!

MARY JONES. Says it's a "sensitive, sympathetic study of a seven-year-old masochistic Mennonite drug addict . . . and the problems he encounters in organizing the Little League baseball team among the Rosicrucians in Venice, California."

MARY SMITH. Hmmmm . . . I see they've started giving away free dishes again.

MARY JONES. But I suppose you'd rather sit home on your ass and watch the fights!

MARY SMITH. I guess they think that'll smooth things over. . . . Ha!

MARY JONES. You've become entirely too color-conscious, John. You're withdrawn.

MARY SMITH. Well, it won't smooth things over with me! It's a perfectly ghastly pattern.

MARY JONES. Why don't you ever take *me* to Roseland Dance City any more?

MARY SMITH. I mean, who wants Betsy Ross staring up at you out of a coffee cup? . . .

MARY JONES. Hmmmm. You know, it says they're equipped to hold balls of any size. Hmmmmm. . . .

MARY SMITH. My God! I mean any time! Much less in the morning.

MARY JONES. Did you ever read about what Catholics used to do to choirboys, John?

MARY SMITH. Of course, as long as they're free, I suppose we could use some of those medium-sized soup bowls for ash trays.

MARY JONES. I'd do a little thinking about that if I were you, John. . . .

MARY SMITH. Uh-oh! I should have known there'd be a catch somewhere! Would you believe it? Only one piece per person!

MARY JONES. I guess that's what ecumenical means. Ah-ha! Now it all makes sense!

MARY SMITH. And besides that, it says you've got to buy a ticket! That's America for you!

MARY JONES. Somebody ought to write an editorial. . . .

BOTH MARYS. The selfish bastards! [*There is a long pause as they slurp their coffee, scratch, and yawn.*] Maid says she saw you slipping out of the house again last night, John. Naked as a jay bird. Who is it this time, John?

MARY SMITH. Oh . . . I know! I know!

MARY JONES. I know all right! Oh yes!

BOTH MARYS. It's that bitch next door.

MARY SMITH. I know a lot more than you think I know.

MARY JONES. You don't give me much credit, but I know a lot. . . .

BOTH MARYS. Oh, yes!

MARY SMITH. You think I'm deaf and dumb?

MARY JONES. You think I'm blind and senseless?

BOTH MARYS. Oh, I know all right. . . . [*Pause.*] You bet your sweet ass, I know! [*Pause.*] You don't shit me!

MARY SMITH. Where have I failed you, John?

MARY JONES. Tell me, John, where *have* I failed?

MARY SMITH. If I only knew, I could try and do something about it.

MARY JONES. I've tried, John. God knows I've tried. . . .

MARY SMITH. You know I've tried. . . .

BOTH MARYS. Everybody knows I've tried.

MARY JONES. Why, John? . . .

MARY SMITH. Why, John? . . .

BOTH MARYS. Why do we torture each other like this?

MARY SMITH. I'm still attractive. . . .

MARY JONES. You used to think I was sexy. . . .

BOTH MARYS. I'm basically against everything you are.
. . . But marriage must be a "fun" thing, John . . .
a "fun" thing.

MARY JONES. Don't you ever think of our child?

MARY SMITH. You don't know what it's like to walk
down the street and have people smile right in your
face.

MARY JONES. I've suffered, John. . . .

MARY SMITH. Oh, how I've suffered for you. . . .

BOTH MARYS. You son-of-a-bitch!

MARY JONES. Why, John? . . .

MARY SMITH. Why, John? . . .

BOTH MARYS. Why, John . . . *why?* Where have I failed
you, John?

MARY JONES. Where, John? . . .

MARY SMITH. Where, John? . . .

BOTH MARYS. Where, John . . . *where?* [*They each take
another long slurp of coffee as both* JOHNS *now lower
their papers, pick up their brief cases, and rise. For the
first time, we see that the two* JOHNS *have been switched.
Both* MARYS *scream:*] John! My God! I thought you
left hours ago! What would my husband do if he caught
you here?

BOTH JOHNS. Shhhhhhhhh . . . [*After kissing their respective* MARYS, *they cross to center stage, come face
to face with each other, tip their hats, and say:*] Good
morning, John.

Both MARYS *collapse on their chairs as both* JOHNS *exit.
The lights black out.*

SCENE II

The same. Enter JOHNMARY JONES *from his house. He carries an enormous bundle of manuscripts which he places on the floor, seats himself and begins to eat.*

Enter MARYJOHN SMITH, *pushing a small baby carriage which she brings to a stop at the edge of the Smith table.*

MARYJOHN. Oh, God! Dried figs, prunes, apple cores, pumpkin rinds, acorns, seaweed flakes, alfalfa blossoms, wormy raisins, turtle egg-rolls, pizza pie, instant hominy, Camembert doodles, salami croquettes, Cuban sugar tits, kosher mountain oysters, candied chicken gizzards, Salvation Army donuts, hot-cross matzoh balls, and poly-unsaturated Pepsi-Cola—*again?!* Oh, there's my little husband, Johnmary Q. Rooney the Eighth. Just wait till he sees *what I've got for him!* The Joneses have such lovely things for breakfast, all made from old greasy Southern red-neck recipes. Just for kicks, I think I shall join him. If there's any time a girl should be with the man she loves, it's when she tells him he's become the father of her child. Yoohoo, Little Annie Q. Jones! Yoohoo! [*She pushes the carriage toward the Jones table, singing.*] "Good morning, good morning good morning! Oh, what a heavenly day. . . . I am as high as an elephant's eye. . . . So that's why I'm going to say. . . ." [*She stops abruptly and places her hands over* JOHNMARY's *eyes.*] Guess who?

JOHNMARY. Stokley Carmichael.

MARYJOHN. You're getting warm. Try again.

JOHNMARY. I give up! Now kindly remove your clammy hands and go away!

MARYJOHN. Oh, you must never, never give up! You're supposed to say, "Well, who . . . pray tell?"

JOHNMARY. Well, who . . . pray tell?

MARYJOHN [*jumping around in front of him*]. It's me! Mrs. Little Annie Rooney the Eighth! The mother of your child!

JOHNMARY. Oh God! I thought you died last night!

MARYJOHN. I have a most delightful surprise for you. But first, let's eat.

JOHNMARY. Why don't you eat your own food?

MARYJOHN [*starting to eat*]. Ummmmm! The coffee's good this morning, isn't it? You know, you really shouldn't put so much sugar in your coffee, Johnmary, it's likely to make you too sweet.

JOHNMARY. You're ruining my appetite!

MARYJOHN. You know, they say at least two per cent of premarital reciprocity is caused by a mixture of sweetness and light.

JOHNMARY. I hate you!

MARYJOHN. You see how aggressive it makes you.

JOHNMARY. I really and truly and most sincerely despise you!

MARYJOHN. Don't beat around the bush, darling. You might wake the surprise.

JOHNMARY. There is no surprise! As usual, you have deceived me!

MARYJOHN. Oh? Well . . . just take a peek in the buggy, Buster! [*She pushes the carriage toward* JOHNMARY.] Say "screw you" to Daddy, darling. Okay, there we are. [JOHNMARY *gasps and covers his eyes.*] Well, there's a pretty how'd you do!

JOHNMARY. What in God's name have you got in there? What is it?!

MARYJOHN. Whata ya mean, "What is it?" How should I know?

JOHNMARY. Well, it's in your pram! And you said you had it!

MARYJOHN [*into the carriage*]. Say, "Wham, bam, thank you, Ma'am!" Your daddy's a sugar dumpling!

JOHNMARY. Please! Please take it away!

MARYJOHN. How can you be that way about our only begotten thing? When one observes a work of art, one must always ask oneself, "What was the creator trying to do?" When you have given up on that, you may then direct your criticisms to how well he did it. Now, you've got to admit, Johnmary, it's *very* interesting.

JOHNMARY. I think I'm going to throw up!

MARYJOHN. Oh, look, Johnny! It's waving at you! And look how all its little eyes have a definite glassy glint of glory about them.

JOHNMARY. I'm sick, I tell you! I'm sick!

MARYJOHN. Little John Maryjohn Smith Rooney Q. Jones Jr. The future kind of euphoria! A monarch of love! Oh, look, Johnny! Look how it's already wagging its regal little tail!

JOHNMARY. No! No! Make it stop!

MARYJOHN. A little blue-blooded barometer of beatified finality! A flower thing!

JOHNMARY. You are a deceiver of youth!

MARYJOHN. We have given the world a glimmer of expectation! We have brought the hope of the future to the living present!

JOHNMARY. Something awful is going to happen! I feel it! I feel it in my stomach! You're not only immoral, but wrong as well!

MARYJOHN. Oh, how happy we'll be, Johnny. We will teach it to laugh. To love love. To relish the complexities of domestication! To scratch our groins. To pinch blackheads out of our chins. And to bake sunshine cakes for the whole wide world!

JOHNMARY [*holding his stomach*]. Oh, I'm too ill to co-operate with anybody! I feel so full of something. . . .

MARYJOHN. Oh, you are, darling! Believe me, you are! Perhaps you're expanding into manhood.

JOHNMARY. But I'm too small for much expansion. I might crack! Or explode!

MARYJOHN. When the time comes, *you'll stretch!* I did.

JOHNMARY. Look, I'm starting to chill. See how my body trembles? A terrible draft seems to be penetrating my very soul!

MARYJOHN. Oh, you're so marvelously disgusting. Your fly's open, stupid!

JOHNMARY. Now I feel hot! And dizzy! My stomach rolls and tumbles. . . . Stand back! I feel as if I were going to shatter into a million pieces!

MARYJOHN [*removing a Coke bottle with a nipple on it from the carriage*]. Here, have a shot of Coke!

JOHNMARY. See, see how the world is whizzing past? Don't you see how fast we're beginning to spin? Look! Look!

MARYJOHN. Oh, yes. Those were my symptoms exactly!

JOHNMARY. Faster . . . and faster and faster! And listen! Listen to that bloodcurdling roar!

MARYJOHN. Hmmmmmm. . . . [*She places her ear against his stomach.*] It does seem to be coming from you all right.

JOHNMARY. Look, Maryjohn! Look how everything is now modulating into a mystifying maze of molecular momentum!

MARYJOHN. Very monotonous. Maybe you'd better lie down.

JOHNMARY. Yes . . . yes! I'm sure I'm either dying or on the brink of a colossal vision!

MARYJOHN. Oh, do try the vision first, love!

JOHNMARY. I think I'm beginning to see the power of man triumph over the power of men!

MARYJOHN. Do you suppose that has anything to do with good and evil?

JOHNMARY. I don't know. . . . Perhaps it would be wise to ask.

MARYJOHN. Oh yes! Yes! Let's do. [*She calls offstage.*] Which of you is *good?*

TWO VOICES [*offstage, from opposite directions*]. *I am!*

JOHNMARY. And which of you is *evil!*

TWO VOICES [*offstage*]. *He is!*

MARYJOHN. Well, it's certainly a relief to get that cleared up.

JOHNMARY. Oh, what a divine revelation, Maryjohn! The venom is indeed being sucked from all the evil hearts and heads of humanity!

MARYJOHN. *Fantastic!* You think I should awaken the thing and let it see too?

JOHNMARY. Oh yes! Wake everybody! Wake the world! Wake the universe! Oh Joy! Oh Life! Oh Beautiful Picture!

MARYJOHN [*placing her hand in the carriage and quickly withdrawing it to the accompaniment of a ferocious growl*]. *Oh my!*

JOHNMARY. Look there, Maryjohn! Look there!

MARYJOHN [*gasping at the sight*]. Oh my God! Not Sunbonnet Sue in a G string?!

JOHNMARY. Yes! Yes! Thousands of Sunbonnet Sues in rhinestone G strings!

MARYJOHN. But not on top of a flagpole!

JOHNMARY. Oh yes! Yes! And how marvelously stimulatingly enthrallingly affectingly *free!*

MARYJOHN. *But not dancing a passacaglia* on top of a flagpole!

JOHNMARY. But what grace! What skill! What precision! What inspiration!

MARYJOHN. What a very dangerous place to go dancing!

JOHNMARY. Oh, the dear, sweet, precious little things. . . . Dance on! Dance on!

MARYJOHN. It makes me nervous, Johnmary! It makes me very nervous! Careful, girls! Watch your step! Careful!

As JOHNMARY *begins to relate the following sights,* MARY-JOHN, *eyes fixed on the spectacle atop the flagpole, suddenly gasps and follows the fall of a Sunbonnet Sue to the ground. She shuts her eyes and covers her ears for the*

*accompanying loud crash. (This action is repeated during
each of the sights related by* JOHNMARY, *and should be
timed so that the crash comes as a punctuation at the end
of each description.)*

JOHNMARY. Oh my God! Look there, Maryjohn! Look
there! Three million one hundred and . . . and . . .
yes! twenty-two! Three million one hundred twenty-two
pink partisan poodles defecating in unison! [*Crash!*]
And there! There! Look over there! All the morning
satellites are singing together! [*Crash! Looking in another direction, he gasps.*] Oh, no! No! Not that! Not
that! They'll never get away with it! It can't be! Can
it be? A coon on the moon?! [*Crash!*] Oh, Lord, look
there! Look over there, Maryjohn! Dragons! Thousands
of dragons! Drinking from Dixie cups!

Again MARYJOHN *gasps and adds a loud anguished scream
as she follows the last of the Sunbonnet Sues to the ground.
After the crash, she slowly removes her hands from her
eyes and begins to sob hysterically.*

MARYJOHN. Look, Johnmary! Look! They've all fallen off!
Those sweet little Sunbonnet Sues have all fallen off
that damn flagpole!

JOHNMARY. Oh no! No! Say it isn't so! Oh, the poor, dear
little sweet innocent little things. . . . [*He covers his
eyes and weeps.*]

MARYJOHN. I guess that's life, Johnny. I suppose we'll
have to get used to it.

JOHNMARY. But they're all gone . . . the flagpole is
empty.

MARYJOHN. If you really look at it realistically, I guess it
wasn't a very practical place to go dancing.

The roar of the M.G.M. lion is heard. JOHNMARY *screams.*

JOHNMARY. Ah! A lion is roaring at me! [MARYJOHN
checks the carriage.] And look! Look, Maryjohn! There's
a beautiful city!

The Twentieth-Century-Fox music is heard.

MARYJOHN. Oh goody! Maybe it's the second feature. Where is it?

JOHNMARY. There! There! In the air!

MARYJOHN. Oh yes! I see! [*She reads.*] "The Human Sea . . . by Cecil B."

JOHNMARY. With . . . with "a cast of billions!"

MARYJOHN. I think I've seen it all already—seen it all.

JOHNMARY. The credits are moving so fast, I can't keep up! Can you read what it says?

MARYJOHN [*reading*]. "From the original hallucination of A as conceived by B and told to C who collaborated with D on an adaptation by E from a poem by F who permitted G to expand it for H who embellished it for I and authenticated it for J who suggested that K do an abridgement for L who paraphrased it for M and superimposed the philosophy of N with the politics of O and a supposition of P with a tangible angle of Q who blackmailed R to sleep with S who had already encouraged T to implicate U in order to subsidize V in honor of W whose valiant and tireless devotion to X made it profitable for Y to employ Z to muck up the original idea of A."

JOHNMARY. Yes, yes. Go on. What else does it say?

MARYJOHN. "We wish to thank all who made this possible."

JOHNMARY. Go on!

MARYJOHN. That's all. It says . . . "The End."

JOHNMARY. What do you mean, "The End"?

MARYJOHN. I mean that every tale has its bottom.

JOHNMARY. But it can't be the end. What about the cast of characters?

MARYJOHN. Maybe it's intermission.

JOHNMARY. You turned me off!

MARYJOHN, I never touched you! It was your vision!

JOHNMARY. You're lying! You're lying! You turned me off!

MARYJOHN. You're ill! You said so yourself. Now lie down and concentrate on the beauty of your pain!

JOHNMARY. But I want to see the rest of it!

MARYJOHN. Don't be naïve! After careful observation, I've come to the conclusion that you are definitely going to have a baby.

JOHNMARY. Don't be ridiculous! I'm not old enough!

MARYJOHN. Then prepare yourself to make medical history! Lie down and concentrate on your bottom.

JOHNMARY. I want to see the rest of it!

MARYJOHN [*forcing him to the ground and sitting on top of him*]. Down, boy! Grit your teeth and start counting!

JOHNMARY. Oh . . . I think I'm beginning to hear the angels sing!

MARYJOHN. Change your concentration to your navel!

She now begins to bounce up and down on his stomach.

JOHNMARY. Ahhhhhhhh . . . Ahhhhhhhhhh . . . Ahhhh-hhhhh. . . .

MARYJOHN [*placing her hand over his mouth*]. That'll be about enough of that! Now come on! Have it and get it over with!

JOHNMARY. Ahhhhhhhhh! Someone's coming! Someone's coming! I can see him clearly!

MARYJOHN [*checking*]. Not yet! Come on now, *grunt!*

JOHNMARY. Oh, it's either an angel or the monster death that I see before me! There! There! Don't you see it? Oh, my God! I fear it is the monster death! Stand back, death! Stand back! I'm too young to die! I'll sell my books!

MARYJOHN. *Grunt!*

JOHNMARY. Ah! He's placing his hand on his golden holster! He's drawing! He's drawing his ruby-studded forty-five! Look! He's taking aim! He's pointing his gorgeous weapon straight at my head! Stand back! Don't shoot! Shield me, Maryjohn! Shield me!

MARYJOHN. Rest, my child. Rest.

JOHNMARY. His finger is moving on the golden trigger! He's pulling! He's pulling the trigger! No! Stop! Don't shoot! Don't. . . .

As the last "Don't" blends into a terrifying scream, the lights abruptly black out. An enormous earth-shaking explosion is heard, followed by the sound of a jet zooming into the sky, with the screams of both JOHNMARY *and* MARYJOHN *fading into the distance. A very jazzy banjo version of "Sitting on Top of the World" fills the air, as the curtain falls.*

SCENE III

Forty days and forty nights later. The stage is completely bare, except for a very large, very organic-looking mound. JOHNMARY *seems to have crashed head-on into it, for we see only his bottom half protruding upward. One leg waves in the air and* MARYJOHN *clings firmly to the other. Their clothes are in shreds and they both appear to have been dipped in a sewer. As the curtain rises, great agonized groans can be heard.*

MARYJOHN. Light! Light! Who turned off the lights? [JOHNMARY *groans.*] Johnmary! Johnmary! Are you still with me? [JOHNMARY *groans.*] Speak to me. Are you all right? [*Again* JOHNMARY *groans.* MARYJOHN *now lets go of his leg and attempts to remove some of the "glop" from her face. Slowly she surveys the situation.*] Ohhhhhh! What hath God wrought? [JOHNMARY *groans.*] Speak a little clearer, darling. I can't understand you. Come out of there and tell me everything's going to be all right! [*He groans louder.*] Now get hold of yourself, Johnmary! [*She attempts to pull him from the mound.*] I think we need to have a *very* serious talk. Come on now! [*She succeeds in pulling him into view.*] There we are! Speak to me, darling! Speak to me! [*Again he emits an agonized groan.*] Are you all right? Speak to me!

JOHNMARY. Ohhhhhhhh. . . . I'm dead. I'm dead. . . .

MARYJOHN. Yes, but are you all right?

JOHNMARY. Why have you desecrated my grave?

MARYJOHN. Oh please, Johnmary. Don't talk like that. I need encouragement in the worst way. Say something to cheer me up.

JOHNMARY. You're dead too.

MARYJOHN. That didn't help much. Try again. Recite your poem about the chicken and the maggot.

JOHNMARY. This smell! What is this smell? This incredible bouquet?

MARYJOHN. Read the card! Read the card!

JOHNMARY. And where are we? Why have you brought me here?

MARYJOHN. I didn't bring you here! *You brought me here!*

JOHNMARY. But where are we? Where are we?

MARYJOHN. You mean you really don't know?

JOHNMARY [*in tears*]. No. . . . And I'm afraid to guess.

MARYJOHN. Promise not to be upset if I tell you?

JOHNMARY. No . . . no. . . . I promise nothing.

MARYJOHN. Now you must try and get a grip on yourself, darling. As I said before, the time has come for a very serious . . . summit meeting.

JOHNMARY. What could there possibly be to talk about *now?*

MARYJOHN. Well, as a starter, I was wrong. I admit it. I was very, very wrong. You didn't have a baby. *But,* nevertheless, I think your dreams may have come true.

JOHNMARY. Oh no! This is not my dream! This is your dream!

MARYJOHN. Oh no! Believe me, Johnmary. This isn't my dream! It's definitely yours!

JOHNMARY. Then where are all the golden streets and lovely mansions that were being prepared for us? Where are all the angels and saints? The righteous and patriotic citizens?

MARYJOHN. Oh, they're all down in there somewhere.

JOHNMARY. Oh my God, Maryjohn! You don't think we might . . . might possibly be in . . . in. . . . [*He covers his eyes and begins to weep.*]

MARYJOHN. No, no, darling! Get hold of yourself. We're not in any of those old-fashioned mythological places! Think transcendental.

JOHNMARY. You lie! You lie! It would have to be hell if you're here! We're dead! [*Again he weeps.*]

MARYJOHN. Oh, knock off that "dead" crap, Johnmary! You're still breathing! You can see! You can speak! You moan and groan just like you always did. And if it's any consolation, you're even more breath-taking than ever.

JOHNMARY. I am?

MARYJOHN. Believe me! So let's face it, little husband. Whether we like it or not, we are still what is generally considered alive. The least we can do is try to think of it as a challenge!

JOHNMARY. But my head. . . . My poor head! I have no energy. I feel lost . . . betrayed. . . . And completely empty.

MARYJOHN. Well, I should think so! My God!

JOHNMARY. My mouth feels caked with . . . with——

MARYJOHN. Yes, dear. I know . . . I know.

JOHNMARY. But there is no taste. Why is there no taste?

MARYJOHN. Offhand, I'd say that may be considered one of its better qualities.

JOHNMARY. Yet this delicately pungent fragrance seems to remind me of some place I've been before. It stifles me.

MARYJOHN. Nonsense! Breathe deeply. It is the essence of man's sweet-scented credulity. The aroma of brand-new-modern-*now!*

JOHNMARY. But it inflames my lungs! I tell you, I absolutely refuse to breathe. [*He begins holding his breath.*]

MARYJOHN [*whamming him in the stomach*]. *Breathe, dammit! Breathe!* Whether you like it or not, Johnmary, the time has come for a seriously assiduous assimilation of your asinine alliterations and allegorical arpeggios into an apprehensible astro-anal agglutination!

JOHNMARY. Don't scream at me!

MARYJOHN. May I point out to you that the wallpaper and pictures have vanished! The cafe curtains and protean beds have returned to nature! Your pipe and easy chair have eclipsed! The honeysuckle and the garden wall have dissolved! The welcome mat is gone! There is no more Coke, Johnmary! *There is no more Coke!*

JOHNMARY [*in tears*]. No . . . no. . . .

MARYJOHN. All the evil things of the world have at last been inundated by the impetus of my Johnny's intestinal initiative. [*She extends her hand.*] Congratulations!

JOHNMARY. But what about the *good* things?

MARYJOHN. Behold, I am with you always.

JOHNMARY. But I don't understand. . . . I don't really understand. What happened?

MARYJOHN. You mean to sit there and tell me, you don't really remember?

JOHNMARY. All I remember is my vision.

MARYJOHN. Oh, that vision was real "high up," Johnmary. But the explosion! Well, I mean to tell you, *it was "something else"!*

JOHNMARY. Explosion? Then I did miss something.

MARYJOHN. Oh no! Believe me, you didn't miss a spot! Symmetrically, I think you should be very pleased.

JOHNMARY. Symmetrically? What are you talking about?

MARYJOHN. Well, darling, as you know, I thought you were simply going to have a baby. But no. Oh no! Not Johnmary Q. Jones the Eighth. You had to be sensational.

JOHNMARY. Have I become a celebrity?

MARYJOHN. Oh, I always knew you had it in you. I just never dreamt you had quite this much. Spread before us are the vintage fruits of my little Johnny's celestial centerpiece. It is unquestionably the most prodigious contribution the world has ever received.

JOHNMARY. Really?

MARYJOHN. Aesthetically speaking, I believe you will be pleased to know that the world itself may now be considered a *total work of art*.

JOHNMARY. Golly!

MARYJOHN. Humanity has at last been laid to rest in a shroud of cohesive crud and centrifugal contentment. . . . The sight of which would no doubt render the philosopher and the poet hamstrung for hyperbole!

JOHNMARY. Oh how happy they must be. I always knew I was destined for daring deeds.

MARYJOHN. Ah, but don't forget, dear heart, behind every daring man, there's usually a darling woman. How else do you think we were propelled here to the fertile fields of fame? When I saw what was happening, I clung to your feet. You shot into the air like a rocket. Had I not been in a position to guide and direct you, you would have no doubt messed up the whole thing.

JOHNMARY. So now you're trying to take credit for my achievement.

MARYJOHN. If it hadn't been for me, we might now be floating aimlessly in a cosmic void!

JOHNMARY. Here void! There void! Everywhere void void!

MARYJOHN. For all practical purposes, I think you should know that we circled the globe for forty days and forty nights.

JOHNMARY. That *is* rather impressive.

MARYJOHN. I thought your creative energy would never cease. From my position, the view was sensational! But my hair! My God! I think you've just ruined my hair!

JOHNMARY. I know your type! You were simply hanging on for the free ride!

MARYJOHN. But I brought you in for a perfect landing. Not a vital organ dented. Although we have traveled many miles, it is as though we had not moved. I have returned us to the exact scene of the blast-off.

JOHNMARY. But where are the photographers, the press and TV cameras? Why is there no one here to celebrate this historic achievement?

MARYJOHN. I'm beginning to think you don't fully comprehend the depth of our accomplishment, Johnmary. It's very, very, very deep. And physically speaking, we seem to be the only two who have come out on top.

JOHNMARY. Really?

MARYJOHN. I wouldn't want to get your hopes up too high, but from all indications, I believe we have, what you might say, inherited the earth.

JOHNMARY. Are you serious?

MARYJOHN. I'm afraid so. . . .

JOHNMARY. You mean, it's really all ours now? To do with as we wish?

MARYJOHN [*singing*].

> "We're sittin' on top of the world . . .
> Just hummin' along . . .
> Just singin' a song. . . ."

JOHNMARY. But how can we really be sure? There's nothing recognizable.

MARYJOHN. Believe me, sweetie, that's only because you have led an extremely sheltered life.

JOHNMARY. But what actual proof do we have?

MARYJOHN. See those big jellylike globs of spectral extinction out there between the wide-open spaces along the hypothetical horizon?

JOHNMARY. Yes. . . . Yes. . . . I think so. Oh yes! They do look very familiar. So solid and content.

MARYJOHN. You see? There's no doubt about it. We're home.

JOHNMARY. Gee. . . . It's good to be back. They say it's where the heart is.

MARYJOHN. What a lovely old sentiment.

JOHNMARY. I wouldn't want anybody to think I'm not greatly honored with my inheritance. . . . But confidentially, Maryjohn, just between us. Now that we've got it . . . what do you propose we do with it?

MARYJOHN. Well, if I remember correctly, the first thing one does in a situation such as this, is call the meeting to order.

JOHNMARY. Oh yes. That seems logical. The meeting will please come to order. How was that?

MARYJOHN. Very good. Now we must elect a leader.

JOHNMARY. Oh, absolutely. That's general parliamentary procedure.

MARYJOHN *and* JOHNMARY. Everybody in favor of ME being Chairman, President, King, Prime Minister, and Prince (Princess) Charming, say "aye"! *Aye!* The "aye's" have it. Congratulations. [*They shake hands.*] Thank you. Now I'll take over from here.

MARYJOHN. Hmmmmm. . . . I noticed you didn't vote for me. How come?

JOHNMARY. You know very well that I am opposed to your political views. However, as the elected leader, I promise I won't start persecuting you until you've ceased to be of value.

MARYJOHN. All right. For the time being, I'll accept that. And I won't start trying to overthrow you until you've made a little progress.

JOHNMARY. Okay. Now let's get moving.

MARYJOHN. Yes, Your Serene Hugeness. But which direction do you suggest?

JOHNMARY. Right, of course!

MARYJOHN. Never! Left or nothing!

JOHNMARY. Then it will be nothing!

MARYJOHN. I see. Then perhaps, due to the texture of the times, it would be noble of His Graciousship to consider compromise. How about forward?

JOHNMARY. Yes. We would find that acceptable. You go first.

MARYJOHN. Oh, no! I'm not going out in that first! You're the elected Kingpin! I'm going to *follow the leader!*

JOHNMARY. But if I should sink, you wouldn't have a leader! Then what would you do?

MARYJOHN. About the same as you would do without a follower. So, press on, buster-charming! [*She pushes him along.*]

JOHNMARY [*after a few cautious steps*]. Excuse me, Knave. But the King seems to have lost his compass. Since you seem to be a native of these parts, you wouldn't by chance happen to know which way is forward, would you?

MARYJOHN. Oh God! I just knew we were going to run into this problem. There's nothing worse for the morale of a follower, than to be lead by a nervous monarch or a timid titan!

JOHNMARY. I know, but it would be helpful if I had something to hold onto. [*He begins to cry.*] Oh why didn't you agree with me when I told you I was dead? Why? . . . Why?

MARYJOHN. Because I want your life, my lily-livered liege.

JOHNMARY. Ah-ha! So that's it. In the name of the high authority invested in me, I arrest you for high treason!

MARYJOHN. Oh shut up, Your Majesty! Don't you realize that we are the chosen two? The two most likely to succeed? As a matter of fact, we are the *only* seed! The only tool, and the only tillers. I fear that whether we like it or not, we are *it*, with nobody to hunt but ourselves. Don't you think it's about time we made some effort to find each other?

JOHNMARY. Such a proposal is totally irresponsible, irrational, illegal, and unconstitutional. It's faith we need at a time like this. Divine guidance is our only salvation. Stand back, I'm going to pray for a miracle. [*He lifts his arms and looks into the heavens.*]

MARYJOHN. Like a super-duper-giant-king-size can of *Drano!*

JOHNMARY. Silence! Oh God . . . almighty or otherwise . . . lend us your ethereal ear. We beseech your pristine paternalism promote its proverbial popularity by producing a particularly prodigious profundity at your earliest possible convenience. Or at least, send us a sign.

A *very large, colorful sign is now lowered into view, directly behind them. It reads:* "Welcome to Fun City."

MARYJOHN. You see? I knew nothing would happen.

JOHNMARY. Don't be so impatient. The Bible plainly states that we must "wait on the Lord."

MARYJOHN. Well, while you're waiting, may I suggest you hold onto your nose.

JOHNMARY. My nose?

MARYJOHN. Why not? At least it's yours, and I presume you know where it is. Don't you?

JOHNMARY. I think so. . . . [*He places his hand securely on his nose, then slowly, he is stricken with revelation.*] My God! Oh my God! God nose . . . I've found my Nose God!

MARYJOHN. I thought you'd like it.

JOHNMARY. But you don't understand, Maryjohn! It's a revelation! A divine revelation! God *has* answered my prayers!

MARYJOHN. Now Johnmary, you know as well as I that it's been there all the time, and you've whiled away many lovely hours picking it.

JOHNMARY. I know, Maryjohn! I know. . . . But spiritually! I'm speaking psychometrically historically! Look! Look where it is! [*He has crossed his eyes and is looking*

and pointing at his nose.] *It's in front of me!* God Nose
knows my nose is in front of me!

MARYJOHN. Where did you think it was, in your navel?

JOHNMARY. But yours is too, Maryjohn! Look! [MARYJOHN
starts to look in her navel.] No, no! Between your eyes!
Look! It's right between your eyes!

MARYJOHN [*crossing her eyes and finding her nose*]. Good
grief!

JOHNMARY. And since it's in front of us, it's obviously
pointing forward!

MARYJOHN. Incredible!

JOHNMARY. All we've got to do is hang onto it and press on.

MARYJOHN. Fantastic! You know, Johnmary, I think we
may have our hands on something of the most universal
significance!

JOHNMARY. How foolish we've been.

MARYJOHN. Oh, yes. . . . It cuts down the smell enor-
mously.

JOHNMARY. I'm already starting to regain my confidence.
At last, we have something we can really get a grip on.

MARYJOHN. Oh yes, Johnny! Yes! I think we've finally
found something smaller than both of us.

JOHNMARY. Man will always find a way.

MARYJOHN. Ain't it the truth.

JOHNMARY. Indubitably incorrigible! Indelibly immortal!

MARYJOHN. Not that I'm complaining, Your Highness,
but have you noticed how deep concentration on the
nose seems to produce a somewhat distorted view of
that which would no doubt seem considerably clearer
under less trying conditions? I seem to be seeing double.

JOHNMARY. I know, Maryjohn! Me too. But that's the most
wonderful part of all! We're obviously starting to multi-
ply! To replenish the earth.

MARYJOHN. How clever of us.

JOHNMARY. From this day forward, I decree that all my
subjects shall have two! Two of everything!

MARYJOHN. My cup dually overfloweth!

JOHNMARY. That is to say, from this day forward, there shall be a minimum of two sides to practically everything!

MARYJOHN. Then it would seem that your intentions are to provoke us with a choice, oh liberal King?

JOHNMARY. That is to say, from this day forward, there shall be a minimum of two sides to practically everything, except perhaps in the one-sided practicality of pre-eminence; as pertaining to politics, power, panic buttons, phosphorescent phalli, perpendicular pedigrees, perforated pilgrims, paraplegic pacifists, peace, and prosperity!

MARYJOHN. Indeed, Your Hugeness. It goes without saying.

JOHNMARY. *E pluribus unum!*

MARYJOHN. Yeah! And all kinds of nice things like that!

JOHNMARY. Progress marches on!

The traditional trumpet fanfare announcing the arrival of the U.S. Cavalry suddenly pierces the air.

MARYJOHN [*after a moment of slightly bewildered silence*]. Did His Serene Bigness hear that groovy horn from yonder hill?

JOHNMARY. It's the call to action! Come! Take up the cudgels and let us press on to paradise! Call out: "Make way for the Monarch!"

MARYJOHN. Yes, Your Collapsible Comradeship. But first, do you not feel it prudent to prepare ourselves for this journey which could possibly prove to be of some considerable longitude?

JOHNMARY. In what way, madam? Erect an altar and make some sort of human sacrifice?

MARYJOHN. Well, sir, to be perfectly honest, I would prefer a good hot shower and a bowl of chicken liver Tetrazini. But! Assuming that you are not a magician, nor yet a completely deified dumpling, I fear that your magnum opus has necessitated the moment to mold the mode of maintenance.

JOHNMARY. In which way?

MARYJOHN. In the interest of cultural sustenance . . . and the placation of our parched palates, let us insure our longevity by masticating a modest morsel of this monumental movement.

JOHNMARY. I don't quite follow you?

MARYJOHN. I mean, dear heart, before we sally forth in this pit of shit, let's eat.

JOHNMARY. Oh yes. That's an excellent idea. I'm famished, Did you pack a lunch?

MARYJOHN. No, Your Serene Husbandry. But rest assured, the menu is completely organic.

JOHNMARY. Excellent.

MARYJOHN. Please be seated. [*They sit.*] As freedom follows fashion, one's footing prescribes the pace. It is the aftermath that determines the alternatives. [*She removes two large spoons from her pocket and hands one to* JOHNMARY.] One for you . . . and one for me.

JOHNMARY. Thank you. [*He polishes his spoon on a piece of his clothing.*] Would you be kind enough to say the blessing?

MARYJOHN. I would consider it an honor and a privilege. [*She clasps her hands, closes her eyes and bows her head.*] "God is a great big, pompous bird . . . and we thank Him for this turd." Amen.

JOHNMARY. Amen.

They now scoop their spoons into the earth, then lift them to the "toast" position.

MARYJOHN. Here's crap in your craw!

They taste . . . then nod approval.

JOHNMARY. De gustibus non est disputandum! [*Enter* MAID JONES *at the extreme upstage right. She is a colossal mess, now dressed in the drenched and dripping remains of what would appear to be the raiment of a queen. Carrying a large toilet plunger, she valiantly probes for an elusive drain. Slowly, she makes her way to the top of the mound and surveys the scene on the ground before her.* JOHNMARY *and* MARYJOHN *remain oblivious to her presence.*] You wouldn't by chance happen to have some salt, would you?

MARYJOHN. Now really, darling! You know you shouldn't put so much salt on your shit. It's not good for you.

A very grandiloquent vocal recording of "The Star-Spangled Banner" now fills the air. MAID JONES raises her toilet plunger and assumes the pose of "Miss Liberty."

MAID JONES [*miming the words*].

> "Oh, say can you see . . .
> By the dawn's early light . . .
> What so proudly we hailed . . .
> At the twilight's last gleaming . . ."

The lights have slowly faded into a blackout. The curtain falls.

THE WHITE WHORE AND
THE BIT PLAYER

A Play in One Act

by

TOM EYEN

To David and Lisa and all the great kids in the ward across the hall—and to all the other lucky people who are no one

CHARACTERS

WHITE WHORE
BIT PLAYER

Author's Note

A play about *one* woman, before and after she made it. The nun-mind—what she imagines herself to be. The whore-flesh—what the world saw her to be. Taking place from the time she commits suicide, by strangulation on her asylum room cross, to the time she actually dies, ten seconds later. The play being all the flashes that appear in clear view of death—and the inevitable struggle (once she knows she is going to die) to live. A play about *one* woman who didn't *quite* make it.

The White Whore and the Bit Player was first presented by Ellen Stewart at the La MaMa Experimental Theatre Club, New York City, on August 28, 1964. The original cast (under the author's direction) was:

WHITE WHORE   Mari-Claire Charba
BIT PLAYER   Jacque Lynn Colton

In subsequent productions at the Caffe Cino Helen Hanft performed the role of Bit Player and J. P. Dodd created the lighting.

THE WHITE WHORE AND
THE BIT PLAYER

TIME: *The ten seconds between the act of suicide and the actual physical surrender of a body.*

PLACE: *A sanatorium room of a famous image, a washed-up blonde, before and after. Before, as she saw herself and after, as the world saw her.*

SETTING: *A large white wooden cross dominates the stage —it can go up to fourteen feet and blink on and off like a cheap neon sign. On right side of cross sits a papal chair for NUN. To the left is a white-silk-covered bed-lounge for WHORE. Thin black poles are placed four feet apart, surrounding stage, cutting off area from audience. Sections of poles may be screened with scrims of wild colors. A large, empty picture frame is seen standing on floor, near cross. There is an ever-present smell of burning incense.*

MUSIC: *The background music changes with mood of emotions. The music at opening is the African Mass (Missa Luba). It switches to the Gregorian chants for most of play except for scenes that do not take place in sanatorium.*

LIGHTS: *Lighting should create a misty, somber illusion for the sanatorium and switch to full stage lighting for scenes from the past.*

THE FIRST IMAGE: *The stage is in complete darkness. Missa Luba begins to permeate through the blackness. Music builds slightly. A light hits the cross, or if neon-cross is possible, it lights itself. A spot hits NUN, pre-set facing audience at stage right. She is praying (Hail Mary) upon a white necklace. Reaching the middle of the prayer, she begins laughing, then begins walking across stage continually praying and laughing. The music swells. A spot hits the WHORE on stage left; she is drowned in white fur and silks. She, too, is praying the Hail Marys and laughing. The WHORE moves to center stage like a bitch in heat, meeting with the NUN face to face as though they were about to kill each other. Upon the moment of face-to-face combat,*

they turn and face the cross, laughing. The Nun *goes to
chair and continues praying.*

The Whore *begins ripping off her costume, now going mad
in time to the African music. She gets down to her white
slip and then bends to* Nun *pleading for her white necklace
beads. The* Nun *gives them to her as a child would relin-
quish a dangerous object to his parent.* Whore *places beads
around her neck and her creation is completed. She progresses to cross as a dancing cannibal muttering her first
word, "I." Reaching cross, she turns and begins reliving
her life for 1/6th of a moment with death clearly in view.*

Whore. "I." I am the light/ the glimmer of dawn/ the
brilliance of high noon/ the beauty of the setting sun/
I am woman/ all women to all men/ my succulent breasts
hanging free/ suspended/ waiting eternally for milk-
hungry mankind.

Nun [*chanting like a priest*]. You ain't going to see me
sucking/ on those teeny-tired/ dir—ty tits/ Amen. [*She
continues to pray Hail Marys.*]

Whore [*ignoring* Nun]. Spotlights dancing/ forming halos
in my hair/ Lenses magnifying my universal beauty/ See,
Mama, I am a star!

Nun [*à la Negro mama*]. Was! You was a star, baby. If
you ever passed English One, you might get your verbs
right. [*Hail Mary, etc.*]

Whore [*not to be stopped*]. Star/ illuminating the heavens
and watched by the multitude/ the people screaming/ we
love you/ love you/ love you/ then tearing/ ripping my
gowns/ proving their devotion. Legions of foreign men
falling to their knees!

Nun. You knew that feeling well, baby doll. You never
went out without your legendary, iron kneepads. [*Hail
Mary, etc.*]

Whore. I?/ I who played Venus with arms to complete
her perfection/ I/ who made Juliet take a weaker sleeping pill so she would be awake when Romeo arrived/
My face was the mirror of the world/ I could transmit

emotion with the flick of an eyebrow/ I could cure the sick with my reflection/ I could——

NUN. Screw! You could screw. [*She switches to a British accent.*] That's all you could do and that's all you ever did. On screen and off. You were a terribly good screw, but a terribly bad plot changer. That Venus flick never did make it!

WHORE. Cars/ Jaguars, limousines/ attended by overgrown, greasy black bucks/ Homes/ here—there—afar/ Pools/ round—square—kidney—bladder/ Hand- and footprints in cement/ Autographs/ Lights!/ *Camera!/ Action!/ White fox/ White gowns/ White pearls/ Purity!* [*Reaching internal orgasm.*] Angelic Virgin sent from heaven to lead the world in love/ *I was a*——

NUN. Whore! [*With a British accent.*] A cheap, masochistic, illiterate, teeny-tired-titted, white whore with a sick bladder swimming pool. [*Reflecting.*] And you should be proud of it. [*She cries for herself and the sins of the world.*] Some people get all the breaks!

WHORE [*coming out of her self-created virginity illusion*]. I was a saint in disguise! Must you always interrupt me? [NUN *cannot be bothered and dials an imaginary phone.*] Couldn't you have at least waited until I said, "saint in disguise"? [*The white phone on the* WHORE's *bed rings.*] *Couldn't you?* [*She runs to answer the phone.*] Well, couldn't she?

NUN [*still in her chair, answering the other side of the phone*]. Ignore that frustrated bitch!

WHORE. It's the most important thing I say to myself now.

NUN. Of course. She's just a nasty nun.

WHORE. Why won't they give me my own room in this sanatorium like they promised?

NUN. They should!

WHORE. I'm not used to the lower classes.

NUN [*rising to center, music stops, and lights go to bright*]. Eighth-grade class!

WHORE [*still on the phone*]. I, the star!

NUN [*singing*]. Twinkle, twinkle, little star, how I wonder who you are. All right, class, we will all rise and sing along with Sister Mitchalina.

BOTH [WHORE *singing flat*]. Twinkle, twinkle, little star, how I wonder who you are.

NUN. Dear! Yes, you. You are still flat. One should not be flat by the time one reaches the eighth grade of St. Francis. We pride ourselves on well-developed pupils. So for your assignment in music tonight, dear, buy yourself a good pair of falsies! Now we will all take our English One books with religious illustrations and turn to page 281, verb usage. You may begin, dear.

WHORE [*reading like a fifth-grade pupil advancing to the fourth*]. The love problems of a political pusher named Napoleon. See Napoleon leave Josephine. See Josephine crying alone on her Louis the Sixteenth bed. Josephine looks up and says, "Uh—oh! I am fucked!"

NUN [*semi-fainting and holding her heart*]. My holy heart! That is not what it says! [*She advances to* WHORE *with murder gleaming in her eyes.*] It says, "Josephine looks up and says, 'Uh—oh! I *was* fucked!'" "Was" is the proper verb. There is no such word as "I am." Everything always was. [*She shakes* WHORE *like a malt.*] Nothing ever is!

WHORE. Do I pass to the ninth?

NUN [*going back to chair*]. I'm afraid, my dear, because of English One, you didn't quite make it. [*She throws* WHORE *a juicy kiss.*]

Music back to Gregorian, lights back down to sanatorium.

WHORE. Yeh! And I suppose you did? You! The Dinah Shore of the B movies. [NUN *takes chalk from the bed and writes on the black wall behind bed, "White Ass Cheap, 5¢ Sale."* WHORE *throws an imaginary stone and begins playing hopscotch.*] You—who sneaked around slyly and gracefully farted when nobody was looking. [*She grabs a microphone from the bed and addresses the world as if at a world première.*] Hi! We all knew it was you. Hi, Robert! You didn't fool any of us. Humphrey!

And when the studio finally found out where the stench was coming from they had you destroyed. Now let's give "Smelly" a great big hand, folks!

Applause is heard. NUN *takes mike from* WHORE.

NUN. Thank you. Thank you. That's enough. Look! They destroyed me before they gave me a chance. I was just a poor young girl from a small town in Indiana. I never saw a contract before. All I knew—it was for sixty-five years minimum and it seemed like a secure job. I didn't see that little clause on the bottom that read, "This contract may be canceled before that period only by natural, accidental, or suicidal death." Well, I just figured it was the standard form. I mean, who am I to stand up to organized procedure? [*She sits, throwing another kiss.*]

WHORE *takes the place of* NUN *in center—about twenty-one now. She is now at contract signing.*

WHORE. No, no—it's fine. Ahhhh—just the time period. It couldn't just be for three years maybe? Five? Yes, yes —I'm sure it's standard but it might be to your advantage, also. What if I turned out badly? I'm not too bright, actually. No, no—by no means stupid, but I do have a habit of screwing things up. Maybe ten? Fifteen? You wouldn't want a dud on your hands now, would you? Twenty! Yea—yea—I'll sign. I need a job! I really have no choice. [*She goes back to bed, rejected but not knowing why.*]

NUN. My choice! I would have made it on my own if they gave me my one choice! Just one part as a heavily scented wanton woman. Just one but they gave them all to you. A wanton woman wallowing in the shame brought on by her own indiscretions, banging merrily against the penis pendulum of time. [*She runs to cross, slightly insane now.*]

WHORE *is now at wall writing in chalk behind chair, "Sister Sue Sucks—Free."*

WHORE. I never banged against any penis pendulums!

NUN [*on cross*]. Sensual/ sinful/ white silk caressing my thighs/ kissing my crevices.

WHORE [*whispering into* NUN's *ear*]. And what would you have done with all your old religious costumes you wore with such Jewish gentility?

NUN. Burn them! Burn them all for a pair of white beads loosely hung around my neck constantly reminding me that one day I will hang from them! Beads just waiting for me to commit one mortal sin so they can strangle me. An easy woman of the cinema world! [*She hops like a horny rabbit over to stage right.*] Fornicating freely in foreign phone booths as a Russian Spyette! [*She hops over to stage left.*] Getting it in some medieval bush in a King Arthur adventure film. [*She hops back to center.*] Reaching my climax on some sacred altar in a quickly made art film about Martin Luther! [*She hops back to cross.*] Or better still—[*She moves up and down on cross.*]—getting humped on the *Titanic* as it sinks into the water tank for the forty-ninth take!

WHORE. [*rising to the rescue*]. Women and children first!

WHORE *begins singing "Nearer My God To Thee" as she pushes* NUN's *shoulders down on cross while* NUN *fights to stay up.*

NUN. Cheap rouge—get me into the lifeboat, Murray! Incandescent eye shadow—save me, Mama, I'm drowning! Hair brushed for hours to look uncombed—someone help me! Breasts freed from binding, suspended, waiting! Hey, somebody get those faggots out of the lifeboats, I'm drowning! Hic!

WHORE [*leaving* NUN *in disgust*]. Cut! Okay, boys, let's clear the set until she sobers up. She's on the hooch again.

NUN [*leaving cross, going to center spot to address the Studio Board*]. No—no, please no more black coffee—and please, no more hopping, horny vestal virgins in those early Roman epics—or sympathetic Jewish land-ladies of the blonde bombshell roomer upstairs who will be mysteriously stabbed in her left tit at midnight. And that religious story! Oh—you know what I'm talking about. My standard. I can't do another variation. I mean, how many sons of the singing nun can you do? She's been singing, dancing, flying, farting, fucking—— What? Oh, I'm sorry if I offended you, you must be Episcopalian! What? You never thought I had it in me? Well —I've had it in me. [*Smiling now like Doris Day.*] You understand now? [*Backing up.*] You'll give me a second chance! Of course, that's what I've been trying to tell you all along! *I am*——

WHORE [*rising*]. A farting flop!

NUN *and* WHORE *are back in sanatorium. A slow-motion cat fight begins between the two.*

NUN. Miscast! [*They do a ballet with tops of their bodies, swaying to and fro in slow motion, trying to choke each other.*] I was miscast! What can you do with such unbelievable roles?

WHORE. They were the same roles they gave Loretta Young and look where she is today!

NUN [*breaking movement*]. Yeh! She's down the hall in the basket room. [WHORE *leaves and goes to the wall on her side and wipes off the writing on the wall.*] But they were wrong for me! I was held down emotionally. That's why the studio had me destroyed.

WHORE. That—that and because you drank so much, you cheap lush.

NUN. So I did there for a while. I'm social—what can I tell you?

WHORE [*sitting on her bed, now like a hard-boiled secretary*]. We do not care for explanations here, dear. Whatever the case, we have decided to have you destroyed.

NUN [*standing in front of the chair and clicking an imaginary phone*]. Operator—operator, I seem to have a bad connection!

WHORE. Have you killed, dear. All those who do not rise to our expectations are killed. You have failed, shall we say, "to put out!" Oh, it will be quite proper—an accident. We have a whole publicity department specializing in unusual deaths. Dear, after all—[*She rises in front of the bed. Both* NUN *and* WHORE *are facing front, driving imaginary cars.*]—it's the only way we can legally get you out of your contract.

NUN [*becoming aware of an oncoming car*]. Hey, mister! Watch it! You're in the wrong lane! [*Blackout.* NUN *screams.* WHORE *laughs. Spot now finds* NUN *sitting calmly in chair, smiling.*] I never touched a drop after that. Cured for good, my doctor told me. It won't get me out of here—but it's nice to know you're well. [*She sees* WHORE *who looks too peaceful on the bed.*] And why didn't you make it? [*No answer except a slight, "Huh?"*] Why did they have to put *you*, the greatest of the white whores of the cinema world, here in the cookie farm?

NUN *begins applauding wildly.* WHORE *grabs a white feather from the bed. Music goes into a wild 20's song.* WHORE *dances to music as though making a film.*

WHORE. It was a line! One small unshowing age line, here under my right eye. I was only thirty-six. A woman has the right to have one small unshowing age line under her right eye at thirty-six. But you see, it violated my contract. One of the conditions was that I would never get any small unshowing age lines under my right eye at thirty-six. It was only one line!

NUN. That—that and because you ate too much. Everyone you could get your hands on. [*She runs over to* WHORE's *bed and goes through her belongings.*]

WHORE. It was only one little line!

NUN [*now becoming the hard-boiled secretary, sitting on the bed*]. We do not accept apologies here, dear. Whatever the case, you must be put away.

WHORE [*standing in front of the chair, clicking an imaginary phone*]. Operator—operator, I seem to have a bad connection!

NUN. Put away, dear! That is, after you finish dubbing

your last film. So please hurry! [WHORE *takes frame near cross and mimics a woman singing. Music plays underneath scene, song used in original production, "I'm Through with Love," sung by Marilyn Monroe. Lights on* WHORE *should be almost violet, making her look like a negative.* NUN *paces across stage like a studio guide.*] All those who do not meet our contractual agreement are put away into a lovely sanatorium run by the Franciscan Order, somewhere in California. [*She becomes an insane director.*] You have failed, shall we say, to keep your body and soul together. More flesh, baby! I want to see more flesh! [*She becomes the polite guide.*] Your surroundings will be most pleasant and your fellow cookies will be among the top echelon of public fame, those who have failed to meet our requirements once they have achieved public adoration. Getting there is only a small part of it! [*Personal, girl-to-girl talk.*] We can't let you stay in the public eye, once you begin ruining your image, now can we, sweetheart? [*She becomes a monster lawyer.*] Our business is based on that image! One line, today! Two, tomorrow! Then, three! We can't market a line drawing! [*She sits, returning to secretary.*] We have been fair. You've had two chances. Two contracts. When you didn't make it on your first religious image—we had you politely killed. You could have left then. You were physically unharmed. But no—you stayed to be molded, and now that you are a figment of our imagination—[*She rises to the frame, facing* WHORE *who is still singing to record in slow motion.*]—our sole creation dedicated to fulfill the sexual needs of the population—we hold the rights to your destruction! *Cut!* [WHORE *freezes.*] Get a lawyer if you want, but the law is on our side. This is your second offense and second offenses are subject to imprisonment. [*She takes frame from* WHORE'S *hand and opens it in front of her like a door.*] A limousine awaits, my dear.

WHORE [*moving now, but back in sanatorium*]. But look, the line's gone! I know I have bags now, but the line's gone. And I've stuck to my diet for two years now. [NUN *freezes, holding onto frame, staring at* WHORE.] Why, I've never been so thin. [*An unseen force draws* WHORE *from behind.*] Where are they taking me? Take me out of here. [*She runs to a pole—with her arms extended.*] Take me out!

NUN [*returning frame to its original position*]. Shhhh! They can't. They've already told the world you're dead. [*She picks up an old, worn newspaper from the bed and reads headlines.*] "Star's Suicide from an Overdose of Sleeping Pills!" [*She sits on the bed and turns to the comics.*]

WHORE [*turning from pole suddenly*]. Ridiculous! I've never taken sleeping pills!

NUN [*finding a large bottle of sleeping pills, throwing five into her mouth with the grace of a boa constrictor*]. Of course you never did—a columnist came to your defense and exposed the way you really died in the *National Enquirer.* [*The phone on the bed rings.* NUN *runs back to the chair,* WHORE *runs to the bed and picks up the phone.* NUN *talks into imaginary phone.*] You died of uremic poisoning, sweetheart. I just read it here in the paper.

WHORE. Oh, really! Save me a copy for my scrapbook. How do you spell it?

NUN [*rising*]. The class will now spell "uremic poisoning." U-R-E—[*She gets sleepy, falling back into the chair.*] What do you think I am? A Fuck and Wagnall's Dictionary!

WHORE [*rising from the bed and crossing in front of* NUN'*s chair*]. Ridiculous! There was nothing ever wrong with my—[*Softly.*]—urine—

NUN. Look! Nothing you can do about it. [*She goes to bed fast, as the sleeping pills are begging to work.*] It's a fact now. As far as the world knows, your urine was sick. [*She lies on the bed as though slowly dying.*] At least the publicity department gave you an excitingly unusual death—[WHORE *comes to the side of the bed and anoints* NUN'*s body with an imaginary sprinkler.*] Me! They could have been more original!

WHORE [*as a priest at last rites*]. Dearly beloved, we are gathered here today—

NUN [*raising herself up for her line*]. The Los Angeles Freeway.

WHORE. To mourn the parting of our holy sister in God—

NUN. I had to die on the Los Angeles Freeway.

WHORE. Who was killed today on the Freeway by a Volkswagen bus.

WHORE *returns to cross, trying out several different sexual poses as though posing for a pornographic holy card.*

NUN [*rising in anger*]. Those god-damn Germans! They gave me the wrong parts! They gave me the wrong death! You! [*She faces* WHORE *on cross.*] You, they gave everything.

NUN *runs to* WHORE—*but* WHORE *runs out, both exchanging places quickly.* NUN *now on cross.*

WHORE. No—no, they took it all away! [*She goes back and forth between the bars.*] They took my youth and gave me immortality! What good does that do me here? They took my friends and gave me admirers—cold, distant admirers. And in return—in return! [*She faces cross,* NUN *returns to chair. An unseen force pushes* WHORE *back to cross.*] They held me down, they opened my legs and let men prick me. Paralyzing me into believing I was *this*! [*She goes into a wild sex pose.*] This —shhhhhhhh. [*She hisses like a tigress.*]

NUN [*rising in front of the chair, trying to imitate* WHORE]. Shhhhhhhh—shit! I wish I could do that.

WHORE [*coming off cross, talking to center spot as though it were a camera*]. They took everything. They even took my story that I wrote on the questionnaire when I went to Hollywood and made me do it in my first films. [*She falls onto the bed.*]

NUN [*quickly taking* WHORE's *position in front of cross, posing like a religious holy card*]. The story of a young religious novice. I was the most beautiful child ever conceived, for love instead of oil was rubbed daily into my baby flesh by a little immigrant woman living somewhere in Indiana—who was granted her only one prize in life at the age of forty-five. The male counterpart to this prize is unknown, but may account for the overdevotion of the mother to her love-baby. And the fields excelled themselves in spring—and at Christmas— diamonds fell instead of snow. But then—upon my fifth Christmas, she had to die.

WHORE [*looking up suddenly from the bed*]. No, Mama, no!

NUN. Desertion! And the good sisters of St. Francis came and took me to their near-by orphanage. And when I was of age, I joined. I wanted to hide in the sanctity of the Holy Church—not knowing it was only waiting to attack me in the form of my Mother Superior—Sister Mary Agnes, a notorious bull dyke (that's a tough Lesbian). But in true Catholic tradition, I overlooked it. [*She moves back to cross.*] I turned the other cheek, I forgave and I went on—[*She climbs on cross.*]

WHORE. No—no, I fled through the now barren fields and the deceiving snow that was only cut glass to the farthest place my feet could run. There, I fled to the first pair of arms waiting, protecting. [*She runs to poles, arms extending beyond them.*]

NUN. Dear Murray.

WHORE. But then it became a surrealistic nightmare! He too, in turn, turned against me.

NUN [*still on cross*]. No, Murray, no.

WHORE. Desertion! [*She backs up from pole.*] So I fled to more arms. [*She runs to opposite pole.*] And then they began grabbing—[*Her own hands grab her body as though commanded by an outside force.*]—and then they turned into legs, thousands of legs—pushing, rotating, pushing—[*The same force sucks her back into the cross. She hits cross with her back, her eyes freeze into a daze. Suddenly her own laughter breaks the daze.*] And when I awoke—[*Her laughter now covers the cry of death.*] I found myself screwed right on Hollywood's door.

The lights go to bright. NUN in chair becomes a sweetly vicious job interviewer.

NUN. The door is open. We are open nine to five, five days a week—to help the poor, tortured unemployed find work. So please—hang up your cross and sit down. [WHORE *sits on the bed. She is now about nineteen.*] Now! What may we do for you?

WHORE. Well—I'm looking for work.

NUN. Of course you are, silly me. What else is there here?

WHORE. You see, I'm slightly desperate.

NUN. Aren't we all?

WHORE. You see, I just left my husband. I mean—he really left me—

NUN. Dear! We do not care for personal problems here. Just fill out this work application form. [NUN *hands an imaginary application to* WHORE. WHORE *makes one gigantic X on it, returns it immediately.*] My—you're very fast, sweetheart. We like quickness here. [*She looks at the application.*] Hmmmm, no previous employer, I see.

WHORE. I've never worked before. You see, I was just married and before that I was in the con—— [*She may say "convent" if* NUN *is not fast enough with her cutoff cue.*]

NUN. Dear! Save your explanations. Whatever your story is —we've heard it before. Just answer my questions. Now, my questions will always be prefixed by a "Why, where, or what." When I merely make a casual remark like, "Hmmmm, no previous employer, I see," *shut up!* Got it?

WHORE [*raising her hands quickly, as though talking to her mother*]. Yes, Mama, I got an A in English today!

NUN [*looking at her strangely*]. Hmmmm, this off-the-street trade. Dear, there is nothing wrong in not having worked before. We specialize in helping the virginal employee. Now, ready? What can you do?

WHORE [*running to* NUN *and kneeling*]. Oh! I can pray!

NUN. Hmmmm, I see we're in for a real treat today. [*She rises and goes to where* WHORE *was sitting on the bed.*] That's very good, but do you type-type-type?

WHORE. Well—I do type, sixty W.P.M. If that's what you mean?

NUN. No good! One must type-type-type. That's one-twenty W.P.M. Perhaps you excel on switchboard. Do you switch by chance?

WHORE [*sitting in papal chair*]. Oh yes! Extremely well! I can switch from this——

NUN [*taking character of nineteen-year-old* WHORE]. —to that, in seconds! See!

WHORE [*taking over character of sweetly vicious job interviewer*]. No good, dear! Switching on one's own is fine for personal variety and self-interest and for confusing one's friends. But for economy's sake, it won't get you a paycheck at four-thirty on Fridays.

NUN [*holding up a baby pacifier, found on the bed*]. Oh, Murray, this is the most beautiful engagement ring I've ever seen.

WHORE [*bewildered, bewitched, and bothered*]. Sweetheart! My advice, dear, if I were you—[*She is now holding up her own pacifier.*]—and who of us is not each other?—is to seek fame. It's the only way someone like yourself—who is unable to do anything well—can get any attention.

Both rise and meet, holding hands.

NUN. Oh—thank you.

WHORE. No—thank *you.*

Both exchange places and characters in one turn.

NUN. No, thank *you* very much.

WHORE [*back where she started*]. No, thank *you* very much for helping me.

NUN. Hardly worth a mention. [WHORE *begins to walk offstage.*] Oh Miss! [WHORE *turns.*] This is a state employment agency. We can't have other people's problems cluttering up our waiting room! [*She shakes* WHORE.] Now, can we? So please, take your cross with you!

NUN *shoves* WHORE *against cross.* NUN *returns to the chair, laughing.* WHORE *begins laughing as she was when employment scene broke into her memory. Gregorian music returns, lights go down, re-establishing the shadows of the sanatorium.*

WHORE. You see—[*She comes off cross to talk to the unseen camera.*]—they changed the ending slightly. It really ends with the heroine dangling by her neck from a cross on the fourth wall of her cookie room—in a Franciscan sanatorium somewhere in California—confessing her sins in her last few seconds before death to her former self —killed long before—an old miscast bit player! [*She sits on the bed, exhausted from the last marathon line.*]

NUN [*rising like a horny volcano*]. Bitch! Now listen here, Peroxide Lady! I was not a bit player! [*She looks into an unseen camera.*] I did cameo roles.

WHORE [*straightening up the four thousand objects on her bed*]. You mean—chameleon, dear. You were invisible.

NUN [*center—into camera*]. If only they'd released my *one* starring vehicle, *The Pregnant Popette*—I would have made it on my own without having been changed. But they said it wasn't commercial. Of course, I knew the real reason. They had to go and preview it for the Ecumenical Vatican Council, and twenty-six cardinals, on the spot, had menstrual attacks. A white dove flew up —and a miracle was declared. I mean—look—things like that don't happen every day! Yes, a miracle was declared, but the film was declared "objectionable for all" and destroyed. I have been censured my whole life, while you freely frolicked in fuck-me movies and the crowds cheered, "New Art Form," "True to Life," "Poignant"—[*She sits down in the chair with the religious pomp of an archbishop.*] "Positively, No One Under Sixteen Permitted Without Their Psychiatrist!"

WHORE *comes to* NUN *and kneels at the side of the chair.*
WHORE *wears a proper scarf over hair and has a lighted
cigarette in her religiously folded hands. Both scarf and
cigarette were obtained from that miracle prop-holder, the*
WHORE's *bed.*

WHORE. Forgive me, Mother, for I have sinned. My last
confession was five seconds ago and these are my sins.

NUN [*making the sign of the cross over her*]. Yes, my child.

WHORE. I have sinned against the church and my conscience by freely frolicking in fuck-me movies. I have
committed the sin of physical vanity. [*She speaks the
next line quickly, to get it over with.*] I have slept with
a man. [*She resumes her normal pace again.*] I have
missed Sunday Mass for the last six years due to my
shooting schedule. And I have tried suicide on five oc-
casions in the last week due to self-indulgence.

NUN. Let us go back, my child— You have slept with a
man? Be more specific!

The following very quickly.

WHORE. He was of medium height.

NUN. Yes.

WHORE. Hair of brown.

NUN. Nice.

WHORE. Protruding nose.

NUN. Delicious! His body, my child—get to his body, fast!

WHORE. Thin.

NUN. No!

WHORE. Athletic?

NUN. I like that much better.

WHORE. Wide strong shoulders——

NUN. Good.

WHORE. —hair that patterned a T on his chest——

NUN. Better!

WHORE. —firm solid stomach——

NUN. Best!

WHORE. —strong, overdeveloped legs——

NUN [*grabbing* WHORE's *lighted cigarette*]. Don't dilly-dally—go on! [*She puffs on the cigarette like a four-year-old Bette Davis.*]

WHORE. I met him on the beach—in back of my summer home—the Pacific!

NUN. Forget the details and get down to the meat of it!

WHORE. He was pre-set there on the sand—naked on a white towel. Not seeing him, I ran into the ocean unclothed. He followed in after—shouting—"I'll save you —*save you!*"

NUN [*covering* WHORE's *mouth with her hand*]. Shhhh! There might be a raid!

WHORE. But I wasn't drowning!—But he said that was all right because, "We never know when we really are." Then he took me back—his massive arms around my breasts, and gently laid me down on the sand and then ——[*Pause.*]

NUN. The weather forecast for the beaches today—is beautiful, for getting laid.

WHORE. That's it—and then he came down upon me and the strength of his chest covered the moon. [*She is now on the floor looking up into the spot.*]

NUN [*reflectively*]. I have waited my whole life for the moon to disappear.

WHORE. And then his pulsating virility groped for my one vulnerable area!

NUN [*as phone operator*]. The confessional you have just dialed cannot be forgiven unless you give the area code!

WHORE [*going insane with the passion of total recall*]. —And upon the discovery of his hand—the screams of my body were deafened by the clash of one giant wave against an enormous defiant rock!

NUN [*going into heat*]. Rock? R as in rip? O as in out? C as in clit? K as in knooky-knooky?

WHORE. Yes—yes, and then like an angry phoenix imprisoned in the hot sand—his organ rose from his body and I could hear——

NUN. Organ? What did you hear? Brahms? Beethoven? Bach?

WHORE [*now on the floor, reliving the final attack of rape*]. I could hear the screams of my naked flesh crying out for forgiveness—but there was no softness—and then the muscle of his body penetrated into the guarded nerves of mine and I could feel—oh how I could feel——

NUN. What? What did you feel?

WHORE. *I could feel——!*

NUN. *What in the hell did you feel!???* [*She is now standing over* WHORE *on the floor.*]

WHORE. *I could——*

NUN. What? *What?!*

WHORE [*making hand motion to imaginary cameraman*]. *Cut! Cut.* [*She jumps up from the floor—*NUN *is frozen from rejection.*] You don't think I'd give you the satisfaction!

NUN'*s body revolves, facing out, in front of the chair. During the quick revolution she becomes herself at sixteen.*

NUN. I wasn't asking for satisfaction——Murray. All I want is a—Murray, I know the light says "walk," but I am not crossing the street or going anywhere until we settle this thing—right here and now! All I want is just one baby, Murray. [*She becomes aware of the lighted cigarette in her hand from previous scene.*] Okay, I'm sorry for smoking in the street. [*She throws the cigarette away.*] I know—I know you hate demanding women but this is America, 1942, and we do have a little more equality. I read it—that's how I know. We've been married for eight months now and I feel a little funny about still being a virgin after eight months of marriage. My relatives are starting to talk. What do you mean, "I have no relatives"? I have Aunt Clara. She's been knitting baby booties for five months now. She's already got thirty-two pairs. No, Murray, I am not going to tell dizzy Aunt Clara to go into the baby bootie business. She's got enough problems. Now please be serious!

I know it was a mistake now. They happen every day. Just take a look around us, Murray. We ain't unique. Look—look at that blind guy over there. You know, we should thank God we're not deformed! What if we didn't have our eyes like that poor blind man? [*She turns in the direction she saw the blind man.*] What? No! I don't have any change. Will you stop begging me? Can't you *see* I'm fighting with my husband? [*She turns back.*] Murray—get back here! I know—I know you'll never leave me because your father doesn't believe in divorce and would only cut you off from his import Chinese silk business—and God knows I have no place to go except back to the convent and that crazy Sister Mary Agnes. I mean, a girl has only so many cheeks she can turn! Murray, you got a dirty mind!—No, I don't care what size—So let's make a compromise, Murray. Just one baby? Look, we have two doors to our apartment. We can get separate locks and divide the place in half with doors—and when your family comes over we can take them down. You know—you'd be surprised how cheap those accordian doors are. *Just one baby*—please. You know, Murray, if it was another woman, I could at least be jealous.

Oh—no—no, don't cry, Murray. Please don't cry. I'm sorry I said anything. It was just that you asked me what I wanted for Christmas and——[*To herself, watching an imaginary man walking away.*]—Good-bye, Murray. [*Shouting slightly, with resignation in her tired voice.*] No, Murray, I don't care what size Christmas tree you get. [*She falls quietly back into the chair and freezes, watching the imaginary man disappear from sight.*]

Music plays "Opera for Music Boxes" Westminster Hi-Fi. WHORE *rises on the bed as* NUN *sits on last line.* WHORE's *next line should come right after and right out of* NUN's *last line.*

WHORE. The biggest tree on the hill, Mama! We'll cut down the biggest green tree on the hill! Only there's no trespassing, Mama. We won't be able to. [*She looks at* NUN *who has been crying from previous scene.*] There —there, now, Mama, don't cry. We'll do what we did last year. Remember? You'll dress me up like the white angel star and stand me up on the table next to the fireplace! Okay, Mama? Now you decorate me. [*She goes under the bed and pulls out small boxes of red and green bulbs and silver tinsel.*] See—I saved all the tinsel from last year. Now you put the shiny bulbs on my ears. [*She puts the Christmas bulbs around her ears.*] Look! See how they pick up all the light, Mama! [*She then takes tinsel and holds some in each hand, and also puts on a head-band of stars and tinsel. She rises now on the bed, kneeling.*] Now you help me up on the table— careful, Mama—don't strain yourself. There we are. [*Her arms are now extended out as an angel, freezing a warm smile like a little child—softly.*] Now say it. Say what you always say—Mama.

NUN. Shine, baby, shine. Show Mama how you can shine.

WHORE. Yes, Mama. Am I shining okay, Mama? Mama, the table's shaking! I'm losing my balance. Catch me, Mama—I'm falling. Catch me! [*She falls down onto the bed, but not off.*] Oh thank you, Mama. I was scared there for a——[*She looks over to* NUN, *who is now bent over in the chair like an old woman.*]

NUN [*closing eyes*]. Death.

WHORE. No, Mama, no! [*She gets back up on her knees, trying to get attention of her mother again.*] Look! See I'm getting back on the table again all by myself—Say it, Mama. [*Loud.*] Say it! I'm going to fall—catch me, Mama—I'm falling! [*She falls on the bed with more panic than before. The* NUN *does not move or open her eyes. Toward the camera the* WHORE *now continues.*] But she never caught me again. Mama had to die. [*She gets off the bed and goes near* NUN.] A note falls from her hand—but I am only five years old—I can't read it. [*Now she runs for poles, with tinsel still in hands, etc.*] I run out into the hall of our tenement apartment, screaming—"*Death—Death,*" but no door opens. I run up and down the stairs, "Death—Death." [*She breaks panic and relaxes, turns, faces the cross from a distance.*] And then with some strange new understanding I've never known before I can read Mama's note and I take it in my hand out into the street—[*She walks to the cross.*]—of the small town in which we live—and I shout it. [*She turns now on cross, facing black vacuum.*] "Please love my baby. It's Christmas. Please love my baby."

And slowly, one by one—the small doors of the little houses open and all the tiny people come out with their arms all extended, saying together, "Of course we will. Merry Christmas. We will." And poor little uneducated Mama, who had never done anything in her whole life, had performed a miracle. By dying, she made an unimportant little town full of lonely people living in small shingled cells come together for the first time. And I run back home—[*She goes to* Nun.]—I pick up Mama's face and I sing one last tribute. [*She holds* Nun's *head in her hands.*] "They will! Merry Christmas, Mama. It's okay. They will!" [*The music box stops.* Nun *awakes and grabs* Whore's *wrists.*] But in the morning, a nasty nun came to take me away!

Nun [*raising herself and* Whore]. Come, my dear. We will go for a lovely walk. [*She takes off her robe.*] Here, take my robe—because it's your favorite weather— It's snowing diamonds all the way to St. Francis' Home for Deserted Children. [Whore *now wears the robe.*] My —what a lovely nun you'll make. Agnes will be very pleased with you.

Whore [*Gregorian music returns*]. Shhhhh! Someone's coming. They must have called him by now. Of all—I knew he'd come.

Nun. Murray? Of course! It's been months! Years? I must look a mess! Is my face all right? [*She is face to face with* Whore.]

Whore. Is my hair?

Nun [*grabbing beads back from* Whore *as though she were going to strangle* Whore's *throat*]. Death!

WHORE. No! Not yet! [*She points to center spotlight.*] When that light goes out—that's when! [*She takes beads off.*] Here—would you like to wear them for him? [NUN *takes them.*] And some cologne?

WHORE *rubs some from behind her ears onto* NUN. WHORE *takes* NUN's *headpiece and puts it on herself.*

NUN [*now in her slip with* WHORE's *beads around neck*]. White beads—dangling, waiting for me to commit one mortal sin so they can strangle me. Free! My mind has been freed, Mama. —And I accept my body now and it isn't too late, for a man still approaches—He's coming back, Mama. And when he opens that one door—the only barrier between us—I shall completely love the man nearing. For I can now, Mama. Completely. I have finally learned to do something. I'm getting my one prize in life now, Mama. Soon! When that door opens——

WHORE [*now complete in* NUN's *costume—sitting in her chair and dressed in her character*]. His hand is on the knob. It is turning. [*Loud.*] Show him, bitch!

Missa Luba returns, building in volume until the end.

NUN [*pulled back one step nearer to cross by force*]. I can't breathe—I'm dying, Mama!

WHORE [*angry as she now has no patience with cowards*]. You can't screw up now! You mustn't die yet! You understand now. You're free. There are so many things you could tell him for both of us. It would get us out of here. His face is nearing! Now!

NUN [*backing up one more step nearer to cross, losing breath*]. I—can't breathe, Murray.

WHORE. Deserter!

NUN [*crying for life in the last second*]. No——

WHORE. Yes.

NUN. No——

WHORE. Yes.

NUN. Death, death—but no door opens.

WHORE. Good.

NUN. I run up and down the halls of my mind screaming——

WHORE. Go on.

NUN. "Why didn't you catch me, Mama?" "Just one baby, Murray."

WHORE. Get to the meat of it, dear.

NUN. And then—with some strange new understanding I've never known before—I can read Mama's note and I take it in my hand out into the streets of the world and shout it——

WHORE. The truth now, the truth!

NUN. "I didn't want her! I didn't want that bastard!"

WHORE. Excellent.

NUN. And then, one by one—all the little people come out of their tiny houses chanting together——

WHORE. Let's hear it.

NUN. "That's your problem, baby! Stop all that noise! It's Christmas now." It's Christmas. [*A force pulls* NUN *backward violently to the cross and her back is heard hitting the wood.*] It's Christmas. Christmas——

WHORE. Good.

NUN. And I fell—and fell asleep there in some strange street with the snow now coming down like glass cutting into my naked flesh. And when I awoke—my blood hardened to my body like cheap paint—I found myself alone, dangling by my neck—[*She is now totally insane.*]—with my breasts hanging free [*Holding them, staring at them as a child would stare at a toy.*]—suspended—waiting eternally for milk-hungry mankind.

WHORE [*rising from chair like a volcano*]. Retake! [*She hits* NUN *in the face.*] What did I tell you about that god-damn line?! It won't sell— It's not commercial! *Those fools want their money's worth!* More flesh, baby —more flesh! Let's sell it! Come on—sell it!

NUN [*now crying alone in the last second*]. Spotlights dancing—forming halos in my hair! [*She hits her own head, as though she might awake. Missa Luba swells with the* NUN-WHORE's *fear.*] See—Mama—I've finally learned to do something. I'm a star, Mama!

WHORE *dances like a vengeful cannibal. She progresses to* NUN *on cross, as in the beginning. She takes the end of beads around* NUN's *neck and begins saying "Hail Marys" —pulling them up to strangle her.*

NUN. No, Mama, no! Catch me, Mama—I'm falling. Catch me, Mama.

WHORE. Cut!

NUN [*turns her head sharply and freezes wide-eyed in death*]. See—Mama—I'm——

Lights fade quickly. Lights come up once more immediately —this time not spotlights but rather several camera flashlights cutting through the darkness showing ten snapshots of the last picture freeze. Time: approximately, ten seconds.

NOTE: *The Missa Luba should be played even until the audience leaves the theatre as it has some very memorable and singable tunes.*

THE OWL ANSWERS

A Play in One Act

by

ADRIENNE KENNEDY

To Edward Albee

CHARACTERS

SHE *who is* CLARA PASSMORE *who is the* VIRGIN MARY *who is the* BASTARD *who is the* OWL

BASTARD'S BLACK MOTHER *who is the* REVEREND'S WIFE *who is* ANNE BOLEYN

GODDAM FATHER *who is the* RICHEST WHITE MAN IN THE TOWN *who is the* DEAD FATHER *who is* REVEREND PASSMORE

THE WHITE BIRD *who is* REVEREND PASSMORE'S CANARY *who is* GOD'S DOVE

THE NEGRO MAN

SHAKESPEARE

CHAUCER

WILLIAM THE CONQUEROR

The characters change slowly back and forth into and out of themselves, leaving some garment from their previous selves upon them always to remind us of the nature of SHE who is CLARA PASSMORE who is the VIRGIN MARY who is the BASTARD who is the OWL's world.

SCENE: A New York subway is the Tower of London is a Harlem Hotel Room is St. Peter's.

———

The Owl Answers was first produced by Lucille Lortel at the White Barn Theatre, Westport, Connecticut, on August 29, 1965. The cast was as follows:

SHE	Ellen Holly
BASTARD'S BLACK MOTHER	Lynn Hamilton
GODDAM FATHER	Bill Moor
THE WHITE BIRD	Ross Parkes
THE NEGRO MAN	Milton Irons
SHAKESPEARE	Michael Warren Powell
CHAUCER	Alex Giannini
WILLIAM THE CONQUEROR	Patrick Gorman

The play was directed by Michael Kahn, lighting Gary Long.

THE OWL ANSWERS

The scene is shaped like a subway car. The sounds are subway sounds and the main props of a subway are visible— poles, fans, lights. Two seats on the scene are like seats on the subway, the seat in which SHE WHO IS sits and NEGRO MAN's seat. The colors of the subway props are black.

Seated is a plain, pallid, middle-aged Negro woman, wearing a cotton summer dress that is too long, a pair of white wedged sandals. Her hair is tightly curled and exceedingly well combed in the manner a great many prim Negro women wear their hair. SHE sits staring into space. SHE is CLARA PASSMORE who is the VIRGIN MARY who is the BASTARD who is the OWL. Scene moves, lights flash, a sense of exploding imprisonment.

SHE WHO IS speaks in a soft voice as a Negro schoolteacher from Savannah would. SHE WHO IS carries white handkerchiefs, SHE WHO IS carries notebooks that throughout the play like the handkerchiefs fall. SHE will pick them up, glance frenziedly at a page from a notebook, be distracted, place the notebooks in a disorderly pile, drop them again, etc.

The scene should lurch, lights flash, hand straps move, gates slam. When THEY come in and exit, THEY move in the manner of people on a train, too. There is the noise of the train, the sound of moving steel on the track.

The WHITE BIRD's wings should flutter loudly.

The gates, the High Altar, the ceiling, and the Dome are like St. Peter's; the walls are like the Tower of London.

The music which SHE WHO IS hears at the most violent times of her experience should be Haydn's Concerto for Horn in D (Third Movement).

Objects on the stage (beards, wigs, faces) should be used in the manner that people use everyday objects such as spoons or newspapers.

The Tower Gate should be black, yet slam like a subway door.

The gates slam. FOUR PEOPLE *enter from different directions.* THEY *are* SHAKESPEARE, WILLIAM THE CONQUEROR, CHAUCER, *and* ANNE BOLEYN, *but too they are strangers entering a subway on a summer night, too they are the guards in the Tower of London. Their lines throughout the play are not spoken specifically by one person but by all or part of them.*

THEY. Bastard. [THEY *start at a distance eventually crowding her. Their lines are spoken coldly.* SHE WHO IS *is only a prisoner to them.*] You are not his ancestor. Keep her locked there, guard. Bastard.

SHE. You must let me go down to the chapel to see him. He is my father.

THEY [*jeering*]. Your father?

SHE. He is my father.

THEY. Keep her locked there, guard. [CHAUCER *locks the gates.*]

SHE. We came this morning. We were visiting the place of our ancestors, my father and I. We had a lovely morning, we rose in darkness, took a taxi past Hyde Park through the Marble Arch to Buckingham Palace, we had our morning tea at Lyons, then came out to the Tower. We were wandering about the gardens, my father leaning on my arm, speaking of you, William the Conqueror. My father loved you, William——

THEY [*interrupting*]. If you are his ancestor why are you a Negro? Yes, why is it you are a Negro if you are his ancestor? Keep her locked there.

SHE. You must let me go down to the chapel to see him.

THEY *stare coldly,* CHAUCER *and* SHAKESPEARE *exit, slamming the gate, scene moves, lights flash.* ANNE BOLEYN *and* WILLIAM THE CONQUEROR *remain staring at her.* CHAUCER *and* SHAKESPEARE *return carrying a stiff dead man in a black suit. The most noticeable thing about him is his hair —long, silky, white hair that hangs as they bring him through the gate and place him at her feet.*

THEY. Here is your father.

THEY *then all exit through various gate entrances.* SHE
*picks up the dead man, drags him to a dark, carved, high-
back chair on the right. At the same time a dark* NEGRO
MAN, *with a dark suit and black glasses on, enters from
the right gate and sits on the other subway seat. Flashing,
movement, slamming of gate, fans twirl. The* NEGRO MAN
sits up very straight and proceeds to watch SHE WHO IS.
*Until he speaks to her, he watches her constantly with a
wild, cold stare.*

The DEAD FATHER *appears dead. He is dead. Yet as* SHE
*watches, he moves and comes to life. Throughout the play
when the characters change and come to life it must give
the impression of logic yet be understood that the other
state actually existed. When the* DEAD FATHER *was dead,
he was dead; when he is the* REVEREND, *he is the* REVER-
END. SHE WHO IS *always watches them as they change,
for this is her mental state. The* DEAD FATHER *removes his
hair, takes off his white face, from the chair he takes a
white church robe and puts it on. Beneath his white hair
is dark Negro hair. He is now* REVEREND PASSMORE. *After
he dresses he looks about as if something is missing, seizes
the gate, exits, and returns with a gold bird cage that hangs
near the chair and a white battered Bible. Very matter-of-
factly he sits down in the chair, stares for a moment at
the cage, then opens the Bible, starting to read.* SHE
*watches, highly distracted, until he falls asleep. Movement,
flash, twirl.*

ANNE BOLEYN *has remained behind during that time where
she stands near a subway pole. She throws red rice at* SHE
WHO IS *and the* DEAD FATHER *who is now* REVEREND
PASSMORE. *They see her.* SHE *exits and returns with a great
black gate (like the gate at Valladolid) and places the
gate where the pole is. It is clear now that she has erected
the gate but she cannot pass through it.* SHE WHO IS *runs
to* ANNE BOLEYN.

SHE. Anne, Anne Boleyn. [ANNE *throws rice at* SHE WHO IS
CLARA PASSMORE *who is the* VIRGIN MARY *who is the*
BASTARD *who is the* OWL.] Anne, you know so much of
love, won't you help me? They took my father away and

will not let me see him. They locked me in this tower and I can see them taking his body across to the chapel to be buried and see his white hair hanging down. Let me into the chapel. He is my blood father. I am almost white, am I not? Let me into St. Paul's Chapel. Let me please go down to St. Paul's Chapel. I am his daughter. [ANNE *appears to listen quite attentively, but her reply is to turn into the* BASTARD'S BLACK MOTHER. *She takes off part of her own long dress and puts on a rose-colored cheap lace dress, the kind of a dress a Southern Negro woman might wear to dress up in, and anything dark on her face.* SHE WHO IS*'s reaction is to run back to her subway seat.* SHE *drops her notebooks. The* BASTARD'S BLACK MOTHER *opens her arms to* SHE WHO IS. SHE *returns to the gate.*] Anne. [*As if trying to bring back* ANNE BOLEYN.]

BASTARD'S BLACK MOTHER [*laughs and throws a white bridal bouquet at her*]. Clara, I am not Anne. I am the Bastard's Black Mother, who cooked for somebody.

Still holding out her arms, she kneels by the gate, her kinky hair awry, eyes closed, she stares upward, praying. Suddenly she stops praying and pulls SHE WHO IS *through the gate.*

The WHITE BIRD, *with very loud fluttering wings, flies down from St. Peter's Dome and goes into the cage.* REVEREND PASSMORE *gets up and closes the cage door.*

SHE. Anne, it is I.

BASTARD'S BLACK MOTHER. Clara, you were conceived by your Goddam Father who was the Richest White Man in the Town and somebody that cooked for him. That's why you're an owl. [*Laughs.*] That's why when I see you, Mary, I cry. I cry when I see Marys, cry for their deaths.

The WHITE BIRD *flies in the cage.* REVEREND *reads.*

The BASTARD'S BLACK MOTHER *stands at the gate, watches, then takes off rose lace dress and black face; beneath her black face is a more pallid Negro face; pulls down her hair, longer dark hair, and puts on a white dress. From a fold in the dress she takes out a picture of Christ, then kneels and stares upward. She is the* REVEREND'S WIFE. *Scene moves, flashes.*

REVEREND'S WIFE [*kneeling.* REVEREND *stands and watches her.* REVEREND'S WIFE *takes a vial from her gown and holds it up*]. These are the fruits of my maidenhead, owl blood Clara who is the Bastard Clara Passmore to whom we gave our name, see the owl blood, that is why I cry when I see Marys, cry for their deaths, Owl Mary Passmore.

SHE *gets up, exits from a side gate.* THEY *come in.* SHE WHO IS *goes to the* REVEREND *as if to implore him. He then changes into the* DEAD FATHER, *resuming his dirty white hair.* THEY *stand about.*

SHE. Dear Father, my Goddam Father who was the Richest White Man in the Town, who is Dead Father—you know that England is the home of dear Chaucer, Dickens and dearest Shakespeare. Winters we spent here at the Tower, our chambers were in the Queen's House, summers we spent at Stratford with dearest Shakespeare. It was all so lovely. I spoke to Anne Boleyn, Dead Father. She knows so much of love and suffering and I believe she is going to try to help me. [*Takes a sheaf of papers from her notebooks; they fall to the floor.*] Communications, all communications to get you the proper burial, the one you deserve in St. Paul's Chapel. They are letting you rot, my Goddam Father who was the Richest Man in the Town—they are letting you rot in that town in Georgia. I haven't been able to see the King. I'll speak again to Anne Boleyn. She knows so much of love.

Shows the papers to the DEAD FATHER *who sits with his hair hanging down, dead. She begins to unbutton her dress fitfully; naturally, since she is the black mother's bastard, her skin is black underneath. The* NEGRO MAN *continues to watch her.* SHE WHO IS *moves about, flash twirling,* REVEREND'S WIFE *prays.* SHE WHO IS *goes again to the* DEAD FATHER, *takes him by the hair, stares into his dead face.* WHITE BIRD *flies inside the cage.* REVEREND'S WIFE

*stops praying, watches, smiles. Scene moves, fluttering of
wings, lights flash.*

DEAD FATHER. If you are my ancestor why are you a Negro,
Bastard? What is a Negro doing at the Tower of London
staying at the Queen's House? Clara, I am your Goddam Father who was the Richest White Man in the
Town and you are a schoolteacher in Savannah who
spends her summers at Teachers College. You are not
my ancestor. You are my bastard. Keep her locked there,
William.

THEY *stare at her like passengers on a subway, standing,
holding the hand straps.*

SHE. We were wandering about the garden, you leaning on
my arm, speaking of William the Conqueror. We sat
on the stone bench to rest. When we stood up you
stumbled and fell onto the walk—dead. Dead. I called
the guard. Then I called the Warden and told him my
father had just died, that we had been visiting London
together, the place of our ancestors and all the lovely
English, and my father just died. [*She reaches out to
touch him.*]

DEAD FATHER. You are not my ancestor.

SHE. They jeered. They brought me to this tower and
locked me up. I can see they're afraid of me. From the
tower I saw them drag you across the court . . . your
hair hanging down. They have taken off your shoes and
you are stiff. You are stiff. [*Touches him.*] My dear
father.

Music: Haydn.

DEAD FATHER. Daughter of somebody that cooked for me.
[*Smiles.*]

He then ignores SHE WHO IS, *changes into the* REVEREND,
takes the Bible and starts to read. The WHITE BIRD *flies
inside the cage. Wings flutter. The* REVEREND'S WIFE *praying, lights a candle. The* REVEREND *watches the* BIRD, *sits
down, watches the* BIRD *flutter, as though he expects something from him . . . as an answer,* REVEREND'S WIFE

lights another candle, then puts on her black face, rose
dress. Some of the red rice has fallen near her, she says
"Oww," and starts to peck at it like a bird. She then sits
up facing front on her knees, eyes wide open, very still,
"Oww," she repeats, "Ow." SHE WHO IS *wanders about,*
then comes to speak to the BASTARD'S BLACK MOTHER *who*
remains seated like an owl.

End music.

SHE. It was you the Bastard's Black Mother who told me.
I asked you where did Mr. William Mattheson's family
come from and you, my Black Mother, said: I believe
his father came from England. England, I said. England
is the Brontës' home. Did you know Black Bastard's
Mother, who cooked for somebody, in the Reverend's
parlor—there in a glass bookcase are books and England
is the home of Chaucer, Dickens, and Shakespeare. Black
Mother who cooked for somebody Mr. William Mattheson died today. I was at the College. The Reverend's
Wife called me, Clara who is the Bastard who is the
Virgin Mary who is the Owl. Clara, who is the Bastard
who is the Virgin Mary who is the Owl, Clara she said
the Reverend told me to call you and tell you Mr. William Mattheson died today or it was yesterday he died
yesterday. It was yesterday. The Reverend told me to
tell you it was yesterday he died and it is today they're
burying him. Clara who is the Bastard, you mustn't
come. Don't do anything foolish like come to the
funeral, Mary. You've always been such a fool about
that white man, Clara.

But I am coming, the Black Bastard's Mother. I am coming, my Goddam Father who was the Richest White
Man in Jacksonville, Georgia. When I arrive in London,
I'll go out to Buckingham Palace, see the Thames at
dusk, and Big Ben. I'll go for lovely walks through Hyde
Park, and to innumerable little tearooms with great bay
windows and white tablecloths on little white tables and
order tea. I will go all over and it will be June. Then
I'll go out to the Tower to see you, my father.

BASTARD'S BLACK MOTHER *has remained like an owl.* THEY *come on and stand as passengers on the subway speaking at random.*

THEY. If you are his ancestor what are you doing on the subway at night looking for men? What are you doing looking for men to take to a hotel room in Harlem? Negro Men? Negro Men Clara Passmore?

In reply the BASTARD'S BLACK MOTHER *laughs a bird laugh. The* WHITE BIRD *flies out of the cage.*

SHE [*runs to the* BIRD]. My dead father's bird: God's Dove. My father died today.

BIRD [*mocking*]. My father died today God's Dove.

SHE. He was the Richest White Man in our Town. I was conceived by him and somebody that cooked for him.

BIRD. What are you doing in the Tower of London then?

The REVEREND *becomes the* DEAD FATHER *who comes forward, takes the* BIRD, *puts him in the cage, shuts the door.*

SHE. My father. [*He turns, stares at her, and comes toward her and dies; it is his death in the gardens.*] What were you saying of William, my father, you loved William so. [*She holds him in her arms. He opens his eyes.*]

DEAD FATHER [*waking*]. Mary, at least you are coming to me.

Music: Haydn.

SHE. I am not Mary, I am Clara, your daughter, Reverend Passmore—I mean Dead Father.

BIRD *flies in the cage.*

DEAD FATHER. Yes, my Mary, you are coming into my world. You are filled with dreams of my world. I sense it all.

Silence except for the wild fluttering of the BIRD'S *wings.* NEGRO MAN *stares, lights flash, sound of steel on the track, movement.*

NEGRO MAN. At last you are coming to me. [*Smiles.*]

DEAD FATHER. Mary, come in here for eternity. Are you confused? Yes, I can see you are confused.

THEY *come on.*

THEY. Are you confused?

One of them, CHAUCER, *is now dressed as the* REVEREND. *He comes, falls down onto the empty high-backed chair, and sits staring into the Bible.*

DEAD FATHER. So at last you are coming to me, Bastard.

BASTARD'S BLACK MOTHER *exits from gate, returns, part owl with owl feathers upon her, dragging a great dark bed through the gate; the gate slams.*

BASTARD'S BLACK MOTHER. Why be confused? The Owl was your beginning, Mary. [*Begins to build with the bed and feathers the High Altar; feathers fly.*]

SHE. He came to me in the outhouse, he came to me under the porch, in the garden, in the fig tree. He told me you are an owl, ow, oww, I am your beginning, ow. You belong here with us owls in the fig tree not to somebody that cooks for your Goddam Father, oww, and I ran to the outhouse in the night crying oww, Bastard they say the people in the town all say Bastard, but I, I belong to God and the owls, ow and I sat in the fig tree. My Goddam Father is the Richest White Man in the Town but I belong to the owls, till Reverend Passmore adopted me they all said Bastard . . . then my father was a reverend. He preached in the Holy Baptist Church on the top of the hill, on the top of the Holy Hill, and everybody in the town knew then my name was Mary. My father was the Baptist preacher and I was Mary. [THEY *enter, slamming, lights flash, stand about passengers, the* NEGRO MAN *stares.* SHE *sits in the subway seat.*]

I who am the ancestor of Shakespeare, Chaucer, and William the Conqueror, I went to London the Queen Elizabeth, London they all said who ever heard of anybody going to London but I went. I stayed in my cabin the whole crossing, solitary. I was the only Negro there. I read books on subjects like the History of London, the Life of Anne Boleyn, Mary Queen of Scots, and Sonnets. When I wasn't in the cabin I wrapped myself in a great sweater and sat over the dark desks in the writing room and wrote my father. I wrote him every day of my journey. [*Pause.*]

I met my father once when my mother took me to visit him and we had to go into the back door of his house. [*Talking to herself.* NEGRO MAN *stares.*]

I was married once briefly. On my wedding day the Reverend's Wife came to me and said when I see Marys I cry for their deaths, when I see brides, Clara, I cry for their deaths. But the past years I've spent teaching alone in Savannah. And alone I'm almost thirty-four, I who am the ancestor of somebody that cooked for somebody and William the Conqueror. [BASTARD'S BLACK MOTHER *looks more like an owl.* DEAD FATHER *dies again.* BASTARD'S BLACK MOTHER *bangs at the gate.* THEY *all laugh.* The NEGRO MAN *stands before* SHE WHO IS. SHE *screams at the* DEAD FATHER *and the* MOTHER.]

You must know how it is to be filled with yearning.

THEY *laugh.* REVEREND *stares into the cage.* MOTHER *bangs at the gate.*

NEGRO MAN [*touches her*]. And what exactly do you yearn for?

SHE. You know.

NEGRO MAN. No, what is it?

SHE. I want what I think everyone wants.

NEGRO MAN. And what is that?

SHE. I don't know. Love or something, I guess.

NEGRO MAN. Out there Owl?

DEAD FATHER. In St. Paul's Chapel Owl?

THEY. Keep her locked there, guard.

BASTARD'S BLACK MOTHER. Is this love to come from out there?

SHE. I don't know what you mean.

DEAD FATHER. I know you don't.

THEY. We know you don't.

SHE. Call me Mary.

NEGRO MAN. Mary?

THEY. Keep her locked there.

DEAD FATHER. If you are Mary what are you doing in the Tower of London?

NEGRO MAN. Mary?

The REVEREND *gets up, goes to the cage, in a silent gesture, takes the* WHITE BIRD *from the cage, holds the* BIRD *in his hand, gazes into its eyes, tugs at his beard; and gazes into the* BIRD'S *eyes. The* BASTARD'S BLACK MOTHER *reappears on the other side of the gate, owl feathers about her, bearing a vial, still wearing the long black hair of the* REVEREND'S WIFE.

BASTARD'S BLACK MOTHER. When I see sweet Marys I cry for their deaths, Clara the Reverend took my maidenhead and I am not a Virgin any more and that is why you must be Mary always be Mary Clara. [*Goes on building the High Altar; the* BIRD *laughs.*]

SHE. Mama. [*The* BASTARD'S BLACK MOTHER *stops building, stares, then turns into* ANNE BOLEYN, *while* CLARA *stands, calling.*] Mama. [*Watches her change to* ANNE BOLEYN, *who goes on building.* THEY *watch.*]

BASTARD'S BLACK MOTHER. What are you doing on the subway if you are his ancestor?

SHE. I am Clara Passmore. I am not His ancestor. I ride, look for men to take to a Harlem Hotel Room, to love, dress them as my father, beg to take me.

THEY. Take you?

SHE. Yes, take me Clara Passmore.

THEY. Take you, Bastard?

SHE. There is a bed there.

The WHITE BIRD *laughs like the* MOTHER.

WILLIAM. And do they take you?

SHE. No, William.

WILLIAM. No?

SHE. Something happens.

WILLIAM. Happens?

CHAUCER. Happens?

SHE. Something strange always happens, Chaucer.

CHAUCER. Where?

SHE. In the hotel room. It's how I've passed my summer in New York, nights I come to the subway, look for men. It's how I've passed my summer. If they would only take me? But something strange happens.

ANNE. Take you, Mary? Why, Mary?

ANNE BOLEYN *builds.* THEY *exit,* CLARA *dressed like the* VIRGIN *in a blue crepe shawl, wanders about, then goes to* ANNE.

SHE. Anne, you must help me. They, my Black Mother and my Goddam Father and the Reverend and his wife, they and the teachers at the school where I teach, and Professor Johnson, the principal to whom I'm engaged, they all say London, who in the hell ever heard of anybody going to London. Of course I shouldn't go. They said I had lost my mind, read so much, buried myself in my books. They say I should stay and teach summer school to the kids up from Oglethorpe. But I went.

All the way from Piccadilly Circus out there in the black taxi, my cold hands were colder than ever. Then it happened no sooner than I left the taxi and passed down a gray walk through a dark gate and into a garden where there were black ravens on the grass when I broke down. I broke down and started to cry, oh the Tower, winters in Queen's House, right in front of everybody. People came and stared. I was the only Negro there. The guard came and stared, the ravens flew and finally a man with a black hat on helped me out through the gate into the street. I am never going back, Anne. Anne, I am never going back. I will not go.

THEY. Keep her locked there, guard.

The NEGRO MAN *comes toward her. She dresses him as God putting a crown upon his head. The* REVEREND *watches them. A light comes into the Tower as though a cell door has been opened.*

SHE. God, do you see it? Do you see? They are opening the cell door to let me go.

NEGRO MAN. See it, Mary?

SHE. They are opening the cell door to let me go down to St. Paul's Chapel where I am yearning to go. Do you see it?

NEGRO MAN. Love? Love Mary?

SHE. Love?

NEGRO MAN. Love in St. Paul's Chapel?

SHE. No, no, the love that exists between you and me. Do you see it?

NEGRO MAN. Love Mary? [*He takes her hand; with his other hand, he tries to undress her.*]

SHE. Love God.

NEGRO MAN. Love Mary?

SHE. Love God.

THEY *bring the* DEAD FATHER *and leave him at her feet.*

THEY [*simultaneously*]. Bastard, you are not His ancestor, you are not God's ancestor.

NEGRO MAN. Love Mary?

SHE. Love God. Yes.

BASTARD'S BLACK MOTHER [*calls*]. Clara. Clara. [*The* REVEREND *watching.*]

THEY. Open the door. Let her go, let her go, guards. Open the cell door.

THEY *exit leaving the gates open.* NEGRO MAN *will not release* SHE WHO IS CLARA *who is the* BASTARD *who is the* VIRGIN MARY *who is the* OWL.

SHE. Go away. [*The* REVEREND *goes back to his chair.*] Go away. [*The* NEGRO MAN *will not release her.*]

The REVEREND'S WIFE *goes on building the High Altar
with owl feathers, prays, builds, prays, stops, holds out her
hand to* SHE WHO IS, *puts up candles, puts up owl feathers,
laughs, puts more candles on the High Altar.*

REVEREND'S WIFE [*calls*]. Owl, come sit by me. [*The* REV-
EREND'S WIFE *does not look at* SHE WHO IS *but rather
stares feverishly upward, her gestures possessing the fervent
quality of Biblical images. Sitting on the High Altar she
holds one of her hands over her shoulder as though she
drew near the fingers of a deity; suddenly her hand reaches
inside her gown and she pulls up a butcher knife.*] Clara.
[*Staring upward, holding the knife.*]

SHE. Yes, the Reverend's Wife who came to me on my
wedding day and said I cry for the death of brides. Yes?

REVEREND'S WIFE. I told the Reverend if he ever came near
me again—[*She turns the butcher knife around.*]—does
he not know I am Mary Christ's bride. What does he
think does he think I am like your black mother who
was the biggest whore in town. He must know I'm Mary,
only Mary would marry the Reverend Passmore of the
church on the top of the Holy Hill. [*Turns the knife
around, staring at it.* SHE WHO IS *goes through the gate.
The* REVEREND'S WIFE *tries to get her to sit on the
High Altar. When she does not the* REVEREND'S WIFE
*then drags the bed, which is the High Altar through the
gate to the center of the scene, arranges it, then goes on
building, owls and feathers, candles.*] We adopted you,
took you from your bastard birth Owl. [*Goes on building.*]

The NEGRO MAN *stands and waits for* CLARA.

SHE. Home, God, we're home. Did you know we came from
England, God? It's the Brontës' home too. Winters we
spent here at the Tower. Our chambers were in the
Queen's House. Summers we spent at Stratford. It was so
lovely. God, do you remember the loveliness?

NEGRO MAN *stares at her, green light begins coming,*
WHITE BIRD *flies out, end of the lights, flashing, fans
twirling, subway sounds.*

BIRD. If you are the Virgin what are you doing with this Negro in a Harlem Hotel Room? Mary?

SHE. My name is Clara Passmore.

BIRD. Mary.

WHITE BIRD *laughs like the* MOTHER. *The* REVEREND'S WIFE *lights candles.*

NEGRO MAN. What is it?

SHE. Call me Mary, God.

NEGRO MAN. Mary?

SHE. God, do you remember the loveliness?

The REVEREND'S WIFE *lights more candles and moves closer with the butcher knife, calling.*

REVEREND'S WIFE. Clara.

The BIRD *flies wildly, the* REVEREND *sits in the chair reading the white tattered Bible. For an instant he seems as though he might get up and come forward but he does not, instead he smiles and goes on reading the Bible.*

NEGRO MAN. What is it? What is it? What is wrong? [*He tries to undress her. Underneath, her body is black. He throws off the crown she has placed on him.*] What is it? [*The* WHITE BIRD *flies toward them and about the green room.*] Are you sick?

SHE [*smiles*]. No, God. [SHE *is in a trance.*] No, I am not sick. I only have a dream of love. A dream. Open the cell door and let me go down to St. Paul's Chapel. [*The blue crepe shawl is half about her.* SHE *shows the* NEGRO MAN *her notebooks from which a mass of papers fall.* SHE *crazily tries to gather them up.*]

Communications, God, communications, letters to my father. I am making it into my thesis. I write my father every day of the year.

God, I who am the Bastard who is the Virgin Mary who is the Owl, I came here this morning with my father. We were visiting England, the place of our ancestors, my father and I who am the Bastard who is the Virgin

Mary who is the Owl. We had a lovely morning. We rose in darkness, took a taxi past Hyde Park, through the Marble Arch to Buckingham Palace. We had our morning tea at Lyons and then we came out to the Tower.

And I started to cry and a man with a black hat on helped me out of the gate to the street. I was the only Negro here.

They took him away and would not let me see him. They who are my Black Mother and my Goddam Father locked me in the fig tree and took his body away and his white hair hung down.

Now they my Black Mother and my Goddam Father who pretend to be Chaucer, Shakespeare, and Eliot, and all my beloved English, come to my cell and stare and I can see they despise me and I despise them.

They are dragging his body across the green, his white hair hanging down. They are taking off his shoes and he is stiff. I must get into the chapel to see him. I must. He is my blood father. God let me into his burial. [*Kneeling.*]

I call God and the Owl answers. [*Softer.*]

It haunts my Tower calling, its feathers are blowing against the cell wall, speckled in the garden on the fig tree, it comes feathered great hollow-eyed with yellow skin and yellow eyes, the flying bastard. From my Tower I keep calling and the only answer is the Owl God. [*Pause. Stands.*]

I am only yearning for our kingdom God.

The WHITE BIRD *flies back into the cage,* REVEREND *reads, smiling, the* DEAD FATHER *lies on cell floor. The* MOTHER, *now part the* BLACK MOTHER *and part the* REVEREND'S WIFE *in a white dress, wild kinky hair, part feathered, comes closer to* CLARA.

MOTHER. Owl in the fig tree, owl under the house, owl in outhouse. [*Calling cheerfully the way one would call a child, kissing* SHE WHO IS.] There is a way from owldom. [*Kissing her again.*] Clara who is the Bastard who is the Virgin who is the Owl.

SHE. My Black Mother who cooked for somebody who is the Reverend's Wife. Where is Anne Boleyn?

MOTHER. Owl in the fig tree do you know it? Do you? Do you know the way to St. Paul's Chapel, Clara? [*Takes her hand.*] I do. Kneel, Mary, by the gate and pray with me who is your black mother who is Christ's Bride. [*She holds up the butcher knife.*] Kneel by the High Altar and pray with me. [*They kneel; she smiles.*] Do you know it, Clara, do you Clara Bastard? [*She kisses her.*] Clara, I know the way to St. Paul's Chapel. I know the way to St. Paul's Chapel, Clara.

Green light dims suddenly, fluttering of WHITE BIRD'S *wings, when the lights grow bright the* MOTHER *has killed herself with the butcher knife and all about is blood, flesh, and feathers, fluttering of* WHITE BIRD'S *wings is loud.* SHE *and the* NEGRO MAN *stand amid blood, flesh and owl feathers, the* DEAD FATHER *stands, arises and sets fire to the High Altar with the candles.*

Music: Haydn.

SHE [*the* NEGRO MAN *tries to kiss her, they are upon the burning High Altar, the* WHITE BIRD *flies out, laughs*]. God, say you know I love you, Mary, yes, I love you. That love is the oldest, purest testament in my heart. Say, Mary, it was a testament imprinted on my soul long before the world began. I pray to you, Mary, God say Mary I pray to you. Darling, come to my kingdom. Mary, leave owldom—come to my kingdom. I am awaiting you.

The NEGRO MAN *tries again to kiss her. The* WHITE BIRD *picks up the dead* MOTHER *and takes her to the top of St. Peter's Dome. They remain there watching. The* REVEREND *reads the Bible, smiling.*

NEGRO MAN. What is wrong?

SHE. Wrong, God?

NEGRO MAN. God?

SHE. Wrong, God?

NEGRO MAN. God?

They are upon the burning High Altar. He tries to force her down, yet at the same time he is frightened by her. The DEAD FATHER *who has been holding the candles, smiles, then falls dead again. The* NEGRO MAN *tries to undress* SHE WHO IS THE BASTARD, WHO IS. *When he touches her, she screams like an owl.*

SHE. Negro! [*Music ends.*] Keep her locked there, guard. [*They struggle.*] I cry for the death of Marys. [*They struggle. She screeches.*] Negro! [*She tries to get out of the room but he will not let her go.*]

Let me go to St. Paul's Chapel. Let me go down to see my Goddam Father who was the Richest White Man in the Town. [*They struggle; he is frightened now.*] God, God call me, Mary. [*She screeches louder.*] God!! [*Suddenly she breaks away, finds her notebook, and from it withdraws the butcher knife still with blood and feathers upon it, and very quickly tries to attack him, holds the knife up, aiming it at him, but then dropping it just as suddenly as a gesture of wild weariness. He backs away from her. She screeches. He backs further. She falls down onto the side of the burning bed. The* NEGRO MAN *backs further out through the gate.* SHE, *fallen at the side of the Altar burning, her head bowed, both hands conceal her face, feathers fly, green lights are strong, Altar burning,* WHITE BIRD *laughs from the Dome.* SHE WHO IS CLARA *who is the* BASTARD *who is the* VIRGIN MARY *suddenly looks like an owl, and lifts her bowed head, stares into space and speaks.*] Ow . . . oww.

Curtain.

ABOUT THE PLAYWRIGHTS

Autobiographical Notes

ROCHELLE OWENS: "Born Brooklyn, New York, 1936. Live in N.Y.C. with my husband, George Economou, who is a poet. I've published poetry in many little magazines and some anthologies. My plays have been performed in Europe and the United States. Won the 1966–67 'Obie' award for best play with *Futz*, which was also seen at the Edinburgh Festival in August–September, 1967. A collection of my plays, *Futz and What Came After*, has been published by Random House. I have just finished a new play about China, called *He Wants Shih*. Presently, I am a fellow in the Yale-ABC Playwriting Program at the Yale University School of Drama."

VENABLE HERNDON: "As an undergraduate at Princeton and as a graduate student at Harvard I worked in comparative literature (French-Russian-English). Since then I have been an advertising copywriter, an editor for *The Chelsea Review*, and, more recently, a screenwriter. My first play, *Bag of Flies*, has (after two agonizing near productions) not yet been produced. *Until the Monkey Comes* was my second. A third, *Independence Night*, is in the works now. An original movie, *Racing Chair*, is scheduled for production."

JEAN RAYMOND MALJEAN: "My playwriting is subsidized by a music teacher (named Jean Raymond Maljean). The inspiration comes from my lovely wife, Virginia, my lyricist when I'm composing musicals, my co-actor when performing, and my co-signer at times. I was born in Brooklyn and frittered away my childhood in Queens. For years I lived in Hicksville, Long Island, where I wrote a column for the *Mid-Island Herald* and directed plays for stock and elsewhere (mostly elsewhere). My full-length satirical play, *Psalms Are Psung on Psunday*, has been optioned for Broadway."

JOSEF BUSH: "Josef Bush/May 4, 1933/Chicago"

URSULE MOLINARO: "Short stories: about two dozen in

269

magazines ranging from *Cosmopolitan* to *Evergreen*. Novels: *The Borrower* (in French translation, Julliard, Paris, 1964); *Green Lights Are Blue* (New American Library, 1967). Short plays: many Off-Broadway productions. Translations (of novels, plays, short stories) by Gascar, Ollier, Butor, Sarraute, Vauthier, Johnson, Lettau, Hesse, Buzzati, Carrega, et al. Subtitles of films by Molinaro, Lelouche, Godard, Luntz, et al. I am now at work on a new novel: *Sounds of a Drunken Summer*."

JAMES PAUL DEY: "Born in Missouri, June 4, 1930. I attended Drury College and the University of Arkansas. In New York, I studied with José Quintero and Herbert Berghoff. *The Redemptor*, my first play, was produced at the Cricket Theatre in May, 1959, along with *What Did You Say What For?*, which appeared in *Players Magazine* and has since been often produced in American colleges and universities. *Passacaglia* was first produced in May, 1965, by the International Theatre Club at the Mercury Theatre in London. I have held three playwriting fellowships to the MacDowell Colony and am a charter member of Edward Albee's Playwright's Unit."

TOM EYEN: "Born Cambridge, Ohio, August 14, 1940 (twenty-four years of age). Schooled Ohio State University, American Academy of D.A. Has written twelve plays, four musicals, and two vanity happenings. A Rockefeller grantee. Summer of 1967 *Sarah B. Divine!* (Part I) invited to Spoleto Festival. Mr. Eyen lives in the Village with four locks on his door."

ADRIENNE KENNEDY: "Adrienne Kennedy was born in Pittsburgh in 1931 and grew up in Cleveland. She attended Ohio State University but found the social structure there so opposed to Negroes that she did hardly any academic work and started writing at twenty. Her writing received no real recognition until she joined Edward Albee's workshop in

1962. Among her plays are *Funnyhouse of a Negro* (for which she received an 'Obie'), *A Lesson in Dead Language*, *A Rat's Mass*, and *A Beast's Story*. Adrienne Kennedy is presently living in London."

The Editor

WILLIAM M. HOFFMAN was born in New York City in 1939. He attended the City College of New York, where he studied Latin. Mr. Hoffman is a playwright, poet, screenwriter, and Dramabook Editor for Hill and Wang.

DRAMABOOKS
(Plays)

When ordering, please use the Standard Book Number consisting of the publisher's prefix, 8090-, plus the five digits following each title. (Note that the numbers given in this list are for paperback editions only. Many of the books are also available in cloth.)

Elmer Rice: Three Plays (Adding Machine, Street Scene, Dream Girl) (0735–5)
The Day the Whores Came Out to Play Tennis . . . by Arthur Kopit (0736–3)
Platonov by Anton Chekhov (0737–1)
Ugo Betti: Three Plays (The Inquiry, Goat Island, The Gambler) (0738–X)
Jean Anouilh Vol. 3 (Thieves' Carnival, Medea, Cécile, Traveler Without Luggage, Orchestra, Episode in the Life of an Author, Catch As Catch Can) (0739–8)
Max Frisch: Three Plays (Don Juan, The Great Rage of Philip Hotz, When the War Was Over) (0740–1)
New American Plays Vol. 2 ed. by William M. Hoffman (0741–X)
Plays from Black Africa ed. by Fredric M. Litto (0742–8)
Anton Chekhov: Four Plays (The Seagull, Uncle Vanya, The Cherry Orchard, The Three Sisters) (0743–6)
The Silver Foxes Are Dead and Other Plays by Jakov Lind (The Silver Foxes Are Dead, Anna Laub, Hunger, Fear) (0744–4)
New American Plays Vol. 3 ed. by William M. Hoffman (0745–2)

THE NEW MERMAIDS

Bussy D'Ambois by George Chapman (1101–8)
The Broken Heart by John Ford (1102–6)
The Duchess of Malfi by John Webster (1103–4)
Doctor Faustus by Christopher Marlowe (1104–2)
The Alchemist by Ben Jonson (1105–0)
The Jew of Malta by Christopher Marlowe (1106–9)
The Revenger's Tragedy by Cyril Tourneur (1107–7)
A Game at Chess by Thomas Middleton (1108–5)
Every Man in His Humour by Ben Jonson (1109–3)
The White Devil by John Webster (1110–7)
Edward the Second by Christopher Marlowe (1111–5)
The Malcontent by John Marston (1112–3)
'Tis Pity She's a Whore by John Ford (1113–1)
Sejanus His Fall by Ben Jonson (1114–X)
Volpone by Ben Jonson (1115–8)
Women Beware Women by Thomas Middleton (1116–6)

SPOTLIGHT DRAMABOOKS

The Last Days of Lincoln by Mark Van Doren (1201–4)
Oh Dad, Poor Dad . . . by Arthur Kopit (1202–2)
The Chinese Wall by Max Frisch (1203–0)
Billy Budd by Louis O. Coxe and Robert Chapman (1204–9)
The Devils by John Whiting (1205–7)
The Firebugs by Max Frisch (1206–5)
Andorra by Max Frisch (1207–3)
Balm in Gilead and Other Plays by Lanford Wilson (1208–1)
Matty and the Moron and Madonna by Herbert Lieberman (1209–X)
The Brig by Kenneth H. Brown (1210–3)
The Cavern by Jean Anouilh (1211–1)
Saved by Edward Bond (1212–X)
Eh? by Henry Livings (1213–8)
The Rimers of Eldritch and Other Plays by Lanford Wilson (1214–6)
In the Matter of J. Robert Oppenheimer by Heinar Kipphardt (1215–4)
Ergo by Jakov Lind (1216–2)
Biography: A Game by Max Frisch (1217–0)
Indians by Arthur Kopit (1218–9)
Narrow Road to the Deep North by Edward Bond (1219–7)

For a complete list of books of criticism and history of the drama, please write to Hill and Wang, 72 Fifth Avenue, New York, New York 10011.